THE THEORY AND PRACTICE OF SELF PSYCHOLOGY

By

Marjorie Taggart White, Ph.D.,

and

Marcella Bakur Weiner, Ed.D.

BRUNNER/MAZEL *Publishers* • New York

Library of Congress Cataloging-in-Publication Data

White, Marjorie Taggart.
    The theory and practice of self psychology.

    Bibliography: p. 197
    Includes index.
    1. Self. 2. Psychotherapy, 3. Kohut, Heinz.
I. Weiner, Marcella Bakur.   II. Title.
[DNLM: 1. Ego. 2. Psychotherapy. WM 460.5.E3 W586t]
RC489.S43W47 1986   616.89'14   86-919
ISBN 0-87630-425-0

Published by
BRUNNER/MAZEL, INC.
19 Union Square West
New York, New York 10003

MANUFACTURED IN THE UNITED STATES OF AMERICA

10 9 8 7 6 5 4 3 2

Foreword

I experienced being asked to write a Foreword to this book with both pride and pleasure—pride in being associated with such sensitive yet scholarly therapists as Drs. Marjorie White and Marcella Weiner obviously are, and pleasure in this beautifully lucid book in which they share the wealth of their theoretical and practical knowledge with their colleagues.

Self psychology is a very young heir to the rich patrimony left us by Sigmund Freud, a legacy that itself came into being just barely one hundred years ago. When measured against the millenia of human history, the emergence of psychoanalysis and its offspring, self psychology, is but a recent moment in the slow development of man's exploration of himself. Heinz Kohut published his *Forms and Transformations of Narcissism* twenty years ago and I think that happy event can fairly be designated the official birthday of self psychology, even though in retrospect it is not difficult to discern in Kohut's earlier writings harbingers of the things to come. Since then a swelling flood of self psychological papers and case reports has begun to fill the book shelves of the cognoscenti. Only now, however, are we beginning to see systematic summary treatments that compare, correlate, and update the young science in comprehensive and comprehensible form.

The present volume is an excellent example of such a systematic presentation. That does not mean that every self psychologist will necessarily agree with every statement in this book and, indeed, I find myself at times at odds with the authors in their therapeutic enthusiasm when, it seems to me, a more cautiously tempered wait-and-see attitude would still have yielded sufficient evidence of the curative powers of self psychology. But such differences are more of style than of substance. Heinz Kohut, I believe, would have welcomed this book and so, I think, should we all.

December 19, 1985   Ernest S. Wolf, M.D.
Winnetka, Illinois.

Acknowledgments

In a very real sense, this book is the outgrowth of the ongoing 15-year-old Seminar on Self Psychology for Practicing Psychotherapists which traversed the rocky road from ego psychology to self psychology, with many reviews of Freud. This is to stress that our vote for self psychology does not arise from an uninformed enthusiasm.

To all Seminar members, our appreciation of their commitment to psychotherapeutic knowledge, wherever it may lead them.

To Ernest S. Wolf, M.D., our thanks for his beautiful Foreword, which convinces us it has all been worthwhile.

To our contributors, both Seminar members and students, our gratitude for their willingness to "stick their necks out" in providing case material.

To Sheridan Sweet, our tireless "word processor lady," we can only bow down. That her other life includes teaching Kant is, we think, significant. To the Park Slope Copy Center, which gave us tender loving care, our continuing appreciation.

To our editor, Ann Alhadeff, who was "always there" and remarkably flexible, as well as prescient in her command of the language, our profound appreciation for her help.

And, finally, to our patients from whom we learned and whose needs prompted this book, our constant gratitude.

Marjorie Taggart White, Ph.D.
Marcella Bakur Weiner, Ed.D.

Contents

Foreword by Ernest S. Wolf, M.D. v

Acknowledgments vi

Preface xi

Introduction xv

1. An Overview of Basic Self Psychology Concepts 3

How self disorders became treatable through Kohut's discovery of the two basic narcissistic transference needs—mirroring and idealizing—and of the narcissistic rage accompanying the disillusionment with either transference need; how the therapist's empathy with the patient's unfulfilled childhood need to be appreciated for his or her developmental achievements, along with the continuing need to look up to a fulfilling ideal selfobject, helps the patient to resume his/her stalemated development as a creative and caring adult.

2. Aggression from a Self Psychological Viewpoint 19

How self psychology can replace the assumption of an innate aggressive drive by focusing on aggression as a disintegration product of an unresponsive environment; how assertive aggression is productive and time-limited; how the modification of the destructive aggressive drive lifts the burden of fear and guilt over untamable instincts from the weary shoulders of humankind and opens the way for hope.

3. Empathy and the Selfobject 35

How Kohut's concept of empathy as a data-gathering approach enables a psychotherapist to place him/herself inside a patient's self-state and gradually understand how and why the patient feels rage, self-contempt, grandiosity, or deep distrust of others, including the psychotherapist; how empathy facilitates the internalization of the psychotherapist as the sensitive, growth-supporting "selfobject" the patient never really had as a child; how these concepts can be effectively applied in difficult cases, based on supervisory sessions.

4. The Grandiose Self: A Wellspring of Rage or
    Achievement? 57

The crucial childhood need for omnipotence in a frightening world; how narcissistic rage arising from failed grandiosity can turn against the self or the world to get revenge; the psychotherapist's difficulties in treating narcissistic rage and the specter of countertransference; how empathy can help therapists in dealing with these difficult developmental problems.

5. Idealization 75

How the child needs to preserve the infantile paradise through idealizing a parent who then becomes a repository of adult values; how the inability of parents (and psychotherapists) to let themselves be idealized can deprive the child and later the adult patient of chances to develop stable values as touchstones for mature living.

6. A Third Chance for the Nuclear Self: A Tripolar Self
    Through a Twinship 103

How Kohut saw the supraordinate self developing, at first on a twofold basis of self-realization arising out of confirming mirroring, together with idealizable goals as a second chance; how a third chance to develop a supraordinate self through twinship can come through empathic experiences with other relatives or friends who were good selfobjects apart from the parents; how twinship offers another chance for the psycho-therapist to be a beneficent selfobject, fostering the development of the patient's nuclear self.

7. Intergenerational Continuity Versus Punishing Guilt . 116

How Kohut gradually recognized that intergenerational continuity was the natural outcome of human development and not the essentially pathological outcome of oedipal jealousy, patricide, and filicide; how self psychology offers as a natural development a "joyful" oedipal complex in which parents welcome their children's movement into healthy sexuality and assertiveness; how psychotherapists can also help patients to experience a joyful oedipal development in the context of a developing cohesive self.

8. Traumatic States: Too Much, Too Little, or the Wrong Responsiveness 133

How some of the most stubborn and formerly untreatable symptoms, including borderline pathology and the negative therapeutic reaction, can be understood in terms of self-fragmentation and the psychoeconomic imbalance brought on by overstimulation; how the perseverative faux pas, self-state dreams, addictions, and somatic symptoms, including insomnia, are found to respond to the therapist's prolonged empathic immersion in the patient's feeling states.

9. Special Populations 155

How self psychology has increasingly demonstrated that difficult patient populations can hope for more help than ever before; how two special populations—the child abuser and the older adult—respond to treatment using self psychology, thereby encouraging psychotherapists to work with seemingly hopeless patients.

10. The Joy of Psychotherapy 174

How Kohut stressed that healthy narcissism can be creatively transformed into wisdom, the acceptance of the natural termination of one's life, and the great gift of humor; how during treatment psychotherapists can also have the creative feeling of providing a responsive environment in which the patient, perhaps for the first time, can know joy; illustrated by a case presentation, how feeling deeply understood can bring about a self-birth and self-growth.

References 197
Index 203

Preface

Our primary purpose in writing this book is to offer insights and guidelines for psychoanalytic and psychotherapeutic treatment to the practitioner working or planning to work with the late Heinz Kohut's concepts of self psychology. By integrating theory and practice, we offer case material from our therapeutic experience, showing how self psychology can be used with a wide range of patients, culminating in outcomes that are not only beneficial but also exciting and sometimes surprising.

We seek to demonstrate how the use of empathy as a scientific tool can provide the patient with growth-producing soil for his or her nuclear self in a formerly arid environment. Illustrations of empathic failures at various points in the treatment show how the unattuned therapist can recreate the devastating experiences of the patient's past. The therapist's acceptance of the patient's idealization without embarrassment or critical "realism" is also shown as one of the ways patients can repair the self-esteem deficits accrued as a child who was not cared about.

By striving to enter a patient's experiential world without preconceived "maturity morality" assumptions, e.g., the desirability and high ethical standing of superindependence, (Kohut, 1979), we become free to explore how our patients can go beyond archaic grandiosity into constructive, healthy narcissism. Current evidence in brain research is also included as validation for the position that self-esteem is positively correlated with an intact immune system.

Aggression is interpreted as a disintegration product of a nonresponsive environment from birth. This concept assumes that the angry baby has a reason to be angry from his* or her standpoint, and that his or her anger, therefore, is not an expression of an innate aggressive drive, pressing for discharge no matter what. In the context of discovering that aggression can dissipate with an empathic approach to how the environment (including the therapist) was unresponsive, the possibilities of alleviating destructive aggression begin to open up, not only for the individual but for the world he or she lives in. Hostilities between nations, for instance, can be looked upon, not as the expectable discharge of an innate drive dooming humankind to eventual nuclear extinction, but rather as understandable reactions to an unresponsive environment, e.g., an environment threatening total destruction. Once the reactions of another individual or group can be understood as an expectable response to the absence of empathy, a real possibility emerges for more sensitive responses to help bridge the felt differences that otherwise seem to often convert possible allies into total strangers.

In considering the joys of psychotherapy, in the last chapter, we describe some of the enthusiastic reactions we have to our work and how the sense of achievement we feel is reflected in the positive feelings experienced by the patient.

In our chapter on traumatic states, we focus on the origins of and suggested treatment to relieve traumatic states, which include faux pas, regressive psychoeconomic imbalances, and negative therapeutic reactions. The treatment approach includes empathic acceptance of the trauma and an effort to internalize benign self-soothing through a good selfobject relationship with the therapist.

Our chapters on the special problems of older adults and child abusers portray how an understanding of humankind that is not constricted by interpretations of innate drives can lead to a view of man as the creatively loving person he can be. This also in-

---

*Although we have generally used both male and female pronouns throughout this book, in those places where the use of both would be awkward, we have used the male pronoun.

cludes, as Chapter 7 shows, a capacity to extend caring to one's children as the next generation and a continuation of concern in wanting them to find their own way. Such reliable, lifelong caring contrasts with the assumption of innate drives, which call for murderous competition between parent and child, with no room left either for the parent's pride in the child's achievement (including sexual fulfillment) or for the child's mature caring for the parents who need assistance, at least in building a "new" retirement life.

Our book is designed to show that self psychological theory has far-reaching effects in the therapeutic interchange between therapist and patient. Especially important is the therapist's continuing concern about the patient's feelings. It is necessary to explore the therapist's inevitable failures to be attuned sufficiently, arising out of the therapist's subjective structures, i.e,. *his* or *her* self-state interfering with his or her empathic comprehension of a particular self-state of the patient. We suggest that in order to restore attunement with the patient's feelings, the therapist needs to understand his or her own blind spots and to appropriately communicate the effects of this discovery to the patient.

Finally, this book is offered as a testimonial of hope for self-realization, certainly for our patients, but also for ourselves as therapists. In our experience, self psychology shows that therapy need not be a stalemated struggle with untamable infantile drives, but rather an awakening to a creative utilization of the nuclear self with which each of us is endowed at birth.

Introduction

An approach that focuses sensitively upon the self of the person, suggesting that the self could be the decisive center of individual experience and developmental possibilities, is the essence of the orientation of the late Heinz Kohut.

Kohut, an outstanding psychoanalyst and past president of the American Psychoanalytic Association, originally focused on developing a theoretical and technical approach to the formerly untreatable problem of pathological narcissism. In the process, he tested and articulated a self psychology that promises to revolutionize the theory and technique of both traditional psychoanalysis and ego psychology.

THE BEGINNINGS OF CONSCIOUSNESS

The concept of the self has long been overlooked. Before mentioning some of the theorists before Kohut who were concerned with the self, we feel it is important to refer to a major psycho-anthropological inquiry into the advent of the self upon the human scene made by Jaynes (1976). His book on *The Origin of Consciousness in the Breakdown of the Bicameral Mind*, which appeared five years after Kohut's pioneering *The Analysis of the Self* (1971), proposed that ancient man had *no* self; the voices of all-powerful gods were thought to direct man's volition and initiative, often through auditory hallucinations.

Using archaeological evidence and the ancient classics (such as *The Iliad*), Jaynes concluded that there is no proof of humankind possessing consciousness—that is, a subjective awareness of one's consciousness of the world—before the third or second millenium. The concept of the "bicameral mind," composed of the orders received from the gods and the part of the mind that obediently executed the orders, broke down with the gradual development of human consciousness arising from the evolving human brain. By 560 B.C. in the time of Solon, the great lawgiver of ancient Greece, "know thyself" became a predominant theme, which was inconceivable in Homer's time, estimated to have been anywhere from the 12th to the 9th century B.C.

However, as the new consciousness of self emerged over the centuries, parts of the bicameral mind melded with self-awareness. Kohut has impressive clinical documentation, quite apart from Jaynes' theory, of the concept of the unconscious infantile grandiose self, characterized by omnipotent godlike commands, and which, if unfulfilled, triggers narcissistic rage and revenge against the offender for whom no pity is felt. As clinicians, we are painfully familiar with this type of pathology, which is openly deployed by borderlines and psychotics but also more subtly evident in narcissistic personality disorders.

TO LOVE OR NOT TO LOVE THE SELF

Jaynes' theory of the historically late evolution of the consciousness of self would explain the puzzling lack of interest displayed by psychoanalysts and psychologists in the concept of the self. Freud (1905, 1911, 1914) was skeptical about overvaluing the love object, but he also warned against caring too much about oneself. In the Schreber case, he saw "megalomania . . . as a sexual overvaluation of the ego" (1911, p. 65).

In 1914 in his paper, "On Narcissism: An Introduction," Freud seemed to relent a little, defining normal narcissism not as a perversion, but as a libidinal aspect of the instinctual self-preservation attributable to every living creature. The "omnipotent" primary narcissism of "His Majesty the Baby" (ibid, p. 91), however, soon turned into object-love which Freud saw as a need both to possess the loved one and to be loved, in order to raise one's self-regard. Classical psychoanalysts today would certainly view this as a narcissistic need for attention. Yet in 1914 Freud thought that such a "happy love" corresponded to the early condition in which there was no difference between object-love and ego libido. From the vantage point of psychoanalytic developmental psychology, this nondifferentiation would be regarded today as a regression to an infantile symbiotic state.

Freud remained pessimistic about the possibility of effectively treating pathological narcissism, as he found such patients unable to develop the customary transference neurosis. He also used the term *ego* interchangeably with the self, while he accorded the *object*, i.e., the other, fully separate existence. The confusion of the self and the ego here is reminiscent of Jaynes' theories.

In the light of Freud's ambiguous valuation of the self, Hartmann's (1950) position is surprising, that is, according an implied equality to the self along with the object. Pointing out that the two terms were often used interchangeably by Freud, Hartmann stressed that the self connotes one's own person or body in contrast to the object. The ego, he maintained, is one of the substructures of the psychic system, and therefore self-cathexis is really the opposite of object cathexis. He noted that when we say ego cathexis has replaced object cathexis, we mean that either self-love or a "neutralized form" of self-cathexis has replaced object cathexis. When we state that libido has been withdrawn into the ego, we mean that there has been a withdrawal into the self.

The senior author, in an earlier paper (1980), noted that with such a seemingly simple terminological change, Hartmann established self-representations as a content of the ego. The senior author also pointed out that the implications of this change seemed far-reaching, not only with respect to narcissism but also in regard to internalization and identification processes. In this connection, the concept of a self-representation implies that what may be psychologically "taken in" from another has to coincide with or extend a core self-awareness, that is, identification is not done with a selfless blank screen. For example, a child who is musical is not likely to identify with a tone-deaf parent. This notion could be seen as a forerunner of Kohut's nuclear self.

The concept of object constancy was first introduced in 1952 by Hartmann, with the suggestion that it must imply for the ego some neutralization of the sexual and aggressive drives. However, he did *not* suggest the comparable concept of self-constancy in this connection, as he had in 1950 when he proposed that the term self-representation could be used, "as opposed" to object-representation, really focusing on the separation of the self- and object-representations. The term opposed clearly implies a conflict between what the self needs and wants, compared with the object.

EGO FUNCTIONING AND THE SELF

Perhaps foreshadowing Kohut's self psychology, which emerged in 1959, and in connection with the growing trend to consider the concept of self as meriting full investigation, Edith Jacobson (1954) stated that "normal ego functioning presupposes a sufficient, evenly distributed, enduring, libidinous cathexis of both object- and self-representations (p. 94). Self-valuation, or even self-love, from this standpoint seems to be put on an equal footing with object-valuation and object-love, a possibility that Freud and Hartmann did not recognize as desirable or even likely. The senior author (1980) has earlier suggested that the implication of Jacobson's position was that with respect to an even distribution of libidinal cathexis between self- and object-representations, we should normally love ourselves as much as others. In contrast to Freud's economy of love, where he saw being in love as having less self-regard and more concern for the love object, Jacobson seemed to indicate that healthy self-esteem was the foundation for enduring love.

In a remarkable and rare recognition for an ego psychological theorist, Jacobson stressed that to approach another person libidinally required not only an overvaluation of the other, e.g., a hypercathexis, but also the spur of a simultaneous, "libidinous hypercathexis of the *self-representations* which will encourage and guarantee the success of the action," (1954, p. 94) (emphases added).

According to Jacobson, such a hypercathexis would include the organs and body parts concerned in the undertaking. The whole self would also be hypercathected, triggering increased self-confidence that would stimulate both the involved executive organs and the action. The concept of increased self-confidence as a vital and essential aspect of successful object relations naturally underlines again the need for healthy narcissism as indispensable for mature object relations.

Jacobson (1954) also limned a realistic concept of the self that would mirror the condition, potentialities, abilities and limits of our bodily and mental ego. This would mean one's appearance, including the anatomy, along with conscious and preconscious affects, wishes, desires, and attitudes. In addition to the psychic representations of all these specific features, "a concept of their sum total, i.e., of the self as a differentiated but organized entity, will simultaneously develop" (Jacobson, 1954, pp. 86-87).

Jacobson's concept of a more or less constant self is in sharp contrast to Hartmann's rather reluctant conceptualization of self-representations as a way of distinguishing these psychic phenomena from object-representations and from the ego. Jacobson's delineation of a realistic concept of the self, including the idea of mirroring as a factor in the laying down of stable self-representations, can be viewed as a precursor of over 20 ensuing years of intensified interest in the self and in narcissism.

A "supraordinate self" was conceptualized clinically by Kohut in conjunction with his modification of drive theory. He noted that whenever a person strives either for pleasure or destruction, despite any conflicts over them, "it is possible to discern a self which, while it includes drives (and/or defenses) in its organization, has become a supraordinated configuration whose significance transcends that of the sum of its parts" (1977, p. 97).

Although Kohut, to our knowledge, never expanded on this definition of the supraordinate self, we believe that the concept implies a full development of the core nuclear self (which the child is believed to have at birth) into an adult cohesive self.

Presumably, the latter will guide the higher forms of narcissism that the person attains, as well as participate in the fulfillment of sexual and assertive needs.

A crucially related concept, the "selfobject" experienced as part of the self (Kohut, 1971, p. xiv), constitutes the responsive environment needed from birth to ensure the reliable development of a nuclear self into a mature cohesive self. Hopefully, the parents will provide the self-soothing experiences needed to internalize a stable self structure. Too often the therapist must become the missing selfobject, owing to parental failures.

One of Kohut's most courageous and seminal contributions was his view of aggression, not as an innate drive demanding discharge, but as a disintegration product arising in reaction to an unresponsive environment inhibiting the development of the baby's nuclear self.

The release of humankind from the conceptual burden of an innate aggressive drive, which at best could only be tamable, has been hailed by Basch (1984) as bringing psychoanalytic self psychology up to date with the current findings of neurobiology, ethology, and cybernetics. In these findings there is no evidence for the aggressive drive, which, as Basch points out, Freud suggested only as a speculation; unfortunately, it turned into a dogma.

THE NEED FOR A RESPONSIVE ENVIRONMENT

Infant research, examining mother-baby interaction from a driveless standpoint and with the latest pictorial technology, is finding a baby emerging from the womb who is not passive, not aggressive, but seeking selfobject interaction. M. Tolpin (1984) points out that this interacting baby has an impressive capacity to respond to the mother, seeking not only food but all sorts of affective acknowledgment, and resorting to various ways of trying to get it before sinking into nonresponsiveness from nonstimulation (cf. Anthony, 1984; Beebe & Stern, 1977; Lichtenberg, 1979; Sander, 1975; Stern, 1977; Spitz, 1957, 1965).

Earlier, M. Tolpin (1983) stressed the need for a self psychological reconsideration of Alexander's (1956) "corrective emotional experience." In connection with the impressive revival capacities of the child, in the face of humiliations, disappointments, and even self-failures, Tolpin cites the case of five-year-old Mike. He learned painfully to ice skate, with his parents' stable encouragement, despite Mike's frequent falls, bruised knees, and wounded pride. His enthusiasm remained high even though neither parent could be there to encourage him when the teacher took the whole kindergarten class to the skating rink. But he returned home, dejected. When his mother asked him what happened, he tearfully replied that his legs didn't work the right way and he couldn't stand up on the ice, to his great shame. His responsive mother inquired further as to what could have happened, since he had been skating so well. Mike said sadly, "You weren't watching."

Tolpin points out that "for the moment, the missing firming function of his selfobjects and the missing firmness of his own ankles and his entire self experience were one and the same thing" (1983, pp. 364-65). What Tolpin calls the "corrective developmental dialogue" (p. 366) shows how the self-selfobject unit works. When the self-confident five-year-old comes apart temporarily because he still needs the selfobject's mirroring gleam, he can also be put back together again with renewed support.

In her observations of child-mother interactions Mahler et al. (1975) found that when focusing on the baby's movements, she and her co-workers could sometimes see "in *statu nascendi* affectomotor self-libidinization, which may be a forerunner of integration of body-self feelings" (p. 221). Both in vivo and in films, there are episodes as follows:

> The 5-to-8-month-old, surrounded by the admiring and libidinally mirroring friendly adults, seemed electrified and stimulated by this mirroring admiration. This was evident by his excited kicking and flailing with the extremities, and stretching with an exaltedly pleasurable affect. This obvious tactile kinesthetic stimulation of his body-self, we believe, may promote differentiation and integration of his body image (Mahler, 1975, p. 221).

SOCIAL FACTORS AND THE SELF

Kohut's concept of the unresponsive environment can be glimpsed from a much broader perspective in his concept of psychotropic factors shaping the self of humankind. Not only clinical evidence but also the poetic, artistic, dramatic, and literary works of, say, an O'Neill, a Picasso, a Proust, or a Kafka, led Kohut to conclude that the changing social environment of the 20th century was profoundly affecting human self-experience. Thus, insufficient stimulation from caring selfobjects is leading to self-fragmentation, inner emptiness, and a loss of direction. Consequently, more patients with self-pathology, for whom the oedipal problem has little meaning because their nuclear selves need development, are coming for treatment.

Goldstein (1984) has stressed the importance of being aware of the psychotropic environment in its influence on both the child and his or her parents. In her impressive summary of ego psychology and its impact upon psychotherapeutic thinking and practice, Goldstein states that "it is critical that more systematic efforts be made to integrate knowledge of racial, ethnic, social class and life-style differences into our understanding of normal ego development and the processes of coping and adaptation" (p. 273). Goldstein points out that changes in ego psychological theory (which presumably could include self psychological findings) may positively affect an "anti-ego psychological and anticlinical bias" now found in women, blacks, homosexuals, Hispanics, and so forth, who feel their difference has been "unjustly" described as psychopathology.

Alice Miller (1983, 1984) has documented society's rather incredible failure to recognize the developmental needs of children, especially as they are now being perceived through infant research and the concepts of self psychology. Miller, without claiming to, validates Kohut's concept of the ways in which society can shape the self through psychotropic factors, including "maturity morality" (Kohut, 1979, p. 12). The latter, as Kohut pointed out, sacrifices evident human needs for empathic responsiveness at the altar of such late-arrival values as self-sufficient independence and scientific knowledge.

Miller shows how uncompromising parenting and "poisonous pedagogy" have demanded that offspring behave like little adults, almost from the womb, with much emphasis on the total control of affects and sadistic punishments, including bodily mistreatment, for the child's failure. Miller believes that the resulting adult pathology of masochism and self-abnegation can only be overcome by helping patients realize the abuse to which they have been subjected at the hands of parents and other authority figures. With respect to Kohut's position on the dispensability of the drives and his recognition of the importance of narcissistic (i.e. "self-state,") issues, Miller (1984) states:

> . . . The awakening interest analysts are taking in narcissistic needs such as respect, mirroring, being understood and taken seriously is making it clear that a large portion of those desires previously thought to be connected with drives can be more fully understood . . . and described much more adequately than with the word, "Oedipal." (p. 146)

Anna Ornstein (1984) in the course of her work with Kohut, has repeatedly emphasized that a self psychological approach must start with empathy in trying to understand the patient's complex feelings. Only when it is clear that this empathy has succeeded in the therapist's establishing his or her self as a needed and acceptable selfobject for the patient can the analyst then risk moving to the next step of explanation. Ornstein asserts that being internalized as a patient's selfobject enables the patient to experience and express disavowed affects, as a result of the analyst "explaining" the patient's inhibitions in terms of the latter's history. This supplements Kohut's point that explanation, after empathy, increases a patient's objectivity about him- or herself and his or her needs (Kohut, 1984).

In the case Ornstein cites, the male patient thought he needed to provoke her in order for her to help him express his bottled-up anger. Through empathy, she was able to enter into his isolation of affects based on his parents' insensitivity to all of his feelings. These included his homesickness when sent away to school at age 11. He was never able to express this feeling to his family because, early on, he felt they never cared about or listened to his feelings. It was the analyst's empathy with his feeling uncared about and never listened to that unlocked his enduring capacity to internalize a responsive selfobject.

Paul Ornstein, who brought together and edited the indispensable collection of Kohut's papers and letters, the two-volume *Search for the Self* (1978), sounded a trumpet call to comprehend self psychology's activating potentials for a new approach to health and creativity, even in the face of the nuclear threat. At the first international conference on self psychology held in Chicago, 1978, Ornstein stressed that Kohut's approach constituted "a new paradigm" and a context for "a new conception of health and illness" (p. 138). Ornstein pointed out that the reactivation of the archaic but still healthy and adaptive grandiose self and/or capacity to idealize through the narcissistic transferences Kohut discovered "offers the only means by which belated maturation and development can take place within the psychoanalytic process" (p. 138).

Ornstein also notes that the concept of the "selfobject environment" and its function in self-structure building and in psychoanalytic success connects the impact of "external reality" (i.e., the sociocultural context) to the status of health and illness in a new way. The integration of the intrapsychic, developmental-genetic determinants of health and illness, both with the selfobject concept and the existing psychosocial determinants, provides the possibility of a "higher-order concept of adaptation that places at its center the unfolding of the intrinsic patterns for creative action laid down in the nuclear self" (pp. 139-140).

In the above connection, Ornstein notes that Kohut urged a broader outlook than the restricted concept of psychic disequilibrium. Indeed, Ornstein points out, Kohut urged that psychological disturbance should not be looked upon exclusively as an illness but *"as a way station on the road to man's search for a new psychic equilibrium"* (Kohut, 1978b, pp. 538-539, emphases added). Ornstein (1978b) stresses Kohut's proposal for "adaptive solution" (p. 156) that may be necessary to ensure the human race's survival in an overcrowded society shadowed by the nuclear threat. Such a solution, we are reminded, involves groping toward an enlarged and intensified inner life including " 'that playful creativeness' " which joyfully turns toward new situations with " 'life-affirming initiative' " (p. 156).

Arnold Goldberg, also an early and close collaborator of Kohut's, in his Introduction to *The Psychology of the Self: A Casebook* (1978) points out that, in the termination phase of the six self psychological analyses summarized in the book, the attainment of the "transformations of narcissism" were marked. In line with Kohut's expectations in terms of matured grandiosity and the idealization of therapists leading to higher forms of narcissism, Goldberg notes that this may be seen in patients now enjoying life with a sense of values and goals important to them: "Some say that at last they can work on their own, others report that for the first time in their lives they feel genuine, or there may be some other manifestations of a firm sense of self. . . . We are most optimistic about the future yield of these new ideas and believe that, so far, only the surface has been explored" (pp. 10-12).

HOPE FOR THE SEVERE PATHOLOGIES

A therapist's insistence that the patient is responsible for his unhappy or failed state of being—for example, that it is his infantile sexual and aggressive drives that unconsciously dominate his life and cause havoc—can bring about borderline and even psychotic reactions, according to Brandschaft and Stolorow (1984). Using Kohut's empathic approach, they show that a diagnosed borderline patient can establish the particular selfobject ties she needs with the therapist, once she feels empathically comprehended in her archaic subjective states. In other words, the self psychological approach of empathy appears to offer a possible path of rescue for the most severe pathologies.

Stolorow stressed "the crucial distinction between psychopathology which is the product of defenses against intrapsychic conflict and psychopathology which is the remnant of a developmental arrest at pre-stages of defense . . ." (Stolorow & Lachmann, 1980, p. 5). He also pointed out that this understanding was used to shed new light on a number of clinical problems heretofore seen primarily from the standpoint of intrapsychic conflicts.

Kahn (1985) has endeavored to link Kohut's self psychology to Carl Rogers' humanistic psychology, looking toward greater consideration of the importance of self-structuralization and the use of empathy in fostering such self-cohesiveness.

The psychotherapeutic ambience, Kahn points out, is what Rogers, several years earlier than Kohut, saw as the most important facilitator of growth, including "empathy; valuing, caring and prizing of the person; and the therapist's realness and lack of facade" (Kahn, 1985, p. 903). Kahn notes that Kohut, "independently, through his devotion to the introspective method of psychoanalysis, discovered the importance of the selfobject needs of analytic patients" (p. 903). He cites Wolf (1983a), who stressed that "an objective analytic neutrality can no longer be defined by criteria that ignore the patient's sense of whether the analyst is or seems to be for or against the patient . . ." (p. 499).

EMPATHY VERSUS STRESS AND THE IMMUNE SYSTEM

There has been an impressive escalation of scientific evidence of the beneficial effects of empathic experiences upon the body's baseline of defense—its immunological system. The destructive effects of aggression experienced as stress have also been shown with respect to the immune system (Ader, 1981; Goldberg, 1981; Pelletier, 1977).

While the evidence is growing that there is a basic thrust for life if there is a possible chance to survive, we have to ask ourselves about what *incites* people to strive for life, even if they are in a concentration camp or are the disfigured survivors of a nuclear bomb attack. The findings of the authors cited above confirm that the sense of having one's feelings cared about can, at a basic level, involve a conviction that someone is truly concerned if one lives or dies. It is our belief that this is the bedrock of empathy. Early experiences of parental insensitivity, coupled with similar, later experiences, intensify this conviction of not counting when confronted with an unempathic society, an unempathic medical establishment and, too often, an unempathic psychotherapeutic establishment.

In relation to some increased medical scepticism about the relationship between one's feelings, including self feelings, and the outcome of life-threatening illnesses, Herbert Spector, a neurophysiologist at the National Institutes of Health, was quoted as saying:

> The ancients knew that the patient's attitude was very important to his recovery, but modern medicine wrote it off as trivial. The new research makes it clear. Attitudes can matter. (*The New York Times*, October 22, 1985, p. C1)

We must be aware of the increasing evidence of the beneficial effects of empathic experiences upon illnesses—for example, cancer and heart disease. The crucial role of a supportive environment in recovery from a serious illness has been dramatically shown on two occasions by Norman Cousins. Faced with a seemingly undiagnosable illness in 1976 (later found to be collagen disease), he took himself out of the depressing hospital, where he felt that the incessant taking of blood samples weakened him, and where the almost reproachful attitude to his strange disease made him feel like a hopeless case. When he got what he needed at home in terms of supportive care from his family, amusing videos, and his usual body-building exercises, he began to recover and then wrote about his experience (Cousins, 1979).

Seven years later, Cousins "saved" his life once again. When, after a serious heart attack, he found the medical establishment to be anxiety-arousing, he refused to be stampeded into a bypass operation which he felt would kill him. Once again, he insisted on handling the illness himself with exercise, sensible diet, and his involving work. He again wrote a book about his experience (Cousins, 1983). Cousins says in conclusion: ". . . medical treatment should seek not just to repair damage and restore vital balances but to enhance the quality of life and to help the patient overcome feelings of hopelessness and helplessness" (p. 236).

Since the 1970s, increasingly complex connections have been shown between the hypothalamus in the brain's limbic system (the target area for our feelings) and our immune system. Simonton (1978), using guided imagery that is focused on the white blood cells as destroyers of the cancer cells, has achieved impressive results, especially since patients have survived after being diagnosed as terminal.

The hope engendered by the imagery approach, offered and implemented by the therapist, appears to activate that part of the immune system that destroys cancer cells. It would seem, then, that a feeling of helplessness, whether in humans or animals, slows down the immune system, whereas a feeling of receiving interest, care, and help from another activates that system.

This finding has been well documented in studies showing the high mortality rate of widowers dying relatively soon after the loss of their wives (Hammer, 1984). Current studies of rats also show that those that could counteract their feelings of helplessness in receiving shocks by pressing levers to stop the shocks, did *not* develop cancer, even though injected with cancer cells (Laudenslager, 1983). The ability to control traumatic experiences, rather than shock itself, appears to underly the stress factor and the breakdown of the immune system.

This new focus on stress appears consistent with Kohut's (1982) final conclusion that he drew from his work with patients and that therapists continue to corroborate: Empathy per se has a beneficial and therapeutic effect upon the person receiving it. This discovery implies, and the latest research upholds it, that the immune system thrives in an empathic, unstressful atmosphere. Thus, the best interests of both one's body and one's mind are related to trying to understand and care for another and also to being able to seek such responsiveness for oneself from appropriate selfobjects.

Trying to empathize with another person, however offensive, different, or anxiety-arousing that person may be, is in sharp contrast to being disillusioned or narcissistically rageful against ourselves for having expected too much or the wrong thing from another. This fury can also include rage reactions at such evident differences as not feeling understood, cared about, or respected. Our own grandiosity and propensity to narcissistic rage are shown in withdrawing from an offending person or a group or a whole people, as if they did not exist.

This disdainful rejection can then be expressed in a traditional flight-or-fight reaction, e.g., these people are so hopeless, stupid, vicious, immoral, or insane that they cannot be dealt with in any way. As a result, we are entitled to act as if they do not exist at all, which is a form of psychological killing, or to attack them, with the purpose of extermination, i.e., war, including nuclear war. To the extent that we feel swamped by helplessness in having these reactions, we are involuntarily arousing our hair-trigger autonomic nervous system and, we know now, inactivating our most basic lifeline, our immune system.

Kohut's concept of aggression as a modifiable reaction through empathy can move us away from the drive concept of aggression which makes a human being into a battleground between sadism and masochism that, at best, can only be tamed. The drive concept of aggression forces humankind to a precarious and tragic position of always having to fend off the destructive instincts, which, unleashed, can now destroy not only the individual but the whole planet and the evolutionary triumph of the human brain. Kohut's concept of aggression, if understood and broadly used, can open the door to a new era, not only of individual growth but also of profound group change.

OVERCOMING THE BARRIER OF DIFFERENCE

In the last paper written before his death, Kohut (1982) stressed that a belief in the possibility of intergenerational continuity and mutuality, rather than the inevitable murderous competition alleged to be normal, is a hopeful and essential part of humanness. Consequently, just as we can strive empathically to understand our children, i.e., the next generation, so can we strive empathically to understand other human beings of not only the next generation, but our own generation and all past generations, no matter how different, difficult, or even repugnant.

Acknowledging that other people possess a human brain, that they have unique selves needing empathy and confirmation, can be enough to help us attempt to comprehend what their unmet needs are and how their experience of unresponsive environments renders them helpless and therefore rageful. Our efforts alone to set aside our own fears and anger to try to understand theirs, despite all the differences, can represent a human act involving the civilized strivings of which we are capable.

The human beings who can appreciate Beethoven symphonies and land on the moon certainly have the capacity to halt the threat of nuclear war. If we can only begin to use our tremendous intellectual and emotional resources in converting our assertive energies into empathic efforts, rather than clinging to the primitive reaction of aggression aimed at the destruction of the other who offends, we can arrive at mutual understanding and cooperation with even the most different human beings.

The considerate and creative acceptance of difference may be the key to the achievement of intergenerational continuity and mutuality. And going back to Jaynes' bicameral self, a definitive acceptance of the crucial importance of humankind's self-consciousness may be another viable path for our human development.

How to understand and use the mirroring, idealizing, and twinship transferences that Kohut discovered in treating difficult, narcissistic patients, what his concept of the bipolar and tripolar self involves, how narcissistic rage differs from familiar anger, and how it can be a force for great evil or far-reaching accomplishments—all are explored in the chapters that follow.

We, the authors, both traditionally trained in psychoanalysis and psychotherapy, have used self psychology in treatment and taught its principles for over 10 years. We offer a body of experience, with abundant clinical material showing how self psychology can be used effectively with patients and taught to professionals. One of the most exciting outcomes of self psychology has been that seriously disturbed people not only emerge from their pathology into happier lives but also become capable of making impressive contributions. These contributions can be to the arts, sciences, or business, but most crucially to the philosophy intrinsic to self psychology: that humankind can be a positive, inquiring, creative, energetic force and that this potential is natural to us all.

THE THEORY AND
PRACTICE OF
SELF PSYCHOLOGY

1

An Overview of Basic Self Psychology Concepts

In the Great House, and in the House of Fire,
On the dark night of counting all the years,
On the dark night when months and years are
        numbered—
O let my name be given back to me!
When the Divine One on the Eastern Stairs
Shall cause me to sit down with him in peace,
And every god proclaims his name before me—
Let me remember then the name I bore!

Egyptian Book of the Dead (3500 B.C.)

In finding a way to treat a disorder (pathological narcissism) formerly thought untreatable, the late Heinz Kohut also conceptualized a higher form of healthy narcissism. He found this to be an indispensable element in human creativity of all kinds. He concluded that healthy self-love generates the wisdom that enables us to accept our own limitations, including our mortality. He also attributed to stable self-esteem the capacity for humor, which is, perhaps, a unique gift of the human brain. Finally, he recog-

nized the possibility that infantile grandiosity can be transformed
into a wellspring for all creativity.

A CRY FOR RECOGNITION

At first, let us listen to the cry for recognition of one's self, of
one's unique identity that echoes down from the Egyptian *Book
of the Dead*, dated 3500 B.C. and not too distant in time from
Jaynes' dates for the advent of the conscious self (see Introduction,
p. xvi). The poet, in confronting the mysteries of time and existence and also in looking at the idealized god who is not fully
recognizing the poet, cries out twice about self-recognition problems. At first he or she seems to be somewhat overwhelmed by
the experience of time and its threat to human existence and how
to contend with this. Implicit in the plea, "O let my name be
given back to me!" is some sense that one's unique identity could
help one wrestle with the terrible problems of time and mortality.

The other portion of this ancient poem deals with what one
could consider to be a very early version of Kohut's concept of
the idealizing transference. For example, the poet is allowed to
sit down with the Divine One, but he also intimates that his
identity is threatened when "every god proclaims his name before
me." This suggests rageful hurt over a blow to one's self-esteem
by a presumed mentor who had invited the poet to participate
but had failed by ignoring him. Such an outrage felt by the self
is the very essence of Kohut's approach to self psychology. He
was the first to recognize that a fragmentation of self occurs when
there is an affront to one's self-esteem that is experienced as unmanageable. Therefore, the rage over the disappointment is
turned against the self, with the possible withdrawal from coping
with life that this implies.

SELF-FRAGMENTATION

A fragmentation of the self is the "I am falling apart" feeling
that everyone experiences at some point in life. It ranges from the
mild embarrassment when one forgets the married name of an

old friend one meets unexpectedly in the street and needs to introduce, say, to one's mate, all the way to the excruciating fear and shame of a doctoral candidate who cannot answer a key question on his or her dissertation.

Kohut established clinically in his books and papers (1959, 1966, 1971, 1977, 1979, 1982, 1984) that anxiety-arousing, terrifying, and totally immobilizing fragmentations of the self can occur in any situation that leads to an affront to an individual's self-esteem. This includes the psychotherapeutic situation where the patient's self can especially feel the focus of attack. We can validate, from over 10 years of working with a self psychological approach, that Kohut's experience of the pervasive phenomenon of self-fragmentation was not unique.

We also have encountered the pernicious and often ominous evidence of self-fragmentation in a patient, triggered by such a standard psychotherapeutic intervention as, "Well, how do you feel about that?" in reaction to some personal experience, idea, emotion, or expectation that the patient presents to the therapist. Far from sensing that the therapist is attuned to his or her feelings, the patient may indicate in a personal, characteristic way that his experience of self-fragmentation is leading him to a desire for total noncommunication, to an impulse to switch to another subject, or at the other end of the spectrum, to an angry denunciation of the therapist's stupidity, and sometimes to a quick exit from the session.

What has happened? The self-fragmentation brought on by the therapist's presumably concerned effort to find out more about the patient's feelings in relation to a particular experience demonstrates several of Kohut's basic concepts. In order to understand how this attempt at attuned feedback could fail, let us look at some of Kohut's discoveries.

NO I-YOU IN PRIMARY NARCISSISM

Early on Kohut (1966) stressed that primary narcissism referred to "the psychological state of the infant" (p. 245). This means that a baby's experience of mother and her services is in a world in

which there is no "I-you" difference. Consequently, the baby
expects to control mother in the way that a grown-up expects to
exercise control over his or her own body and mind.

We are now confronted with the existential problem of what
happens when the inevitable occurs, namely, when mother cannot be controlled by baby and may have to keep him or her waiting
for the breast and all the other allied services. As parents, we
know that the baby is rageful when the service is imperfect. But
Kohut, in 1977, did not conceptualize this narcissistic rage as an
expression of the baby's instinctual aggression, as Freud thought.
Instead, Kohut saw the baby's rage as an understandable reaction
of disintegration, the fragmentation of a self encountering an unresponsive environment, e.g., slow mother or even absent mother.

THE GRANDIOSE SELF

But what underlies this narcissistic rage is crucial for later development. On the basis of his successful analytic work with presumably untreatable narcissistic personalities, Kohut delineated
two kinds of narcissistic transferences in which the adult patient
repeats with the analyst what the baby did with imperfect mother
and father. The first solution is for the baby to feel him- or herself
as all-powerful and in charge of the good world. The second
solution is to perceive the other person, presumably one or both
parents, as all-powerful (Kohut, 1971). The feeling of the baby's
total control is similar to that which Mahler et al. (1975) attributes
to the toddler in the practicing subphase when he or she stands
up and walks. This is also Kohut's concept of the grandiose self
with its accompanying narcissistic rage. This rage is elicited by
every disappointment over what is experienced as a recalcitrant
part of the almighty self and, specifically, the imperfect but un-
differentiated mother.

How would this concept of the grandiose self manifest itself in
treatment, together with the narcissistic rage attendant upon the
slightest disappointment in the self? It could, for example, express
itself in an all too often overlooked issue—the shame over needing

treatment, which is certainly experienced as an affront to the unconscious grandiose self wanting to be perfect. An interchange could take place, such as the following excerpt from a supervisory session with a male patient.

Patient: I feel so ashamed and hopeless that I have to spend so much time and money coming for this treatment which, in the end, promises me nothing anyway. I don't see how you've helped me so far, and I don't see why I should need this treatment anyway. Why can't I just manage my own life?

Therapist (seeking to be supportive from an ego-psychological viewpoint): Well, the fact that you are coming here and paying for this treatment suggests that a part of you feels you deserve whatever assistance you can get to achieve a better life.

Patient (because his unconscious grandiosity and narcissistic rage have not been acknowledged): You know, I feel that's a lot of do-goodish jargon. It doesn't deal with the big question of why I should need this crazy treatment at all.

Therapist (if attuned to the self psychological concept of the grandiose self and its rage at any imperfection): Well, I can see how you might resent my suggesting you need assistance because I sense you have always felt you should be able to handle anything demanded of you.

Patient (more surprised than angry): Yeah, well I guess . . . I have always felt I should be able to do anything I wanted to do, although I often wound up doing the superhuman feats others, especially my parents, demanded of me.

Here, the patient is responding to the therapist's empathic recognition of the existence of the unconscious, infantile grandiose self and its endless demands upon the conscious self and ego, together with the masochistic defense against the omnipotent grandiosity, i.e., "I shouldn't demand for myself really, but I must be all-powerful to make them love me by fulfilling their needs." The therapist, instead of focusing on the narrow, reality-based issue that the patient is doing something for him- or herself by coming to therapy, is tuning into the deeper unconscious demands of the grandiose self, which are draining off the energy needed by the conscious ego and whatever exists of the cohesive self to serve the needs of the grandiose self.

The therapist, by moving toward the unconscious grandiose self in an accepting way, is beginning to provide the patient with the mirroring he never received from an indifferent mother. The patient obviously still needs this recognition from a selfobject that would encourage his healthy ambition based on the grandiose self's demands, hopefully modified by experiences with reality which lead to transmuting internalization (see below).

THE IDEALIZED PARENT IMAGO

The second solution to narcissistic rage is for the baby to try to maintain "the original perfection and omnipotence by imbuing the rudimentary you, the adult, with absolute perfection and power" (Kohut, 1966, p. 246). Here, Kohut was describing the early, idealized parent imago which showed an especially close relationship between idealization and narcissistic needs. The idealized qualities that the child so adores in the parent imago become internalized when the parent unavoidably but bearably frustrates the child. These qualities and functions then gradually come to be supplied by the child through transmuting internalization. The experiences of this optimal frustration also help to tame and guide the soaring ambitions of the grandiose self.

The child's need to idealize the parent imago presents itself in treatment, as it does in life, with the question, "Will you be there when I need you? Can I count on your strength and your caring when I feel in despair and helpless?" The child who finds out, all too abruptly and too soon, that he cannot count on mother's idealized strength to be there for him always—for example, mother may be sick, on drugs, or absent—feels he has only himself (i.e., his grandiose self) to count on if there is no other reliable caretaker available.

In treatment, the patient's search for the idealized parent imago is revived, perhaps after a long suspension of belief that he or she could find such an ideal. The therapist, hopefully, can recognize and encourage the "vulnerable tendril of idealization" (Kohut, 1971, p. 221) rather than trample on it again, as the parents did. Such a failure could arise out of either the therapist's counter-transference anxiety about being put on a pedestal or the realistic anxiety that he or she cannot possibly live up to the patient's infantile expectations and is, therefore, bound to disappoint the patient once more.

It is easy for the therapist to overlook the patient's need to feel that his or her idealistic expectations are acceptable, given his or her childhood experience, and above all that the therapist is empathic with those needs. It is in this context that the patient's angry disappointment and anxiety over vacations or even weekend absences can be understood. Consider the following dialogue:

Patient (male or female): Well, the holiday season is approaching, and I suppose you are going to attend that conference in New York and leave me to my own devices for a week.

Therapist: Yes, I had planned to mention it in today's session, as a matter of fact. But you know, you have been able to weather these separations for a couple of years now, so perhaps it won't be as difficult as you expect this year.

Patient: Oh, sure! Well, my parents always took off for the Caribbean or sometimes a conference in Europe, right after Christmas, leaving me and my brother and my dear cousins. I used to dream that they would take a longer time and let me come along or that they would go in the summer with me, instead of shipping me and my brother off to camp. So when they finally got around to inviting me, it was too late. I had my own friends and commitments by then, and I didn't care any more about being with my parents.

Therapist (still focusing on the reality of the patient's improved ability to bear what the therapist regarded as separation anxiety): But wasn't it good that you could develop your own friends and interests and not feel left out by your parents anymore?

Patient: And I guess you're saying I should do the same thing now—develop my own support system and not care when you go on vacations. I have to warn you, though, that when that happens, I stop caring about you or needing what you have to give me, and I'm likely to stop coming, whether you think that I'm ready to leave or not.

Therapist (sensing that his intervention has not had the soothing effect he had hoped and wondering if an idealization issue was involved): I guess you would like me to arrange for you to go with me on this holiday trip, just as you would have liked your parents to have arranged it.

Patient: Well, sure, I think my father could have afforded it at least once. He was a college professor, and it would have been great to go with him and my mother to London at Christmastime. I loved Dickens and English history. I think he could have showed me a lot, taken me to interesting places. I felt sad that he never thought of what fun it would be for both of us—and my brother too.

Therapist (realizing that his empathic approach had brought up a disappointed idealization issue with important self-feelings attached, but also anxious that he might be stirring up an expectation he could not fulfill): Well, for us to have experiences like that. . . . But we can imagine here what it would be like to go to London together.

Patient: Oh, I know it wouldn't be possible. I think I would even feel too self-conscious being with you in a nontherapeutic setting. But I imagine you would be stimulating to walk through London with. I bet you know a lot about English literature.

Therapist (smiling): Well, thank you, that's a nice idea. (Here the therapist lets himself be idealized a bit, with undoubtedly some relief that the patient's grasp of reality is enough to keep him from starting to demand in actuality what the therapist suggested having a fantasy about.)

The important outcome of this therapeutic interchange is the emergence of the patient's repeated experiences of being disillusioned about his father's sensitivity to his needs, e.g., the de-idealization of a parent imago and the patient's expectation that the therapist, in leaving him at a holidaytime, has the same insensitivity. When the patient experienced the therapist's empathy about his sense of being ignored, it became possible to partly satisfy his need for idealizing the therapist as a parent imago through fantasy.

THE NEED FOR MIRRORING

Attuned parental responses to the child's needs include calming, merging, mirroring, nourishing, and stimulating reactions, together with the superior values and ideals that the parental selfobjects represent. All the foregoing were found by Kohut to be internalized as the basis for higher forms of narcissism including creativity, humor, and the positive acceptance of our self-worth and healthy ambition. Kohut (1984) concluded that the dynamic striving for our ambitions and our ideals, as well as our "twinship" longings for someone with whom to share our enthusiasm and feelings, constitutes the human being's three basic choices to realize the tripolar nuclear self (see Chapter 6).

The need to be remembered, noticed, and admired permeates the ancient poem introducing this chapter—"He holdeth fast to the memory of his identity." Kohut (1971) came to believe that this need for positive recognition—namely, to be mirrored—is essential to the development of healthy self-esteem, not only for effective functioning, but also for achieving the higher forms of narcissism so essential to humankind's contributions to civilization. It is still bewildering that this whole area of human needs should have been neglected and demeaned over the centuries, bitingly illustrated in the Oriental proverb, "Praise to the face is a disgrace."

But the clinical findings are mounting that sadism toward the self and the latter's basic need for applause and sensitive responses had its origins in the long-standing historical failure to realize the complex early needs of children and the consequences of unknowingly brutal treatment by parents down through the generations. We have found this sad phenomenon in our own practice, along with Heinz Kohut, Alice Miller, Lloyd de Mause, and an increasing number of psychotherapists who are turning to self psychology to understand the grim consequences of un-attuned parenting and what can be done to redirect pathology into healthy development.

THE NEED FOR EMPATHY

Kohut's fresh emphasis on the concept of "experience-near em-pathy" (1959, 1982), with which he launched his exploration of self psychology, was also his final message in his last paper. It is the absence of empathy with the growing child's needs for attuned responses that has made possible the tyranny and human destructiveness of which we are so painfully aware (see Chapter 9). As an information-collecting, data-gathering activity, Kohut (1982) proposed that empathy is a necessary precondition to being successfully attuned and is therapeutic. He stressed that if a mother's reactions to her child are to be experienced as respon-sive, empathy must guide her. He then went on to emphasize that in clinical experiences "empathy *per se*, the mere presence of empathy, has also a beneficial, in a broad sense a therapeutic effect—both in the clinical setting and in human life in general" (p. 397).

Kohut's clinical work with empathy in relation to "untreatable" narcissistic personalities led him to the possibility of a different way of looking at human development. This involved a cohesive self with stable self-esteem, rooted in tamed grandiosity and re-liable ideals, and focused on the joyful experience of development including sexual longings and the possibility of an empathic pa-rental acceptance of the sexual, competitive child of the oedipal period.

THE SELFOBJECT

Empathy and the joyful experience of good-enough parenting bring us to another basic concept of self psychology—the selfobject. The new term, selfobject (i.e., without a hyphen) is designed to denote a newly conceptualized view of a relationship between a self and an object (i.e., another person) where there is either a total or a partial lack of differentiation of the self from the other. As Ornstein (1978a) describes it, ". . . such an object is related to only in terms of the specific phase-appropriate needs of the developing self, without recognition of the separateness of the object and its own center of initiative" (p. 60).

Clearly, if a child is fortunate enough to have a reliable, loving selfobject in the mothering person, who is able to provide the mirroring essential for the child's self-acceptance of healthy ambition, then problems of fragile self-esteem and pathological narcissism are not so likely to arise. However, there can be a grave problem if one or both parents also prove unworthy of idealization, which involves Kohut's earlier concept of the second chance offered by the bipolar self, that is, ideals in addition to or instead of ambition.

What the psychotherapist is offering to the patient is a second chance to believe in and then to internalize a good, reliable selfobject which the patient never had. This may become a major area of conflict in the treatment and one of the most disheartening countertransference feelings for the therapist, i.e., that he or she has not had any effect at all. However, if the therapist reviews how the patient was at the start of treatment and how the patient is now, quite often the therapist may be very heartened at how much progress has actually occurred.

It is important, then, to remember that the patient may be fighting off any awareness of dependency on the therapist because this is the line over which the patient is unconsciously determined not to step.

THE NEGATIVE THERAPEUTIC REACTION

Self psychology has discovered that the formidable "negative therapeutic reaction" (Freud, 1923a/1961) may often be a self-protective defense against another disillusionment by a hoped-for selfobject, a disillusionment that the patient is convinced will bring on an irreversible fragmentation of his vulnerable self (Brandschaft, 1983).

The therapist who empathically realizes this terror will not feel a terrible transferential rejection or hopelessness at the patient's understandable dread at trusting once again. He or she will be able, patiently and delicately, to provide the empathic understanding of the patient's narcissistic rage. Through such empathy with the patient's rage and the cataclysmic terror of abandonment underlying it, the capacity to trust and, thereby, to depend on the analyst as a reliable selfobject can grow. So, as Brandschaft discovered, Kohut's approach can offer a real possibility for a developmental way out of the tragic impasse of the negative therapeutic reaction (see Chapter 8).

AGGRESSION AS A DISINTEGRATION PRODUCT

Kohut (1977) not only saw the traditionally rejected self-love, (i.e., narcissism) as the soil from which higher forms of narcissism spring, such as creativity, humor, and the acceptance of mortality; he also proposed that human aggression was not an innate instinct but a disintegration product of a nonresponsive environment.

Just as the child needs enough oxygen to breathe freely, so he or she also needs an empathic milieu of a responsive selfobject. An injury to the self is always involved when destructive rage is aroused, especially narcissistic rage. This arises from an affront to the infantile grandiose self, which expects to exercise complete control over a presumably responsive environment (e.g., mother) only to find her unempathic and even threatening to the self's basic needs.

The child then experiences the urge to destroy the failing selfobject. However, his rage, arousing counteraggression from mother, may be turned back on himself, leading to self-loathing and despair, which may very well lead to compulsive masochism. This outcome, so destructive to the development of healthy self and object relations, can unfortunately recur in psychotherapy when the patient experiences empathic failures by the therapist. This may be in the form of interpretations that are experienced as criticism and therefore as blows to both self-esteem and the unconscious grandiose self. Self-loathing and despair can also recur if the therapist reacts to the patient's aggression as an *unwarranted* reaction and becomes defensive.

CASE VIGNETTE

The following clinical vignette from a supervised case shows how a self psychological approach to a patient's aggression changes the therapeutic relationship. Early in treatment, Hilda K., an attractive woman in her thirties, with professional and sexual problems of incapacitating indecision, expressed disappointment that the female therapist had forgotten a fact about Hilda's half sister mentioned in the previous session. This patient's annoyance over the therapist's memory lapse so early in treatment made the therapist think that Hilda might expect perfection from her in terms of remembering every detail. Trained in drive theory and inexperienced in self psychology, the therapist also assumed that this "unrealistic" expectation was a narcissistic demand for attention and a defense against Hilda's repressed anger at not always being the center of attention.

This assumption seemed to be corroborated by the fact that the detail the therapist had forgotten was the specific disease —rheumatic fever—that had made the half sister an invalid from the age of three until she died at age 15. The therapist had attached little importance to the disease itself, again assuming that Hilda *must* have been angry at the little intruder who became the center of attention. Presumably, the therapist thought, Hilda had defended herself against her jealous rage by a reaction formation of overconcern. From a self psychological viewpoint, the therapist would be much more concerned about the state of the patient's self-esteem and the possibility of developing a selfobject transference than about the patient's aggression toward her half sister.

Therefore, the therapist had said to Hilda: "You're angry that I don't seem to give you all the attention you feel you deserve." This interpretation certainly took account of the patient's obviously vulnerable self-esteem, and presumably the compulsive need for perfect attention in order to shore up her sagging self. But the interpretation also sounded like a criticism for wanting too much attention, like an unreasonable, hungry child. At any rate, this is how Hilda reacted to it. She did not openly deal with the therapist's interpretation but complained about her boy-friend's insensitivity to her feelings, especially in regard to flirting openly with other women.

No Clear Reaction to an Interpretation

The therapist might have focused on Hilda's failure to react specifically to her interpretation and Hilda's changing of the subject as a *transference reaction* to what the patient experienced as the therapist's *lack of empathy* in continuing to criticize her on the very delicate and complex issue of self-esteem. However, it was early in treatment, and the therapist decided to defer getting into the transference until a little later when there would be more clear-cut material on transference feelings, especially in regard to Hilda's anger at all women. Meanwhile, the patient canceled the following session and had not paid her bill.

In the supervisory session, the therapist was advised to go back to the interpretation she had made and to suggest that perhaps Hilda was upset about it so that possibly this was reflected in her missing the next session. The therapist was also asked to apologize to the patient, in the event that Hilda had thought the therapist was being critical of her in regard to wanting attention. It turned out that Hilda was able to say, with deep feeling, that she had felt hurt and misunderstood by the therapist's suggestion that she became angry over not getting enough attention. Hilda stressed that in fact she was angry and hurt because her half sister had been the most important person in her life until she died at age 15 and that everybody else had neglected the half sister. And here the therapist was doing the same thing. In this way one of the most important aspects of Hilda's self problem, her anger at not being listened to with respect, came out early in treatment.

Some Difficulties with a Self Psychology Approach

The therapist's empathic exploration of Hilda's anger helped her eventually to trust the therapist to the point that therapy became possible. Until that time, she had not been able to trust any woman. So the therapist's capacity to look at anger from the self psychological standpoint and to turn a criticism into an empathic exploration helped therapy to continue.

How did the therapist herself react to the supervisor's suggestion to try to clarify with the patient why the interpretation about the patient's anger at the inattentive therapist was experienced as criticism? We touch here upon some of the difficulties of using a self psychological approach from the therapist's point of view. Self psychology, as we have begun to indicate, requires a more intensive monitoring of the specific effects of a particular interpretation, especially with regard to the positive or negative impact on the patient's self-esteem.

In the example given, the therapist assumed that the patient's anger at the therapist was a traditional transference reaction, displacing onto the therapist her infantile anger at being forgotten about because of the sick, intruding half sister. However, upon exploration, it turned out that the patient felt misunderstood, not heard, just as she had been ignored by her parents when she tried to make them more concerned about her half sister's chronic illness. So her anger was one of indignation and disappointment at the failure of the parents she needed to idealize and trust, just as she needed to idealize and trust the therapist if she were to internalize the therapist as the really caring selfobject she never had.

However, this kind of delicate delineation and understanding of the patient's complex feelings cannot be achieved if the therapist brushes aside the patient's negative reactions as the "resistance" that has to be "worked through." True, in this instance, the patient did become resistant, i.e., anxious and angry over *again* not being listened to so that she mistrusted the therapist upon whom she needed to depend.

But it is to prevent this kind of impasse, which has produced therapeutic failures where there might have been successes, that self psychology calls upon the therapist continually to ponder the impact of his or her intervention and to explore this impact if it seems to have distanced the patient. The therapist is also called upon to set aside interpretive approaches that make the patient feel misunderstood and might trigger dangerous regression. This involves the therapist's admission that his or her interpretation or sometimes what is experienced as a moralistic attitude is off the track in the sense that it makes the patient feel accused rather than empathically understood. As we shall see in the following chapters, the process of self psychology can be a searching and regenerative process for the therapist as well as the patient.

2

Aggression from a Self Psychological Viewpoint

This chapter will focus on the exciting, regenerative implications, both for individual development and for civilization's survival, of Kohut's concept of human aggression as a disintegration product of an unresponsive environment. This approach relieves humankind of the impossible burden of an inborn destructive drive, which has always been conceptualized as demanding a senseless discharge, and now threatens the very existence of the planet, through a nuclear war over the basic differences among people.

Everyone is, in some sense, different because each person has different life experiences (Atwood & Stolorow, 1984). Mature object relations require the acceptance of differences in others, including those we love. Not least among the offending differences can be the other person's capacity for independent initiative, which may leave us feeling ignored or not understood.

We are so accustomed to the idea that the human infant comes into the world with his or her aggression ready to go off like a loaded gun that we often don't consider the possibility of aggression being a reaction to a provocation rather than an inevitable discharge. This is particularly true of the psychotherapeutic situation where we may easily assume that a patient's angry outburst or sullen silence arises from infantile demands that no longer can

19

be fulfilled. While it is our unenviable task to help a patient eventually tone down his aggression, before Kohut it was not likely
we would consider the patient's "resistive" aggression as an appropriate reaction to our probing scalpel.

AGGRESSION AGAINST UNATTUNEMENT

Yet Kohut placed the responsibility for the triggering of aggression on the limitations of parents or substitute selfobjects (psychotherapists, for example). He said that "man's destructiveness
as a psychological phenomenon is secondary . . . and that destructive rage, in particular, is always motivated by an injury to
the self" (1977, p. 116).

The patient's angry reaction to therapeutic probing, so often
dismissed as "resistance" by the therapist, is generally experienced by the patient as the therapist's empathic failure. After all,
whether the therapist is being idealized or is unconsciously regarded as an obedient part of the patient's self (like his hand, for
example), in either case the therapist should *know* how the patient
is feeling and not have to ask!

We can imagine what a baby feels if his mother insists on forcing
the bottle into his mouth when he really is nauseous. This could
be the same despairing feeling of psychic abandonment that a
patient feels when a therapist does not say hello when the patient
comes into the office. For the therapist, then, to interpret the
patient's despair as anxiety over sexual feelings toward the therapist will certainly inflict a narcissistic injury upon the patient's
self that can trigger more rage against the treatment per se.

But this kind of empathic failure can also lead to a negative
transference reaction. In the preceding example of the baby who
is force fed, the initial reaction involved an injury to the cohesion
of the self, especially if it proved to the child how unattuned his
or her selfobjects were to his feelings. What the child needs from
his or her selfobjects, in terms of mirroring his ambitions and
achievements and in terms of being an omnipotent ideal, becomes
a guideline for how the psychotherapist can become a good selfobject to the patient, a second chance or a "new edition" of self-

object experience, as Kohut put it (1971, 1977). Hedges (1983) notes that "the working through of selfobject transference involved 'picking up where the original selfobject left off.' Classical working through is not considered a new edition but rather is thought to involve the attainment of insight through interpretation" (p. 66).

THE SELFOBJECT MODEL FOR PSYCHOTHERAPY

If aggression is no longer to be regarded as an innate drive, then how does a self psychologist deal with a patient's aggression? Drawing upon Kohut's concept of a selfobject sensitively attuned to another's empathic needs, we can hope that the therapist, presumably having arrived at psychological maturity, can assess the patient's needs. Like an empathic parent, the therapist can then welcome the patient into the therapist's psychological structures. In this way, a patient's homeostatic imbalance can be relieved, just as a parent can relieve a child's emotional upset.

Kohut noted that including the child into the selfobject's own psychological organization is of the greatest significance since it helps the child to "consolidate his nuclear self" through "transmuting internalization," as we described in Chapter 1. The idea that the mother tames the child's aggression by neutralizing it through love is not as accurate as saying that the baby's anxiety and his anger, arising from his sense of the disintegration of the former, more complex psychological unit of unquestioning assertiveness, have touched off unempathic resonances within the mothering person. Therapists also need to guard themselves against unempathic reactions which may be triggered by difficult patients (Weiner & White, in press).

HOW AGGRESSION DISAPPEARS

Perhaps a therapist can usefully bear in mind, as a prototype of the empathic selfobject, the way a calm mother can soothe a child. "The child experiences the feeling states of the selfobject

. . . as if they were his own" (Kohut, 1977, p. 86). Thus, the child's mounting anxiety, whatever touches it off is followed by a signal of stabilized mild anxiety and then by calmness and the selfobject's absence of anxiety. The psychological disintegration products the child has started feeling now disappear through merger with the empathic calmness of the mothering person.

Kohut believed that mild empathic failures of marked discrepancies between empathic resonance and actual need satisfaction were not psychologically harmful and could foster transmuting internalization of the selfobject so long as the selfobjects react to the child with "a full range of undistorted empathic responses" (1977, p. 87).

However, if the selfobject's empathy is too dull or absent or, worse still, if the selfobject panics and reacts with hypochondriacal, manic, depressive, or other rejecting responses, then the child not only misses the needed wholesome merger, but also is either drawn into a noxious one or tries to escape by walling himself off from the threatening selfobject. Kohut (1977) concluded that the outcome in all these cases is either a failure to develop reliable tension-regulating structures for the taming of affects including anxiety, or the growth of faulty structures, e.g., the tendency to overreact affectively, including the development of panic states.

HEALTHY ASSERTIONS

If aggression is a disintegration product of an unresponsive environment, and empathy with the disintegration experience or the lack of fulfillment is the most effective way to restore constructive calmness, then what happens to constructive aggression, first proposed by Hartmann, Kris, and Loewenstein (1949) and later developed by Erikson as the concept of "aggressivity" (Blanck & Blanck, 1974, p. 351)? Kohut also dealt with this potentiality, describing it as "the preceding broader and more complex psychological unit of unquestioning assertiveness" (1977, p. 87). Kohut saw this assertiveness as a part of the primary psychological configuration that constituted the experiencing of the connection between the self and the empathic selfobject.

The senior author, in a lecture* on *The Restoration of the Self* (Kohut, 1977) said:

> Nondestructive aggressiveness is seen as being there from the start, in the service of establishing and maintaining a rudimentary self—the nuclear self. . . . This healthy assertiveness, as it can be termed, is mobilized by optimal frustrations, i.e., nontraumatic delays in responsiveness by the selfobject. This normal assertiveness subsides when the goals striven for are reached.

Gunther (1980) distinguishes Kohut's concept of assertiveness from aggression by defining assertiveness in regard to one's general self goals as a kind of "elementary building block" (p. 186). This approach conceives of assertiveness as an innate urge toward action, without specific aims. Assertiveness, therefore, is seen as basic to any action of a cohesive self.

SCIENCE SHOWS NO AGGRESSIVE DRIVE

Science has made significant advances since Freud first indicated the lack of reliable information on human instincts. Basch (1984) reminds us that biology, ethology, cybernetics, and control theory, none of which was developed in Freud's day, now permit us to reevaluate Freud's speculations.

Basch points out that cybernetics and control theory have replaced Freud's "mechanistic discharge theories" as ways of explaining the ups and downs of the behavior of living systems. Basch goes on to say:

> . . . The notion that the motives for or the meaning of thought and behavior depend upon an energic force of libidinal or aggressive nature, in neutral or unneutralized form, has been repeatedly and tellingly rejected by biologists, neurophysiologists, and physicists, as documented in the

---

*Presented at the 1984 Lecture Series of the Society for the Advancement of Self Psychology, April 14, 1984, New York, N.Y.

psychoanalytic literature by Kubie (1963), Holt (1965), Rosenblatt and Thickstun (1970), Peterfreund (1971), and others (Basch, 1984, p. 30).

THE TREATMENT SITUATION

All that has been said thus far about adequate or inadequate empathy from the selfobject, of course, applies to the treatment situation where, hopefully, the therapist is working toward eventual internalization of himself or herself, either as an attuned selfobject in the self psychological approach or as a benign superego from the standpoint of the traditional psychoanalytic approach. In either case, the therapist is likely to feel that he or she is often walking a tightrope in relation to the patient's aggression and especially with respect to narcissistic rage, which we will discuss later. But to handle aggression as a disintegration product in relation to an unresponsive environment rather than as an innate drive demanding discharge poses a new problem for psychotherapists, whether narcissistic rage is involved or not.

CASE VIGNETTE

We present below a case where the treatment problem was whether to focus on what appeared to be a need to discharge innate aggression, from the instinctual drive standpoint (Hartmann, Kris, & Loewenstein, 1949), or to use Kohut's empathic approach, including trying to decipher the meaning of a traumatic situation for a patient. We shall now continue with the case of Hilda K., cited in Chapter 1 as an example of how a therapist's confrontational approach to a patient's anger almost drove the patient away. Because of the complex issues involved, we will recap some of the details already presented. The therapist had assumed that Hilda's anger at the therapist's inattention in regard to Hilda's half sister's early illness indicated a demand to always be the center of attention, unrealistic expectations of the therapist's impeccable memory, and a reaction formation against Hilda's own jealous rage against the younger sibling intruder. So the therapist had told Hilda she was angry at the therapist's not giving her all the attention Hilda felt she deserved. Hilda had reacted to this very early transference interpretation as if she was being criticized for wanting too much attention, like a naughty demanding child. It proved to be characteristic of Hilda that she did not verbalize these angry feelings to the therapist but complained about her lover's insensitivity to her feelings. However, she missed her next session and did not pay her bill.

The therapist was helped, in supervision, to apologize to Hilda at the next session, for what may have seemed like a critical interpretation. Hilda acknowledged that she was hurt by the therapist's suggestion that not getting attention would anger Hilda. She emphasized that her half sister had been important in her life until she died at 15 and that everybody else had neglected the sick little girl, and ironically, her therapist now seemed to be doing the same thing. In this way, one of Hilda's most important self-esteem problems, her angry disintegration at not being listened to, came out early in treatment.

The fact that supervision with a self psychological focus had helped the therapist to clear up an empathy failure on her part that almost led to the patient's departure does not mean that similar breaches of understanding on the therapist's part did not recur often enough to make the treatment a very demanding experience for the therapist. She sometimes fell into the trap of assuming that the patient's aggression, either verbalized or acted out, was a discharge through the transference of the intense aggression Hilda had felt in her deprived, unhappy childhood. It was necessary, again and again, in supervision, to help the therapist consider whether the patient's aggression was a disintegration product arising from an unresponsive environment, as Kohut proposed. The therapist in this case would be the unresponsive environment, triggering the aggression by somehow not comprehending what the patient was feeling and responding to it empathically enough.

A Pull to the Oedipal Interpretation

A major problem was the familiar one of the therapist's prior training in traditional psychoanalysis and ego psychology. Although the therapist was very interested in self psychology, she almost involuntarily slipped into perceiving the patient's problems in familiar Freudian terms. Hilda was 35, dark-haired, slender, attractive, and single. At the outset, she seemed to present a classical picture of mixed neurosis with sadomasochistic tendencies, obsessive work problems, and hysterical seductiveness. Previous treatment with another therapist had not helped Hilda to resolve her ambivalence of several years toward her boyfriend who was equally uncertain about wanting marriage or separation. Her doctoral dissertation in biology also seemed to be as up in the air as her relationship with her lover. Yet Hilda had obtained her B.A. and M.A. in a demanding field and was holding down a difficult though not sufficiently remunerative job.

While recognizing Hilda's fragile self-esteem and her rage at not having her infantile need for empathic attention understood, the therapist found herself often focusing on the sadomasochistic power struggles Hilda had with men in sexual relationships and with her advisers over her thesis. This seemed to be a regressive defense against traditional hysterical anxiety over marriage involving an unresolved oedipal complex. Hilda's preoedipal history, however, was so traumatic that her therapist found it increasingly difficult to focus on Hilda's ambivalent transference reactions as an expression of unconscious oedipal competition. Given this possibility, the therapist would unconsciously represent to the patient her mother as a rival for her father.

Hilda's mother had died of heart failure when Hilda was two. Her father—a cold, critical man—had then left her with an unloving foster family for a year, as she found out later. At three, she was brought to a new home with her father and her stepmother, who was always a rather shadowy figure. Her stepmother soon became pregnant and Hilda's half sister, Wendy, arrived when Hilda was about four. Hilda recalled little about her feelings over Wendy's arrival but remembered how upset she was when Wendy showed more and more signs of chronic illness, e.g., in her mobility problems, social withdrawal, and taking frequently to her bed.

The Grandiose Nurse

Hilda apparently became a "nervous Nellie," a little mother toward Wendy, accusing her father and stepmother of neglecting the difficult, ailing child and of not loving her enough. Since Wendy was later diagnosed to have rheumatic fever, the therapist assumed that Hilda had been right, that the parents, for whatever reason, had shrugged off Wendy's serious condition, hoping she would "grow out of it." It would have been easy for the therapist to confront Hilda with the possibility that her hovering concern over Wendy was a defensive denial of Hilda's rage at no longer being the center of attention.

However, in trying to understand and empathize with Hilda's feelings in supervision, the therapist came to realize that Hilda was gradually daring to trust the therapist with an important secret, namely, that it was only through her caring for her half sister that she had been able to have any positive feelings about herself. Inevitably she had experienced terrible helplessness and unlovability at age two when her mother dropped dead of heart failure, coupled with the lack of attuned caring she experienced with the foster family, her own father, and her stepmother. In caring for her half sister and demanding recognition of her serious illness, Hilda was unconsciously fulfilling some of the demands of her infantile grandiose self who felt frightened and ashamed when she could not save her mother's life. But with her half sister, Hilda felt she had another chance to prove to herself (and therefore to others) that she was not only lovable but all-powerful.

By coming to understand the self-sustaining aspects of the grandiose self, the therapist was slowly able to empathize and to help Hilda empathize with the full meaning of her relationship with her half sister. It was through this empathy that the therapist was able to encourage and support Hilda's physical and psychological emergence from the self-sufficiency by which she had kept lovers and friends—all good selfobjects—at a distance, including the therapist. The full emergence of this capacity to trust and depend upon another human being as a necessary prelude to full self- and object-love came when the therapist tried to understand some of Hilda's feelings about the death of her half sister.

Hilda reported that Wendy died from rheumatic fever when she was 15 and Hilda, 17. She added, rather offhandedly, that she was regarded as being very close to her half sister, caring for her as if Hilda were her own mother. But after the half sister died, Hilda said she was criticized for hardly ever speaking of Wendy. When the therapist, genuinely puzzled, asked Hilda what she thought might be involved in her silence about Wendy after her death, the truth began to surface.

The Patient Becomes Evasive

Hilda immediately became evasive and said she didn't remember what she felt. Recalling Hilda's similar evasiveness about her feelings in regard to the therapist's summer vacation during the first year of treatment, the therapist suggested that to let herself be aware of any feelings about needing anyone, including Wendy after she died, would confront Hilda with reexperiencing some of the terrible panic and helplessness she had known as a child after her mother's death.

In the session following this interpretation, Hilda brought in the following dream, which she had had the night after the session:

> I had left your office after a session and instead of going to my apartment, I suddenly found myself in a plane taking off for Europe. The plane began to lurch and the stewardess, obviously frightened and looking as if she might faint, told everybody to get the parachutes under the seat, that the plane might crash. I jumped out of my seat and rushed forward to where the pilot was sitting hunched over the controls as if he were sick or dead. I pushed him out of the way, took over the controls, and brought the plane safely back to Kennedy airport. Both the stewardess and the pilot recovered and embraced me warmly, and I was applauded as a heroine.

The therapist thought this was a remarkably undefended dream of wished-for grandiosity combined with a rescue fantasy. Hilda's own fear of dependence, which the therapist's interpretation in the session that day had obviously pushed into her preconscious, had been projected upon the stewardess, frightened and fainting at the prospect that the plane upon which they all depended might crash. The pilot, too, presumably representing Hilda's early disillusionment with her indifferent, abandoning father who could not provide her with values stable enough to serve as a strong direction-giver (Kohut, 1977), had to be replaced by her grandiose self who would finally win applause for her daring and heroic rescue feat.

These possibilities seemed present in the manifest dream content. But the therapist had given Hilda an interpretation at the previous session, directly linking Hilda's terror over her mother's death and her father's leaving her with strangers to the defensive denial of any feelings after Wendy's death. What could this dream be saying about fears of dependency and disillusionment, not only about the therapist—for example, Hilda leaves the therapist's office at the beginning of the dream, but also about later childhood experiences involving these painful feelings?

A Frightening Plane Trip

Hilda's first associations were to the stewardess being frightened and fainting, which reminded her of how "frightened to death" she was when she took her first plane trip. She did not elaborate but went on to stress how wonderful she felt in the dream about being able to prevent the crash. The therapist thought, as she later reported in supervision, that there might be some special anxiety connected with her first plane trip, which Hilda defended against by a regression to infantile grandiosity.

The therapist asked for further associations to her first plane trip. At first, Hilda said she didn't have any. Recalling that the child at the grandiose level of development needs mirroring, that is, some kind of responsive attention (Kohut, 1971), the therapist decided to disregard what could be the patient's defensive resistance and asked her what had frightened her on that first plane trip. Hilda hesitated and then said slowly, "I thought I wouldn't make it." The therapist said, "You mean you were afraid you would crash?" Hilda replied, "I guess everybody is afraid of that, especially on the first trip. But what I was really worried about was that I wouldn't get back in time." She paused and smiled wistfully, adding, "I don't know what else to talk about," as she often did. Clearly, her resistance was quite strong. The therapist then remembered how much encouragement she had needed in treatment for the verbal expression of positive feelings connected with her self, and yet in the dream she was basking in narcissistic grandiosity. Perhaps, the therapist thought, the omnipotent wishes included a hope that the therapist could read her mind so Hilda wouldn't have to put anxiety-arousing feelings into words. Recalling also that her interpretation before the dream had connected anxiety about Wendy with early parental losses, the therapist thought there might be a childhood memory embedded in the dream. So the therapist continued: "I imagine it would have felt wonderful if you could have flown that plane yourself to get it there on time."

Hilda's face lit up briefly and then she said grimly, "It was too late even before I got on the plane. They didn't call me at camp until she'd been sick for two days." The therapist assumed that Hilda was alluding to Wendy's last illness, which had occurred when Hilda was 17 and at a time when she could have been in summer camp as a counselor. If this were the childhood memory alluded to in the dream, then it probably involved a regression to an omnipotent rescue fantasy that she had had, not only in connection with her mother's sudden death but all through her childhood as she mothered and nursed Wendy. Although Hilda had not directly connected Wendy with that first plane trip, the therapist, in the interest of empathy, decided not to ask who "she" was but simply to assume it was Wendy. She figured that to be wrong would be more bearable for Hilda than to have the therapist seem completely unattuned at this point. So the therapist said, "You were away at camp when Wendy got so sick?"

"Yes," Hilda said harshly. "Those goddamn fools—they couldn't face how sick she was. They couldn't admit that she needed me until. . . ." Her voice faded away and the therapist finished the thought with, ". . . until it was too late." She nodded, pounded the arm of her chair, and almost snarled, "If only they had called me the day before, I could have gotten to her sooner and I might have. . . ." She could not continue; she appeared to be choking with anger. Again, in order to preserve whatever selfobject connection she had with the therapist through the telling of this terrible experience, the therapist finished her thought, "You believed you could have saved her." Hilda looked suddenly embarrassed, her eyes filled with tears, and she started to cry soundlessly, as perhaps she had been forced to cry without making any noise as a lonely, motherless toddler.

The Pain of Helplessness

At last some of the pain over her helplessness was surfacing. The therapist said softly, recognizing the developmental need both for mirroring missed in the past and for empathy: "It's wonderful that you could love her so much." Here the therapist sought to accept the verbalized, acknowledged grandiosity and to connect it with her lifelong yearning to be loved in the way that she had tried to love Wendy by providing the total responsiveness Hilda had never known. Hilda's need to express her love for Wendy had also been complicated by her father's disapproval because of his own possessiveness toward Hilda. Sick little Wendy offended his narcissism. Hilda was, therefore, enraged at his final interference in not telling her soon enough about Wendy's illness so that Hilda, in her grandiose fantasies, could have saved the girl's life at the last moment with her love.

When the therapist said how wonderful it was that Hilda could love Wendy so much, Hilda stopped crying and said thoughtfully, softly, "She was the only person I've ever felt really close to. It wasn't only that she was as vulnerable and hypersensitive as I was . . . and still am. She was bright and could share some of my interests, even though she was younger. I would read to her —novels, poetry, even Shakespeare. It seemed to make her feel better physically and it helped her in school. She missed a lot of school because of rheumatic fever but she graduated with honors from elementary school and would have gone on to high school that fall if. . . ." She sobbed deeply, then added, ". . . if she hadn't died that summer. I couldn't talk about her afterwards because I couldn't tell anyone, especially my family, what Wendy meant to me."

A Twinship Relationship

The therapist, thinking that Hilda's relationship with Wendy could have been like a "twinship" selfobject relationship (see p. 103), said: "I guess it felt like losing part of yourself." Hilda nodded, crying soundlessly again. "Yes," she said when she was able to speak. "She was like a twin, like me in many ways, except I was the stronger physically. But she had a great spirit in spite of her sickness and a mind hungry for knowledge and beauty. Our parents didn't understand her any more than they understood me, and they never tried to. That was why we needed each other so much. Because no one else around us even tried to understand what we were feeling, let alone what we needed! I didn't want to go to camp as a counselor that summer but my father said I had to earn money that way or I couldn't go back to high school for my senior year. And I felt I had to be in high school to look after Wendy during her first year there. After she died, nothing seemed to matter. In a way, I've just been going through the motions ever since, doing what seems to be expected, in my work and even in relationships with men."

The therapist realized that a combination of grandiosity, narcissistic rage against herself for Wendy's loss, and long-delayed mourning had prevented Hilda from being able to look for a good selfobject relationship, like the twinship she had had with Wendy. It was this complex of disintegration feelings that barred the way to Hilda's spontaneous development of a second cohesive self, given an appropriately responsive human environment. Recognizing that she had to accept the far-reaching implications of Wendy's love and loss for Hilda and empathize with the difficulty of trying to find another "twin" rather than to challenge whether it was really a mature objective, the therapist said gently, "Life must have seemed so empty for you since you lost her."

In focusing on the loss of Wendy, the therapist was trying to be attuned to Hilda's conviction, now becoming conscious, that she could have and should have saved Wendy's life either by not going to camp, by intuitively knowing that she was sick and returning, or at least by making the plane go faster, by taking over the controls, as in the dream. The therapist also wanted to convey subtly that insofar as she could, she would try to be a selfobject "twin" for Hilda, sharing her enthusiasm and her disappointments, even if the therapist could not always fully resonate with the content. With a renewed hope that such a sharing and reciprocity, as the basis of a twinship selfobject relationship might be found again, Hilda's considerable talents could begin to function better in the context of a developing cohesive self.

A Pivotal Session

From a supervisory standpoint, this session seemed pivotal in the development of a stable, selfobject transference which more and more assumed the characteristics of a twinship relationship (see Chapter 6). There was this important difference, however. As Hilda realized she could find some of the empathic and enthusiastic responses to her feelings and interests from the therapist, she was able to take more chances in exploring what some other people had to offer, including men, and begin to find that other people could be responsive to her, even though they were not exactly like her. This is not to say that the going was easy. She still withdrew whenever she felt criticized or overlooked, especially in social situations, and her aggression toward the unresponsive environment made it difficult for her to fight back or try again. She made considerable progress on this score with her doctoral thesis and finally obtained it about a year after the "pivotal" session. It seemed that Kohut's concept of healthy assertiveness (1977) was more accessible to Hilda in arguing for the validity of her ideas than in trying to win acceptance of herself as a person worthy of respect and love. However, she is no longer immobilized by her infantile grandiosity, self-rage, unresolved mourning, and ambivalence about the feasibility of any project she, the doomed one, might undertake.

It seems very clear from this vantage point that if the therapist had pursued the tack of confronting Hilda's aggression over not receiving the perfect attention and understanding she longed for but didn't expect (her narcissistic needs), Hilda would have left treatment shortly after the first "confrontation." Or she would have gone through it as another futile exercise, with the empty triumph of having defeated the therapist through a negative therapeutic reaction. However, given the therapist's ability to take a self psychological approach in empathizing with Hilda's "unrealistic aggression," a desperately needed selfobject transference could be developed, thus giving Hilda a real second chance to develop a cohesive self.

3

Empathy and the Selfobject

A situation in which we are listened to by another seemingly sensitive human being who is seeking to understand us and explain us to ourselves is a situation that offers us "the most crucial emotional experience for human psychological survival and growth: the attention of a selfobject milieu" (Kohut, 1984, p. 37).

As we noted in the first chapter, Kohut, in the last paper before his death (1982), said, "I must now, unfortunately, add that empathy per se, the mere presence of empathy, has also a beneficial, in a broad sense, a therapeutic effect—both in the clinical setting and in human life, in general" (p. 397). In his use of the term "unfortunately," Kohut expressed the struggle between his wish to be the pure, detached scientist and his own cumulative proof that the empathic observer affects the very situation he or she is trying to understand.

THE INFLUENTIAL OBSERVER

In the 19th century, total objectivity was the major ideal of psychoanalysis, involving the separation of the influence of the observer from the observed, especially in relation to countertransference. However, the 20th century has not only brought us, from the physicist's standpoint, the profound insight into the important effect of the observer upon the observed in any situation; it has

35

also brought us increasingly profound and illuminating insights into the effects of loving and unloving parenting upon the expanding or stultified growth of children. We are including here such psychoanalytic theorists as Anna Freud, Heinz Hartmann, Erik Erikson, Margaret Mahler, Edith Jacobson, René Spitz, Anna Ornstein, Alice Miller, Louis Sander, Marion Tolpin, John Mack, Joseph Lichtenberg, and T. Barry Brazelton.

Nevertheless, it was Kohut who turned the searchlight on the lifelong importance of the child's nuclear self and how it is responded to by the baby's human environment in a situation where the human responsiveness is as essential as oxygen to the sustaining of life. It is this metaphor that highlights the importance of the selfobject as the source of self-sustaining emotional oxygen involving a recognition of the baby's needs. For the mother, hopefully, the task is not too difficult if she can recognize what her baby needs at a particular moment and respond to it appropriately, whether it is to play, cuddle, nurse, or calm the baby's fears.

In self psychology, when the term selfobject is used, this means that the therapist ultimately has the task of trying to become the good selfobject to a patient whose impaired self indicates the deficiencies of his original selfobjects. Therefore, if the therapist accepts this requirement, it means that he or she will have to empathically try to understand where the adult patient failed to receive the emotional oxygen he or she needed to develop a healthy self and how a strange adult, the therapist, can begin to fulfill this void.

TO EMPATHIZE OR NOT TO EMPATHIZE

Most therapists, in our view, would prefer to think of themselves as empathic, even though "empathy" might be modified to "no gratification." On the other hand, the patient either seems in danger of insatiably wanting more and more gratification, owing to original deprivation, or, conversely, needs to learn to tolerate frustration because he was given too much. In either of these cases, the therapist can be in a quandary about how much and what kind of, if any, empathy he should give to the patient. However, leaving aside these usual indecisive soliloquies of the therapist who is less committed to empathy than to exploring the unconscious, let us consider the therapist who is really concerned about empathic self psychology.

Here is a supervisory case of a therapist experienced in and disposed toward being empathic who is treating a very depressed woman. This patient had previously been a successful singer in nightclubs and in Broadway musicals but had had to give up her singing not only because of chronic laryngitis but also because of endless conflicts with her managers. She had come to treatment in connection with a chance to do a television talk show and was overwhelmed with a depressive conviction that she would lose this chance, just as she had lost so many others. Here is a replay of the therapeutic interchange around the issue.

Therapist: I can understand how anxious you must be about losing this really big chance to get into a different field but, after all, you have shown yourself to be such an experienced performer, right at the top.

Patient: Yeah. Thanks a lot. (pause) You don't seem to realize that it can't ever be the same. Who needs this?

Therapist: Well, I understand that this talk show is not the same as being on Broadway. Still, you sang in nightclubs for quite a while before you made Broadway.

Patient: You remember that I sang, and I remember that I sang, and for a singer there is nothing in the world like singing. I suppose it's like a dancer dancing. Just talking words, no matter how many people are listening, is not the same.

Therapist: Well, I can understand what you're saying, but still we have to be realistic about the chances we get.

The patient missed the next session and then took a "vacation" from therapy because of pressing work problems. She did not return for another year, but the fact that she did return indicates that she felt some empathy from the therapist. What the patient later explained and the therapist came to realize was that he did not and perhaps could not empathize with what it means to be a singer unable to sing anymore for a living. As she put it very movingly, "It is like taking the voice from a bird."

This kind of empathy requires what Freud first said of empathy, that it is a "feeling into" the other person. We can try to imagine what it is like for a singer not to be able to sing anymore for her living but, if we are not a singer, we cannot imagine the expressive loss and the blow to one's self-esteem. Still, if we can imagine what it would be like to lose a precious skill we have—for the therapist, for example, it would have to be talking and hearing—we can then imagine what the loss and rage would be for a singer. Here we are not concerned with the economic or career loss but rather with the experiential, creative loss that would go back to the nuclear self of childhood. To tune in on this would be real empathy.

GRATIFICATION

There is a hint in the therapist's response to the patient, before the patient left treatment for a year, of his understandable concern that she could spoil the realistic chance she had to resuscitate her career with a television show. Yet, the patient felt misunderstood enough to leave treatment for an extended period, with the implication that the therapist's focus on reality triggered narcissistic rage in the bereaved singer. We use the word "bereaved" advisedly, because we are confronting the fact that the loss of a self-fulfilling talent such as singing can be as great a loss as the failure of a love relationship, including the death of the loved one. So, when an important talent is frustrated or even completely blocked, we are entering into an area of profound feelings. But our focus here is on gratification, and what does gratification have to do with the therapist's overconcern with a reality situation that would then block his or her capacity to empathize with a major loss that his or her patient is suffering?

We have to go back into history to consider what Freud is *supposed* to have regarded as the proper scientific stance of the psychoanalyst. Yet Freud, like all great thinkers, has too often been imprisoned in a striking early stance, even though he modified this later. There is, in our opinion, no other issue where this is more true than that of how much, if any, gratification is to be given to the obviously needy patient, whatever his or her aggressive state. Probably one of the most widely quoted positions of Freud is his 1912 version of the neutral, reality-oriented, nongratifying analysts who should "model themselves during psychoanalytic treatment on the surgeon, who puts aside all his feelings, even his human sympathy, and concentrates his mental forces on the single aim of performing the operation as skillfully as possible" (p. 115).

Freud justified this "emotional coldness" in terms of creating the most desirable conditions for the doctor to protect his own emotional life and provide the patient with the most help he or she might be given during this time of treatment.

Let us remember that Breuer, Freud's rather reluctant collaborator in the birthing of psychoanalysis, became terrified at the emergence of a demanding sexual transference from his patient, Anna O. When she indicated that she wanted to have his child, he dropped the case and psychoanalysis. It is, therefore, understandable that Freud was, early on, fearful of hard-to-manage feelings from patients.

The Surgeon or the Affectionate Doctor?

Yet Freud was a great scientist because he was a great questioner, even of his own most authoritative pronouncements. Still on the subject of gratification from the analyst to the patient, one year after the "be a surgeon" order to psychoanalysts, Freud (1913), in his next paper on technique, "On Beginning the Treatment," backtracked in relation to the timing of interpretations by the analyst: "It remains the first aim of the treatment to attach him to it and to the person of the doctor" (p. 139).

Freud goes on to point out that the only thing to be done is to give the patient time. If the analyst shows a serious interest in the patient without too many mistakes, the patient is likely to form a connection that will identify the doctor with one of those

people who treated the patient affectionately. If, however, the
therapist takes up any attitude apart from "sympathetic understanding" e.g., a moralizing posture, or if the therapist seems to
take the part of a person opposing the patient, therapeutic success
may be forfeited.

What to Give the Patient

At about the same time, in February 1913, Freud wrote to Binswanger about the problem of countertransference, which Freud
considered to be one of the most difficult ones technically in psychoanalysis. In this letter, Freud said that "what is given to the
patient must be consciously allotted, and then more or less of it
as the need may arise. Occasionally a great deal. . . . " (Binswanger, 1956, p. 50). Freud also set down the crucial maxim here:
"To give someone too little because one loves him too much is
being unjust to the patient and a technical error" (Binswanger,
1956, p. 50).

Eight years later, in 1921, Freud added a footnote to his chapter
on "Identification" in *Group Psychology* in which he said: "A path
leads from identification by way of imitation to empathy, that is,
to the comprehension of the mechanism by means of which we
are enabled to express any attitude at all towards another mental
life" (p. 110). As Ernest Wolf, one of Kohut's collaborators, points
out:

> . . . Thus, Freud stated unambiguously that if we moralize
> instead of empathize, we will forfeit the proper development
> of transference. Further, he said that empathic comprehen-
> sion is the only means by which it is possible to have any
> opinion about another's mental life. (Wolf, 1983a, p. 310)

We have traced Freud's position on empathy and gratification
from his emphasis on surgical emotional coldness in 1912 to his
advocacy of sympathetic understanding in 1913 and his embracing
of empathy in 1921 as the only way to comprehend the mental
life of another human being. Our purpose here is to underline

the changes brought about in the attitudes of some analysts in response to their patients' strongly negative reactions to surgical coldness.

Is empathy per se, when defined as beneficial and therapeutic, a gratification? Two dictionary definitions (*Thorndike*, 1956; *Reader's Digest*, 1967) state that to gratify is to "give pleasure or satisfaction to" and both suggest "satisfy" as a synonym. The more recent definition (1967) defines "satisfy" as follows: "to supply fully with what is desired, expected or needed." The earlier one (1956) defines "satisfy" as "give enough to" and also "put an end to (needs, wants, etc.)." We are, perhaps, being pedantic in trying to clarify what gratification and satisfaction are held to mean in common parlance, and yet the very word "gratification" evokes guilt, anxiety, and defensiveness among psychoanalysts.

EMPATHY AND INTERNALIZATION

If a trained mental health practitioner is willing to try to help a patient reduce his or her anxiety, low self-esteem, and feelings of helplessness and abandonment by love objects, there has to be at least relief from pain and some restored hope for the future. This relief and hope can be seen as fulfilling minimal needs in living and thus offering satisfaction, since the therapist would be the supplier of what is both needed and desired. Like all suppliers of needs, the therapist would gratify the person seeking relief from the hunger of an unmet need. Therefore, in this basic way, the therapist gratifies the patient. Modell (1975) recognizes the implicit gratification in the analyst's constancy, reliability, and perception of the patient's unique identity. Thus gratification can be seen as a necessary part of how the therapist offers him- or herself to the patient as the potentially good selfobject the patient has never had. The internalization of this good selfobject is necessary for the patient's arrested development to proceed, as Kohut and his co-workers found in treating their own patients.

In Kohut's last paper (1982), he explained why, 23 years earlier in 1959, he had concluded that psychoanalysis needed to employ the introspective-empathic stance. He cited his discomfort with

Alexander's emphasis on the biological aspects of the drives, including regressive drive-fueled inclinations toward dependence. Kohut also regretted Hartmann's focus on the sociopsychological concepts of adaptation and dependence.

As Kohut pointed out, analysis has become a kind of moral system through the influence of these ideas. As a result, psychoanalysis has become less a scientific understanding based on the exploration of dynamic and genetic relationships, and more an educational approach aimed at predetermined goals that are "unacknowledged and unquestioned" (Kohut, 1982, p. 399). Not only is the patient led toward these goals, according to Kohut, but the patient even tries to reach them, owing to a similarly "unacknowledged and unquestioned dimension of his transference" (p. 399).

Stressing that he also subscribes to the knowledge and independence values of western civilization, Kohut (1982) adds that the unacknowledged influence and presence of these values distorts the analyst's perception and interferes with his ability to permit his patients to develop in accordance with their own nuclear program and destiny. Kohut (1982) asserts that these two values have interfered with our recognition of the self's key position as well as its vicissitudes in the human psychological make-up. Above all, knowledge and independence values have confused the era-specific psychopathology of contemporaneous man.

HOW MATURITY MORALITY INTERFERES WITH EMPATHY

The imposed value of knowing as much as possible about ourselves, including our most hideous traumas, plus the expectation that we should be as independent as possible, regardless of how this may interfere with good object relations, would be examples of "maturity morality," which Kohut felt was often used unthinkingly but destructively in the therapist-patient relationship.

For the therapist to assume that the patient automatically understands and accepts the therapist's maturity morality and to demand an accounting if the patient's reactions do not jibe with the therapist's expectations can too often leave the patient feeling totally misunderstood and uncared about. Such an attitude can also propel the patient permanently out of the door, leaving the therapist convinced that the patient was "untreatable" because the former had certainly done nothing to precipitate the patient's leaving.

Failures in empathy are experienced by many patients much as they were experienced by the child early in life: as outrages perpetuated upon a self seeking an open, responsive environment in the same way that one seeks fresh air to suck into a living organism. Ruptures with the human environment are felt as threats to the self.

CASE VIGNETTE

A supervisee provided a moving example of such an empathic rupture. He had first met the patient, Marie, at a meeting of a parents' organization where he had given a talk. She had approached him afterwards, expressing her appreciation of his presentation. She then added that she was quite dissatisfied with the therapist she had been seeing for two years and indicated that she would like to see him. The supervisee was aware that there might be complex feelings connected with Marie's wish to change therapists, so he said he could arrange a consultation to explore the advisability of their working together. He also thanked her for her appreciative remarks about his talk.

When Marie came in for the consultation, she confirmed the supervisee's impression of her as an attractive woman in her mid-thirties—tall, slim, and intelligent-looking. She was married, with a small child, and worked part-time in advertising where she appeared to be doing a competent job. The supervisee did not notice her physical limitation—a slight limp from a childhood bout with polio—until she mentioned having had polio. She also explained that she had a problem buying shoes since only special types, though sold in regular shoe stores, could fit her.

Obviously taking much pride in her appearance, Marie reported spending considerable time in seeking and getting shoes that were also attractive and matched her outfits. At this point, the supervisee found himself wondering how appropriate a discussion of her shopping habits was in a consultation about whether she should start treatment with him. However, since Marie was talking about shopping for something related to a childhood illness that undoubtedly was traumatic, he decided not to interrupt. Marie went on to say that recently a favorite type of shoe for her had been taken off the market and replaced by updated styles that were difficult for her to wear. She had complained about this to her previous therapist, Dr. J., who had, with a slightly superior air, asked her why she didn't have the customary "special" shoes made for herself.

The Trauma of a Childhood Handicap

Marie told the supervisee that she had reacted with horror to this suggestion, saying to her previous therapist: "But I spent years as a child, wearing just that kind of awful-looking shoe and waiting for kids to ask me why I was wearing those 'old-lady' shoes. Or sometimes, they would just point and whisper. When they laughed, it was the worst! I still shudder when I think of all those awful years and how hard I fought to learn to buy regular shoes and to look like everyone else!"

The supervisee found himself very moved by Marie's eloquent description of the painful humiliation she had suffered because of her childhood handicap and of her struggles to overcome it. He wondered how her previous therapist had tried to compensate or apologize for his insensitive suggestion. He did not have to wonder long, because Marie told him.

"If only you weren't so vain!" her previous therapist had said, shaking his head disapprovingly. At this point, Marie said she started to cry. It was not so much the painful memories of the past as it was the great disappointment she felt in him at not understanding her feelings.

"I suddenly felt as though I were miles away from him, as though he had never been there for me at all. I began to think of other comments like this. Suddenly, my anger welled up and I thought, 'What am I doing in therapy with a man like this? He doesn't really understand what I'm saying at all!' "

Marie looked at the supervisee, sighed, and said, "It was then I was sure I had to change therapists. I left the session and called him the next day to say I simply could not continue. When he asked me to come in to discuss it, I said I had been thinking about it for quite a while and would prefer not to. And that was that."

The supervisee said, "I can understand how you felt." He was relieved that he had not been unempathic in asking her what the purpose of her shoe-shopping discussion was, given the pressure of time in an initial consultation. He realized particularly that it was not so much the previous therapist's failure to tune in on her childhood suffering as it was his flagrant disapproval of her "vanity" that had made Marie feel completely uncared about. To imply that she was pathologically narcissistic in her natural desires to be admired and thought attractive "like everyone else" was to deny her inborn right and need to be exhibitionistic, as if her childhood handicap had permanently deprived her of the appreciative mirroring she so desperately needed to compensate for her childhood traumas. Fortunately, Marie's childhood experiences seemed to have given her enough healthy mirroring and ambition to strive to overcome her handicap and make the most of her assets. Yet her self-esteem was sufficiently vulnerable, not only because of the polio trauma but also because her father had suddenly disappeared in an impetuous separation from her mother.

A Maturity Morality Therapist Versus Vanity

Marie's expectations for an empathic father figure to be there for her who was reliable and sensitively attuned had been severely undermined by the disappearance of her father and had, inevitably, made it difficult for her to trust other men to be dependably loving. She had come to treatment mainly over this problem, with an unconscious conviction that her childhood problems had driven her father away and continued to discourage other men. Marie was easily convinced that what she experienced as Dr. J.'s remoteness and insensitivity to her feelings was all she, poor maimed Marie, could ever expect until she became what Dr. J. and other "acceptable" men expected her to be—whatever mysterious way of being that was. But Dr. J.'s gauche maturity morality in criticizing her for her "vanity," when she was struggling so hard to compensate for her handicap, made her suddenly realize that the gap in understanding between this therapist and her feelings was too huge. Whatever he wanted to develop her into, she wouldn't want to be anyway.

Marie had found the supervisee's discussion of parent-child problems at the parents' meeting sufficiently appealing to overcome her cynicism about ever finding a therapist she could trust to be even minimally sensitive. In the consultation, she also found him empathic enough to start seeing him on a regular basis. As the treatment has progressed, she has found him sufficiently responsive to her feminine insecurities to dare to believe again that she might find a man whom she could trust with her love. A most delicate listening and imagining task is called for in a consultation with a patient who has become disillusioned with a previous therapist. The empathic approach requires that we strive to stay solidly on the side of the patient and not let ourselves be tempted to "understand" why the previous therapist might have had difficulties. The supervisee turned toward a confrontational approach in wondering whether he should question all the talk about shoe-shopping. If he had not stopped to think of what a lame leg from polio could do to the patient's feeling of desirability as a woman, he might have disillusioned her as much as Dr. J. did, perhaps permanently. If we always try to think of how what we say will feel from the patient's standpoint, such an effort at empathy will rarely mislead us.

EMPATHY AND DIAGNOSIS

The foregoing case vignette gives an example of the very delicate listening and considering that are needed when a patient, either leaving or having definitively left a previous therapist, is consulting a prospective new therapist. In this section, we plan to explore empathy as a diagnostic tool.

Self psychologists are often accused of nearsightedness, that is, they only look at the self-state of a patient and nothing more.

While this is generally true and goes along with Kohut's (1977) exciting concept of the supraordinate self as being the ultimate touchstone of our existence, nevertheless, Kohut certainly leaves the door open for object-relations problems. We see this particularly in his expansive approach to the oedipal experience as having the normal potential of being joyous rather than an experience burdening a child with guilt forever (unless he or she has a successful psychoanalysis, which may finally lay the ghost of Oedipus to rest).

Where Does the Patient Want to Go?

It is important in the tentative and gradual diagnostic process, which hopefully all therapists and analysts undertake, that consideration is given to the various possibilities of where a patient is now and where a patient wants to go (if, indeed, the patient has any concrete ideas about this). What level of growth a patient consciously wants to achieve and seems capable of achieving may vary appreciably from where a therapist may realistically believe that the patient has the capacity to go. If we are still locked into Freudian drive theory or realistic ego psychology, then we may feel pressured to think of the patient as a neurotic with a blazing or submerged oedipal problem. Or we may think that the patient has had an accrual of preoedipal developmental deficits which hamper normal ego development, including object relations. In either case, the self of the patient is not considered by the therapist any more than the patient probably considers it. In our experience, the patient who comes in with an urgent "I" problem forces us to consider the "I," even though we may, with our maturity morality objections to flaunting narcissism, object to so much emphasis on the self as opposed to object relations.

We are proposing, as we believe Kohut proposed (1977, 1984), that the first diagnostic criterion to be considered is the state of the self. If we remember that the baby comes into the world with a potential nuclear self which will develop in terms of how the caretaking environment responds to the baby's needs—and we are including early tendencies such as motoric, verbal, active, and passive—then we can realize that the patient before us may be struggling to develop a real nuclear (that is, a cohesive) self, or that the patient is way beyond this and is seeking an oedipal understanding that could have been joyful but turned into self-hate for sexual and angry feelings.

CASE VIGNETTE

Let us take the case of Sandra S. who entered into treatment with a supervisee at the age of 35. She originally sought treatment for feelings of extreme isolation, "not feeling understood and having no one there for me." Her mother had died when she was two and a half years old, and she was then placed in an orphanage. Although she remembers little of the orphanage experience, this is not an indication of developmental deficit, since she had experienced the trauma of her mother's death and the trauma of being removed from her home and put in a strange environment—the orphanage. In the more traditional and developmental approaches to psychotherapy, there seems to be a tendency to dismiss the trauma of early loss of love objects, as well as the trauma of being in a totally strange environment. Somehow, a well-functioning ego by the age of two and a half should be able to rise above such stress and traumas and proceed with the requirements of living.

This seems to have been the attitude of Sandra's stepmother, whom her father married seven years after Sandra was placed in the orphanage. She was taken out of the orphanage and into the father and stepmother's new home at almost 10 years of age. Her experiences of her stepmother were like Cinderella's, with physical abuse and exploitation being a daily experience.

Whether she feared her father's regret or his anger at her complaints, Sandra could not tell her father about the abuse, who she felt "did not know what was really going on." She kept all of it to herself, especially after her stepmother warned that "if you tell your father, it will only be worse for you, and besides, he wouldn't believe you." Sandra's rationale to herself for her sad situation was that her father had remarried to "give me a home and did not really love *her*."

This idealization of her father remained with her until the day he died, when Sandra was 27. Her stepmother lingered on a few years in a nursing home. After her father's death, Sandra moved into a hotel to live the life of a single, isolated woman. Her major area of satisfaction came to be her job as a secretary. In treatment, she told about each incident at work in full detail. Narcissistic wounds such as the boss's casual attitude toward her or a peer's caustic remark were reported with great intensity of feeling and pain. She accepted these feelings as her due and evaded exploration of them. Years later, and still in treatment as a necessary part of her survival, she often said: "You always believed me. You were and are my lifeline."

The therapist accepted this idealization appreciatively, saying, "Naturally, I realized that your pain at others' insensitivity to your feelings was real and is real to you. It has been a terrible experience for you, just as your experiences with your stepmother were." In empathizing with her helplessness in standing up for herself, the therapist gave her the attuned responses she never received from either parent, while not undermining her idealization of her dead father as a possible defense against oedipal guilt. However, a colleague to whom she was referred when her therapist had to go away on an extended trip was not so sensitive to her needs.

The Danger of a Standby Therapist

This second therapist questioned the reality of Sandra's co-workers' attacks on her, thereby fulfilling her stepmother's prophecy. She reacted with rage to his probing and canceled the rest of her sessions with him. Her own therapist apologized when she returned and promised that she would never again refer the patient to anyone who was not a competent self psychologist because of the big differences in the empathic approach.

This patient very nearly left the therapist permanently, just as the patient was moving toward daring to want a man of her own. Although in her early forties, Sandra had had little experience with men. Attractive, with a shapely body, she nevertheless felt she was "old, unattractive," and mostly "like a child of 13 in my knowledge of men." The therapist acknowledged that, though an adult, she naturally felt like a young adolescent due to her lack of experience.

For the first few years in treatment, men and sexuality were hardly ever mentioned. After about five years, Sandra started to pay more attention to what she wore and also told the therapist that she sometimes masturbated. The therapist commented that it was good that she could use her own body for pleasure. She then told the therapist that she even experienced orgasm. The therapist reinforced how good it was that she could enjoy ecstasy and joy within herself. A short time later Sandra spoke of wanting to be with a man and yet of her terror of dating. She told the therapist that sometimes, if a man at a business lunch with her boss spoke to her in a flirting way, she floundered. Once or twice when this had happened, she had even vomited.

The therapist empathized with her feelings of terror. Recently, when she had gone to buy a painting for her home, the store owner, Joe, had offered to come and hang the painting in her apartment. Aware of what the message was, Sandra had agreed. She mentioned to the therapist that she thought he was interested in her. Sandra said she had to call him to make the appointment but was terrified of doing it.

The therapist asked if she wished to call Joe with the therapist sitting beside her during the session. Sandra was delighted and said she wanted to. She knelt on the carpet near the therapist's phone, took the therapist's hand and with her other hand dialed and spoke into the phone. The therapist let Sandra hold her hand and concentrated fully on her. She appeared relaxed and her voice was pleasant, warm, and appropriate as she made the appoint- ment with Joe. After speaking a few minutes, she hung up and threw herself down on the chair. She let out a long sigh and said, "I did it but I'm so nervous. I'm jumping all inside myself. I don't know if I can take this."

Wondering if Sandra's anxiety had anything to do with the familiar fears over sexual desire and/or oedipal longings for her father, the therapist asked Sandra what she was thinking of just then, even though she knew Sandra might be offended that the therapist did not immediately know what underlay her seemingly calm and appropriate manner on the telephone.

However, Sandra did not seem to expect the therapist to read her mind on this occasion. She sighed and said: "I'll be OK, I think, until he finds out I'm a virgin. What do I tell him then? How do I explain that I have a body of a 44-year-old woman, that I've been in therapy for years just to learn to talk to a man, and that I'm a virgin and have never had sex with a man?"

A Patient's Fear of Arrested Development

The therapist's self-monitoring about possible oedipal aspects underlying Sandra's anxiety led to a diagnostic decision that Sandra's fears of being ridiculed and rejected by her potential new boyfriend arose from her shaky image of herself as a desirable woman and not from superego guilt internalized from her harsh stepmother. The therapist sensed that Sandra was embarrassed over what she thought of as her retarded sexual development and feared that her potential lover might be turned off by this discovery, as if there were something hopelessly abnormal about Sandra's arrested development. The therapist found herself in a dilemma that is all too familiar to self psychologists: namely, whether to slow down a patient's rising enthusiasm or even passion with reality-based warnings that the patient's hopes might not be realized or to risk the patient's possible disillusionment while encouraging the patient to search for self-fulfillment.

The therapist decided to respect Sandra's inevitable worry that the man might just lose interest if she proved too sexually inhibited. On the other hand, the therapist also empathized with Sandra's fear that if she pretended to be more experienced than she actually was, this man might discover that she was a virgin and be angry at her for deceiving him. The therapist conceded, regretfully, that both eventualities were possible, thus underlining delicately that even a good selfobject like the therapist could not totally guarantee that sexual experience and attraction would always lead to love and happiness. This is a painful discovery that adolescents and young adults, too, make over and over again, especially in these days of the sexual revolution. What Sandra was embarking on now was really her late adolescent-early adulthood developmental phase that had been so cruelly arrested by her fragmented self—the untimely death of her father and her intimidated idealization of him, which had made a natural, joyful oedipal experience unreachable.

The Right to Say No to Insensitivity

Above all, the therapist did not want to interfere with the delicate opening up of Sandra's passionate femininity. While recognizing the validity of Sandra's worries about losing her potential boyfriend, the therapist suggested that Sandra go slowly at first to see whether she cared enough about him to want an ongoing relationship. Here the therapist was emphasizing something that is so often lost sight of: namely, a woman, no matter how inexperienced and uncertain she is in her dealings with men, does have preferences and dislikes. The therapist was thereby communicating to her that Sandra had the right to say, "No, this man is not really understanding enough for me to lay bare the painful facts of my life. I've had enough humiliation and disappointment already." At the same time, the therapist was conveying to Sandra that, again like a good selfobject, the therapist would be there to help her plan what to tell the man if she decided she wanted to risk it.

Since the therapist's office was in her home, the patient knew that the therapist was in a long-term marriage and was, therefore, more experienced as a woman in anticipating masculine reactions. While this acknowledged expertise on the part of the therapist could have felt like a know-it-all parent telling a child exactly how to do her homework rather than helping her over the hurdles, the therapist emphasized the mutuality of the discussions Sandra and the therapist could have, stressing that it would always be up to Sandra to make the final decision on what she wanted to say. This careful respect the therapist was showing for Sandra's autonomy and her complex feelings seemed to relieve Sandra's anxiety. In a burst of emotion, she said, "I'm sick and tired of being alone. I want someone there for me. I want a man to hold me, to kiss me, to tell me he cares. Other women have this. Why not me?"

The patient's forthright demand for love and sexual gratification represented a triumph for the therapist's delicate approach. The terrible ambivalence for Sandra over whether to turn away once more from a man who seemed to care for her just because he could not possibly accept *her* feelings and *her* self represented, of course, a reenactment in the transference of Sandra's crucial self-fragmentation that she experienced with her stepmother. Having lost her mother at two and having lived in an orphanage until almost age 10, Sandra had had very little lovingly reliable experience with a selfobject. Conceivably, with caretakers or other children in the orphanage and possibly with her mother for the crucial first two years, she had experienced enough appreciation of her own very extensive abilities to handle many difficulties, so that self-expectations intensified her unconscious grandiose demands that she should be able to bring everything off perfectly.

Unfortunately, in her experience, especially with women, she had failed miserably. She not only had not been able to keep her mother alive (Weiner & White, 1983) but also had not been able to make her stepmother care for her instead of mistreat her. Finally, Sandra had not been able to get a trustworthy green light to approach her father to ask for consideration and love. Whatever her own mother's relationship with her father had been and whatever her father's problems, Sandra had not felt cared enough about by him to expect spontaneously that he could take her side against her stepmother.

The Therapist as Stepmother

Given Sandra's experience, whenever an issue of a triangular relationship emerged, the therapist, and perhaps especially a woman therapist, would certainly be suspected of abandonment (e.g., her dead mother) or of retaliation (e.g., her stepmother). Sandra could construe these imagined reactions as punishment for her wanting some love either from the mother figure or the father figure in the triangle. But the masochistic defense against wanting perfect love from everyone—the infantile grandiose expectation—is to believe that one will only be loved if one provides everything the other person wants, that is, the reverse of the infantile grandiose expectation.

It was this masochistic reaction that Sandra was sinking into when she felt the long-frustrated stirrings of feminine sexuality arising in response to a man who was spontaneously attracted to her. But the situation was particularly complicated by the fact that the therapist, her good selfobject, was a woman. Could Sandra finally trust a woman to help her, to be there for her in a triangular relationship, which conceivably might finally take Sandra away from the therapist? We understand that we are moving now from self relations into object relations but this is inevitable and desirable in treatment from a self psychological view. It is moving toward the goal of being a whole person.

In consideration of all these issues riding on the therapist's reaction to Sandra's chance to have a sexual relationship, the therapist proceeded both cautiously and, from a conservative psychotherapeutic standpoint, incautiously, in order to help Sandra confront and deal with this major self- and object-related issue of feeling entitled to heterosexual gratification. To date, the supervisee reports that Sandra is involved with Joe and is trying to break through her own lifelong anxiety about making demands for herself when she is with Joe, friends, or even her employer.

THE THERAPIST AS A SOURCE OF GRATIFICATION

Since we are all (for many explicable and some still inexplicable reasons) interested in the "incautious" or questionable tactics of a therapist (or of anyone else), let us first consider the "incautious." From a traditional Freudian approach or an ego psychological approach, the therapist is not supposed to touch the patient because presumably any physical contact will amount to infantile gratification that will get out of hand, which can only mean sexualized.

When the therapist encouraged Sandra to telephone her potential new boyfriend right then, in the session, Sandra responded
"with delight" by kneeling on the floor near the telephone and
taking the therapist's hand, while with the other, she held the
telephone and made the call. From a self psychological viewpoint,
this was a wonderful expression of her need to keep her connection with her good selfobject, the therapist, while reaching out
for another selfobject for sexual fulfillment! The fact that the therapist did not reject her open expression of need for physical contact through her taking the therapist's hand would seem to be a
total—physical, verbal, and emotional—reaffirmation on the therapist's part that the therapist gave her blessing, so to speak, to
Sandra's reaching out finally for a man's love.

The fact that, as the therapist subsequently reported, Sandra
was able to go on to develop a cohesive self that included a delicate, sensitive, sexual womanly self would seem to be sufficient
proof that sometimes, in treatment, if a patient spontaneously
makes an affectionate, touching gesture, the therapist needs to
accept it. We say "needs to" because if a therapist, out of countertransference reasons of his or her own inhibitions cannot, then
there may be a serious problem for the patient of reexperiencing
in the treatment a rejection of his or her physical self, which had
proved so destructive to the development of a cohesive self feeling
confident of being lovable.

Touching a patient is still a profound therapeutic issue. This
was movingly presented by Kohut in his last address before he
died to the 1981 Self Psychology Conference in San Francisco. He
was very concerned about justifying himself for having extended
a finger to be held by a very depressed patient who was fearful
of dying and of having the coffin lid closed over her. Kohut had
felt that this gesture was responded to by the patient as if she
were a toothless infant suckling the mother's breast. There is no
doubt that Kohut, himself very ill, was identifying with the patient
in the fear of death. Nevertheless, his strict training as a psychoanalyst made him ambivalent about the justification for his
daring to touch the patient, even though her response, as he
described it, was of a starving infant.

In the case of Kohut's patient and in the case of Sandra, they both needed the physical empathic touch of the therapist to re-assure them that they were not alone, would not be left alone if they pursued whatever they wanted to do, and would be em-pathically responded to whatever their needs were. Between Ko-hut's patient's desperate fear of loss of existence and Sandra's desperate fear of never being sexually loved as a woman, there is a whole span of developmental growth. Nevertheless, it would seem we all need some reassurance that the empathic human milieu of a good selfobject is there for us. And it may well be that the power of a loving human touch, so needed and so recognized by an infant, is what many adults need in their moments of self-anxiety and self-despair. If the therapist is somehow inhibited about the acceptability of a mere human touch, then wouldn't this be experienced as a rejection and a travesty of the therapist's offering himself or herself as the good selfobject the patient never had?

We are dealing now with the intricacies of empathic expression. In the case of Sandra, the therapist's empathy throughout treat-ment helped her to grow into a warm, sexually interested, self-confident woman, an outcome naturally gratifying to both the patient and the therapist. We deliberately use the word "gratify-ing" because we believe that the outcome of treatment should be gratifying to both participants in the therapeutic adventure.

Empathy is, as far as we know, the unique human capacity to feel oneself into another's psychological life and to attempt to understand it and, on the basis of that understanding, to attempt to participate in it. From the therapist's position, the attempt is to share in the other's psychological life as a development-en-hancing selfobject, to compensate for the inadequacies of the pa-rental selfobject. In the larger sense, beyond therapy, empathy is what we all need in trying to feel and understand the psycho-logical lives of those who are close to us or whom we must un-derstand professionally if we are to work effectively with them.

4

The Grandiose Self:
A Wellspring of Rage
or Achievement?

When Kohut proposed in *The Restoration of the Self* (1977) that human aggression was the disintegration product of an unresponsive environment, he included his concept of narcissistic rage under this rubric. In an earlier presentation, "Psychoanalysis in a Troubled World" (1970), Kohut saw the infantile grandiose self not only as the source of narcissistic rage but also as a wellspring of humankind's healthy ambition and remarkable achievements. In the same paper Kohut then asked, almost 15 years ago, if self psychological concepts could curb the narcissistic rage that can now destroy the human species and the planet with nuclear war, and could help to harness the energies inherent in human grandiosity for the preservation of humankind.

In a limited sense, the concepts and techniques of self psychology have demonstrated for well over two decades that narcissistic rage, entrapping the infantile grandiosity in regressed pathological narcissism, can be tamed and the grandiosity drawn upon to fuel constructive ambition in the cohesive self through the therapist's attunement to the patient's archaic needs for mirroring (Atwood & Stolorow, 1984). The taming of narcissistic rage has been achieved by what Kohut described in his posthumously published book, *How Does Analysis Cure?* (1984), as "the two-step interventions of the analyst—the experience, over and over again, of understanding followed by explaining . . ." (p. 206).

By "understanding," Kohut of course means empathy, which we described in the previous chapter. In his posthumously published 1982 paper, Kohut described empathy not only as a mode of gathering data through vicarious introspection into the selfobject needs of another, but also "as a powerful emotional bond between people" (p. 397).

He then cited chilling examples of the fear of the "loss of the empathic milieu" that keeps the self alive through emotional attunement. He referred to the fear of death and of psychosis, of the loss of earth as home by astronauts fearing their corpses would circle in space forever, of the ghastly psychological effects of having faced dehumanized extermination in the Nazi concentration camps, and of the artistic versions of exposure to no empathy in Kafka's *Metamorphosis* and O'Neill's *Long Day's Journey into Night*.

A comprehension of narcissistic rage through empathic immersion is what the analyst, using self psychology concepts, undertakes. He or she is trying to help a patient regain access to the infantile grandiosity that, released and accepted, can power the ambition of the nuclear self. Kohut discovered, through both analytic failures and successes, that one of the major transferences spontaneously developing in patients with self deficits was a need for mirroring, that is, empathic encouragement for the patient's interests or achievements. When this "gleam in the mother's eye" (Kohut, 1971) was not forthcoming, the patient characteristically reacted with narcissistic rage, which might take the form of an icy unresponsiveness or a relentless attack on the analyst's shortcomings, and presumed areas of sensitivity, such as age, professional achievements, physical appearance, taste in decor, or any personal or professional failures the patient might know of.

NARCISSISTIC RAGE: THE NEED FOR TOTAL CONTROL

Narcissistic rage, in whatever form it occurs, is characterized by an urge to revenge oneself, to undo an offense, and a drivenness to accomplish these goals, which allow no respite to those affronted by a narcissistic injury. As Kohut noted in his ground-breaking paper (1972), these features characterize narcissistic rage in all its forms.

Thus, the "enemy" is experienced as a "recalcitrant" aspect of an enlarged self over which the narcissistically prone person expected to exercise full control (Kohut, 1972). To be made aware that the other individual is different or able to be independent is an offensive blow to those with deep narcissistic deprivations.

Kohut notes:

> . . . The archaic mode of experience explains why those . . . in the grip of narcissistic rage show . . . the unmodifiable wish to blot out the offense . . . against the grandiose self and the unforgiving fury that arises when the control over the mirroring selfobject is lost or when the omnipotent selfobject is unavailable. (cited in Ornstein, 1978b, p. 645)

If the observer—for instance, a parent, teacher, friend, and, above all, a therapist, can be empathic enough, he or she can perceive the broader significance of the frequently trivial irritant that set off the narcissistic rage and can strive to understand rather than give way to counterattack or rejecting withdrawal.

The vast implications of Kohut's stark description of the breadth and depth of narcissistic rage are still difficult to comprehend fully. Since this issue will be further explored later in this chapter, for now, let us return to the therapist struggling with his or her feelings over the seemingly unremitting and inappropriate attacks by a patient in the throes of narcissistic rage. It is so difficult not to gnash our professional teeth when a patient works us over for weeks both before and after we take a much-needed vacation. At least *we* feel we need it but we feel helpless in having that need accepted by the patient, who only cries, curses, or is stonily silent over the outrage at being deserted.

Sometimes we are surprised at an equally enraged reaction to an emergency change in an appointment. Perhaps we may then remember that this seemingly unwarranted rage is an understandable reaction if the patient assumes that the therapist is out of order as a recalcitrant part of the patient's body or mind. As a participant in the unconscious grandiosity, which has long been a powerful but undelineated manipulator of the patient's self, the therapist is to be the obedient genie for the patient, carrying out and even anticipating every request.

"But this is infantile!" a reality-attuned therapist will protest, while wondering perhaps if this reaction reflects his or her countertransference. "An infant does need this kind of understanding and help, but an infant also needs to find out very quickly that he or she has to wait, that mother is not a magical human being."

GRANDIOSITY: REASSURANCE VERSUS HELPLESSNESS

As therapists using self psychology discover, the patient raging at them is still unconsciously in the twilight zone of grandiose reality, desperately needing the reassurance that he or she will not be left helpless in a frightening world. Such reassurance is the essence of all the myths of humankind, both religious and political, and babies through the millenia have been suckled on these myths. Indeed, as Miller also discovered (1981, 1983), parents have often turned to the brightest and most responsive baby as if he or she were a parent to meet their frustrated needs and did not require much parenting at all. The centuries-old recourse by the child to imagined grandiosity is seemingly inevitable in such cases, but the exploited child's grandiosity, so ridiculed by adults, has to be covered up with the exquisite self-abnegation we have termed masochism.

So pervasive and difficult to treat, masochism cannot be understood unless it is seen as a desperate barricade against the unleashing of narcissistic rage against oneself, often through suicide. Without the spurious sense of self-worth from fulfilling the demands of others, our "exploitees" would at least sink into inertia, then into deep depression and perhaps suicide. They are living proof that a healthy, cohesive self requires the early "mirroring" from the mothering person that gives the vital boost to healthy ambition and self-esteem.

THE NEED FOR APPLAUSE

Kohut was the first psychoanalyst to spotlight the importance of applause for the young child and the continuing need that all adults have throughout life for appreciative responses from some selfobjects. In 1972, he stressed that "the overcoming of a hypocritical attitude toward narcissism is as much required today as was the overcoming of sexual hypocrisy a hundred years ago" (p. 620). He added that "we should not deny our ambitions . . . our wish to shine" (p. 620) but rather recognize these narcissistic needs as legitimate. Only then can the wellsprings of infantile grandiosity and exhibitionism develop into stable self-esteem.

Kohut (1971) had maintained early on that the grandiose self constituted a normal stage of development as well as a regressive defense against the too-early or too-abrupt disappointment in the omnipotent parent imago. This is in contrast to Kernberg's (1975) position that narcissistic grandiosity was a regressive fixation. Mahler et al. (1975), however, in her extensive observational studies of normal mothers and children, confirmed the regular appearance of a "practicing" subphase (of the larger separation-individuation phase). In this phase the toddler emerges from crawling to attain the uniquely upright posture of the human being, with the attendant feelings of omnipotence, elation, and the confident expectation that the world is now and forever shall be his or her oyster. Kohut also underlined the feelings of triumph and certainly the basis for healthy, ambitious aspiration, which are implicit in the attainment of the upright posture, when he said

> . . . Is it the "upright posture" (Straus, 1952) which, as the newest acquisition in the sequence of developmental steps, lends itself most aptly to become the symbolic act that expresses the feeling of triumphant pride? (Kohut, 1977, pp. 12–13)

He goes on to suggest that the "flying dream and the fantasy of flying" could be regarded as expressing the human delight of the race in the upright head position—*"re-experienced by each new generation of toddlers"* (*Ibid.*, emphases added).

THE RIGHT TO FEEL GOOD ABOUT ONESELF

We are emphasizing that the grandiose self, as described by Kohut, was and is seen as a normal developmental stage. Not only Kohut but also outstanding exponents of the psychoanalytic developmental approach and of the more traditional Freudian approach take this position. It reflects the view that the phallic stage of development, with its exhibitionistic needs (ages three to four with genital development), is recognized as important.

In our own experience as analysts and in working with supervisees, as well as in the oral and written accounts of other analysts, we have found that empathy for the manifestations of the grandiose self, especially in the transference, encounters emotional obstacles. It seems that understanding can more easily be summoned up if the therapist can remind himself or herself that this sadistic, insatiable, hypersensitive, volatile, self-destructive, and object-destructive patient is, basically, a child, tragically deprived of his inalienable right and need to feel good about himself.

With one particularly difficult woman patient, a supervisee needed to remind herself, sometimes at every session, of how unresponded to, humiliated, and punished this patient had been, in order for the therapist to summon up her empathy for the narcissistic rage the patient directed at the therapist. The therapist sometimes wanted to yell back at her, to tell the patient she had no right to treat her so contemptuously, and, at the very least, to defend herself, to contradict her distortions, and to set the record straight. Whenever the therapist attempted to do the latter, the patient's rage rose to fever pitch, with screams that made the therapist worry about possible eviction. One day, when the therapist gathered herself together for the announcement of her Christmas vacation, which always elicited verbal mayhem, the patient remained ominously silent. Then she suddenly darted toward the closed casement window before the therapist could stop her and thrust her hand toward a windowpane.

Horrified, the therapist hoped against hope that she had not really broken the glass. Then she saw a piece of glass lying on the floor near the window. The therapist feared the patient would try to use the glass either on herself or the therapist. Had the patient already cut her hand, the therapist wondered? Since she was standing near the window with her back toward the therapist, it wasn't possible to see what had happened to her hand. Trying to grab for something empathic to say as the only possible thing that could calm the patient, the therapist asked, "Did you hurt your hand?" That immediately made the patient feel that the therapist wasn't as afraid of her as she was concerned about the patient's feelings and well-being. The patient turned, and without saying anything, held her hands out. They were not cut because the windowpane that fell out had a crack in it and gave way at her first pressure.

The therapist said, "I'm glad you didn't cut yourself," and quickly stooped down to pick up the broken glass and get it safely in a wastebasket before the patient's mood could switch back to rage. As the patient watched, she said with real concern to the therapist, "Be careful with the glass. Don't hurt yourself." This was one of the first expressions of concern she had ever made about the therapist personally, and it was felt as the first tentative movement away from consuming narcissistic rage to an awareness of the therapist as a somewhat separate person with feelings that needed to be considered.

Certainly there were often regressions back to the rageful, temper tantrum infant. But the therapist never felt again the cold pitilessness or the narcissistic rage that only wants murderous revenge for the failures of empathic response from a punitive selfobject and that leaves the patient feeling so uncared about as a human being.

Kohut gave us some important guidelines in connection with the somatization problems of patients in the grandiose self phases of the transference, which, like the child's development, alternate with idealization of the therapist. In reviewing the implications of Kohut's concept of the supraordinate self in relation to bodily parts and physiological and mental functions, he suggested that "a person's ability to experience the pleasures of body parts and single functions is enhanced by the security provided by the organizing schema of his total body-mind self" (p. 748), including the "presence of a strong nuclear self" (1974, p. 764).

THE TERRORS OF SOMATIZING

The patient who is fixated at the grandiose self and in a state of narcissistic rage is overwhelmed with terror at any indication that he or she does not have total control over his or her body-mind self. For example, a headache, nausea, constipation, or impotence, let alone a mysterious malady, can plunge the person into what seems like suicidal despair. It may really be the confusion and fright that a 10-month-old toddler feels when he or she has one of the common ailments of infancy: "Why can't mother make me feel well and if not mother, why can't I do it myself?" The early terrors connected with serious illnesses, and operations especially, have usually been attributed both to separation anxiety from the mothering parent and to the child's fear of his or her aggression toward the mothering person's failure to protect him or her from such devastating experiences. Many psychoanalytic hours have been spent in trying to help the adult patient, still grappling with these early terrors, to "accept" the realistic necessity of these awful experiences—that it was neither mother's fault nor the child's badness that brought on these traumas, but the inevitable vicissitudes of life (Kramer, 1955; Mahler, 1971).

RAGE AT THE SELF

What has been overlooked here is the narcissistic rage directed at the grandiose self as the toddler's last hope (and, unconsciously, as the fixated adult's last hope) to overcome life's terrible assaults on his or her body and mind.

Kohut (1972) suggests that certain self-mutilations and suicides may be seen as expressions of narcissistic rage turned against the imperfect and therefore shameful self. He suggests that in self-mutilation, unacceptable parts of the body-self are experienced as an agonizing burden which must be removed (e.g., the rejected, therefore evil, penis). Suicides arising from narcissistic rage express the failure of the libidinal cathexis of the self. Kohut says that characteristically such suicides are not triggered by guilt feelings but by torturing emptiness and deadness or by deep shame.

Self-Rage at Physical Imperfections

Self psychology's recognition of the power of such unconscious grandiose expectations enables a therapist to deal much more empathically with the wearying and frustrating complaints of patients who endlessly blame themselves for their somatic disorders. However, they become angry or contemptuous of the traditional interpretations that they are experiencing their repressed and guilt-arousing impulses in a physical form; or the transferential interpretation that they are exaggerating their discomfort in order to gain sympathy from the therapist as they once sought their mother's sympathy; or that they need to develop more adult tolerance for the vicissitudes of life, including physical illness.

None of these interpretations goes to the heart of the matter, of course, if the patient is unconsciously enraged at him- or herself for the imperfection of having any physical problem at all. However, an interpretation along the following lines may help the patient to feel somewhat understood: "It seems as though ever since you were little, you've felt your body had to be perfect in order to feel completely safe. So it's no wonder you're enraged at your body for frightening you so with all this pain."

The patient may look utterly amazed at this interpretation, especially if the therapist has not been using a self psychological approach. He may shrug it off as though he has not heard it and turn to other topics. He may even deny it, although a moment before he was castigating himself for being a hypochondriac. In the best circumstances, he will agree, with a note of relief in his voice, that a dreadful situation was finally beginning to be understood.

Parents' Anger at Sickness

Often, associations will follow about parents' anger when the patient was sick or hurt himself as if he could somehow have prevented it. Sometimes, the mother or grandmother will be remembered as going into a panic at a cut finger or a stomachache, and the patient would find himself having to calm them down, forgetting about his own problem. Or his reputation for being a frail child would lead to embarrassing scenes of being overdressed or kept in from some occasion that was too "much for him, given his delicate condition." Such humiliation caused him not only to turn on himself but also to conceal from himself and others all but the most lethal signs of illness, along with compulsive efforts at physical endurance and stoical attitudes toward pain.

It may take considerable time for the patient to become aware and to let the therapist become aware of the extent to which unconscious expectations of self-perfection have dominated his attitudes toward his own body and mind. If the therapist empathically accepts these feelings, not as ridiculous, but as a natural part of early development which became an indispensable protection, given the unfeeling reaction of his parents to his various physical problems, then the patient will gradually begin to accept them and relinquish them both as unnecessary and as dangerously immature.

Grandiose expectations of one's physical and mental invulnerability can often lead to dangerous self-neglect and even death, as, for example, with the abuse of drugs, alcohol, or dangerous sexual practices, which might have been avoided if appropriate treatment had been sought earlier. As the patient is gradually helped to accept his own narcissistic rage toward his fallible body and mind, which leads to alleviation of the rage, he is also gradually internalizing the empathic therapist as the responsive self-object.

PATIENT'S RAGE AT THERAPIST

It is inevitable, however, that in the process of working through his narcissistic rage at himself for his physical and mental vulnerability, the patient will begin to express some of his rage and disappointment at the human shortcomings of the therapist. This may appear as a sudden attack when, say, the therapist keeps him waiting a couple of minutes before his session, with the intimation that the patient before him was being given extra time and, therefore, special consideration.

The therapist, feeling relatively confident that transmuting internalization of himself as a caring selfobject is proceeding positively, may he be caught off guard by the patient's sudden criticism and may slip into defensiveness. A disclaimer that the therapist had taken a telephone call in the session or even a puzzled question as to why the patient would think the therapist would give more consideration to the other patient is enough to trigger the narcissistic rage that was described earlier.

If the therapist is somewhat aware, as Kohut suggested, of how a seemingly minor incident can touch off narcissistic rage, then he or she will realize that even a two-minute wait is enough for the narcissistic rage to erupt. Expressing an understanding of this affront may be enough to calm the patient, who may then feel that finally someone has awareness of what he experiences as his hypersensitivity and its inevitable rage.

However, if the therapist persists in his defensiveness, that is, his "reasonable" explanation, it is likely that the patient will become more enraged, feel misunderstood or even ridiculed for his own sensitivity to nonexistent slights. The session then may turn into a tug-of-war silence or a precipitate leaving by the patient. Such a breach of empathy on the part of a therapist beginning to be internalized is enough to catapult the patient back to the distrust with which he entered treatment, based on years of feeling misunderstood by parents, friends, lovers, and other therapists—the distrust that has been difficult enough to overcome, even with a more empathic therapist. What may seem like a minor misunderstanding can turn into a dangerous withdrawal of trust and a prelude to premature termination unless the therapist is able to spotlight when and how the rift occurred, understand it, apologize for it explicitly, and use it to explore earlier, far-reaching attunement failures.

CASE VIGNETTE

For instance, the patient, Charles C., who was upset by waiting two minutes for the therapist, must have had some specific feelings about being kept waiting. Perhaps Charles's arrival a few minutes early for his appointment made the two-minute extra wait for the start of his session seem even longer. When this was explored in session, it turned out that the patient was feeling positive, almost high, because his obsessing over his insomnia and migraine had subsided. He was feeling a new confidence in the skill and especially in the sensitivity of the therapist, in contrast to his previous ambivalence.

The feeling of new confidence reminded Charles of the time when, at 13, he had finished a painful ordeal with the dentist, an ex-Marine with all the toughness that connotes, who had complimented the patient, surprisingly, on his stoical self-control. The patient had come home, not only eager to tell his impressionable mother about this, but also to remind her of her promise to take him to a Horowitz recital as a reward for completing the dentist ordeal. At that time, the patient's musical talent as a pianist and his dedication to becoming a concert artist had augured well for a future which somehow slipped away into the shadows of "having to be like everyone else and do what was expected."

On that particular afternoon, however, as he came home from the dentist, relieved that the physical ordeal was over and even high in his feelings about the "poor slob dentist's back patting," Charles was especially looking forward to the Horowitz recital two days away. But on his arrival home, his mother was not to be seen until she finally emerged from his younger sister's bedroom with the monosyllabic information that his sister had slipped on the ice and sprained her ankle.

"Well, I'm sorry, but a sprain's not so bad," he had stammered out. "She just has to keep off it for a few days. You know, I finished with the dentist today and he said I really held up under it. And you promised to take me to hear Horowitz the day after tomorrow. . . ."

His mother had sighed, as if this reminder were the last straw and she was about to collapse. She looked at the patient with a tragic face and said, "How can you be so selfish, thinking about a recital and your old teeth when your sister is having a terrible time?"

A Mirroring Failure and the Loss of a Career

At that point, Charles had shrugged off his disappointment at his mother's failure to understand him. He had gone for a long walk during which he had unconsciously tried to halt the regressive fragmentation of his self-esteem through compulsive physical exercise, a symptom with which he was still struggling in treatment. In retrospect, perhaps that experience at age 13 of not being adequately mirrored by his mother, who had never been able to meet his needs once his sister, a year and a half younger, had appeared on the scene, began his final turning away from music as a career. The therapist (a supervisee) had wondered if the patient's involvement with music had been mainly to impress his mother rather than a genuine talent—perhaps a defensive structure to cover over the deep self-deficit her inadequate mirroring had left him with.

It was hard to know because Charles continued to play and study, although not with the same intense focus as before. But he stopped attending recitals and concerts and eventually decided to become a chiropractor, specializing in athletic injuries, which seemed like a desperate effort to please his mother at his own expense by going into a profession that conceivably could have helped his sister on that memorable day.

As the therapist explored this background of Charles's rage over having to wait, both patient and therapist developed a new perspective on the patient's deprivation in terms of adequate early mirroring and respect for his artistic ambitions and ideals, his needs being shunted aside at his sister's every accident and including a broken promise as to the reward he was going to get for *his* ordeal. Naturally, it seemed to him that the therapist's empathy with his newly relieved physical problems was too much to believe. So he was primed for the therapist's delay and seeming preference for the other patient before him. However, if the therapist had not empathically investigated the breach, the patient's tenuous connection with the therapist as a good selfobject might have been broken and overlooked. This would have intensified the difficulties of reaching the patient's grandiosity, narcissistic rage, and a failed cohesive self, defended against with a masochistic vertical split.

The Vertical Split

Kohut saw the vertical split as a kind of disavowal of the grandiose self. The person, as in this case, presents himself as fate's victim along with the implication that he could have really made it if only *he* had tried harder, but his incentive failed him. A therapist may feel pressured to focus on reality, that is, there are no victims of fate and perhaps, given his talents, his expectations were too high. This, of course, would be experienced as a criticism, giving rise to narcissistic rage.

It is often difficult for therapists to believe that the person presenting himself masochistically is really that sensitive to any criticism since he denigrates himself so endlessly. The traditional therapeutic approach has been to see the complaints and self-reproaches as a bid for attention, with the hope that feeling sorry for oneself will bring gratifying empathic responses from others. This interpretative approach does aim at the narcissistic component underlying the masochistic self-abasement. However, the narcissistic component is usually regarded as a phallic exhibitionistic wish, unconsciously defending against the despair and rage of oedipal defeat. But, as we saw in the previous case example of Charles, masochistic self-abnegation proved to be the only stance that worked for him in dealing with an unempathic and unmirroring mother.

Charles's father was too detached to compensate for the self-deficit accrued by Charles in his desolate childhood. A compulsive conformity with "what mother seemed to want" stimulated in Charles the grandiose hope that somehow he would be able to share center stage with his younger sister, especially through his real musical talent. In this way, he would not always have to defer to what mother thought his younger sister should have. It became clear, in the course of treatment, that Charles's mother had unconsciously identified with her daughter and was settling old scores by giving to the daughter at the expense of her son. Unfortunately, Charles also stimulated in his mother her resentment of her older brother and her detached father, only too reminiscent of her husband. So Charles's grandiose self-expectations that he could somehow magically win his mother over were bound to fail. Such a failure would prove to Charles that he was totally unlovable and deserved to die, that is, representing the turning of his narcissistic rage against himself rather than against the mother who failed him. In this sense, his masochistic way of life—his hypochondria, his disparaged profession, and his self-flagellation for having failed as a musician—were outlets for his narcissistic rage against himself and, possibly, a protection against suicide.

Internalizing the Therapist

Charles feared reexperiencing the helplessness he had known as a child in being so ignored or unfairly criticized by the one person whose caring he so desperately needed. It became clear that Charles could not contain the narcissistic rage he still harbored toward his failed self as a defense against his mother's sadism until his self-esteem had been heightened and solidified through internalizing the analyst as a reliably empathic selfobject.

This internalization would have to include not only the analyst's empathic acceptance of Charles's narcissistic rage as it emerged masochistically against himself and grandiosely against the therapist; the internalization would also have to include Charles's enduring belief in the reliability of the analyst as a caring selfobject, despite the inevitable shortcomings of the therapist as a human being with his or her own problems and a life to live apart from Charles.

It was the development of this belief in the overall caring of the therapist that made it possible for Charles to develop reliable self-esteem and self-constancy. This awareness that the therapist cared about him, including his core self, enabled Charles to then accept other people's needs as a fact of life rather than an existential affront to Charles's very being. Through this internalization of the therapist as the caring mother-father he had never had, Charles could release the locked-up energy in his infantile grandiose self and use it for his own growth in a more self-fulfilling life, which came to include loving other people despite their imperfections. Charles was also able to return to his music, both for private self-fulfillment and as an acceptable exhibitionistic bridge to other people.

DEALING WITH NARCISSISTIC RAGE

The positive outcome of Charles's case will hopefully encourage therapists to use the self psychological approach in dealing with narcissistic rage, either as it is concealed in a masochistic self-stance or as it is overtly focused on the therapist in an unrelenting attack for all disappointments. Above all, the patient with a fragmented self blames the therapist for the "outrage" of being a separate person and having a private life.

Even so, it is not easy for the therapist to take the rage empathically, that is, to try to understand why a particular disappointment on the long list is coming up now and what genetic significance it has. Yet it is not easy to handle the outpouring of passionate love or vitriolic hate, which we have become accustomed to in focusing on pathological oedipal problems. The therapist needs consistently to remember the infantile context of the narcissistic rage and the early fear over the patient's experience of the therapist as a separate person with the inevitable indications that the therapist is not completely available as a benign selfobject. Then the therapist will not slip too often into indignation that the patient is as demanding as a little child. Rather the therapist will be deeply aware that the patient's needs for mirroring as a support for his healthy ambition were not accepted at the phase-appropriate time.

As Kohut suggested, it is not inconceivable that just as we long throughout life for the omnipotent parent imago, hopefully modified into a nurturing selfobject, so we are as prone to long for the feeling of omnipotent elation in which we control the universe again, hopefully modified into healthy ambition as an essential aspect of the healthy bipolar self (Kohut, 1977). Suppose we follow Freud's dictum to explore the myths of humankind in order to gain insight into the human unconscious. Kohut (1982) did this in proposing the myth of Odysseus who saved his son's life rather than the myth of Oedipus who, out of alleged inborn fearful rivalry, was almost killed at birth by his father. From a myth-exploring stance we can ask how the existential base of the healthy development of human ambition became corroded with the terrible intimidation inflicted by self-destroying religions and governments, aimed at destroying "dangerous" individualism.

THE GRANDIOSE GODS

If we can speculate that the mythical gods were conjured up by human beings with evolving high-level brains in order to give themselves some sense of efficacy in a terrifying thunderstorm of a world, then we can also understand how those who were able to seize power over other humans identified with the grandiosity projected upon the gods. We can then not only empathize with the rage arising out of helplessness which our patients heap upon us, but also glimpse the parental sadism projected upon the revengeful gods.

The theme of revenge for a wrong, so blatant in narcissistic rage even against nonhumans (e.g., Moby Dick) is nowhere better illustrated than in the concept of hell as an eternal torture house. Alice Miller (1983) has charted one way for all people to begin to understand the potential peril the world now faces in terms of social dissolution, including nuclear war, because of the centuries of sadistic parenting that have turned out more and more grownup "children," burning for revenge.

Let us not denounce grandiosity or try to stamp it out but rather be aware that infantile grandiosity, only if suitably tamed by appropriate mirroring, can produce mature developmental fruit, healthy ambition, and cohesive self-esteem.

The censure of grandiosity may, if we come to understand it, shed some light on the curious vacuum of awareness in relation to the concept of the self. Even psychoanalysis is still predominantly focused on the quality of object relations as a measure of mental health, with the implication that if one's relations with other people are all right, then one's self-relations are bound to be gratifying. Self psychology has definitively demonstrated that many people can have a façade of smooth object relations and a desert within as far as feeling any reliable and growing self-esteem.

But, as Kohut (1977) pointed out, poets, playwrights, composers, and artists have known of the bitter struggle for self-realization at least since the fifth century B.C. in Greece. So the cry for identity, for acknowledgment of one's existence, for applause over one's achievements and attributes echoes down the centuries, even from a paleolithic cave of 25,000 years ago—the Pêche-Merle in the Dordogne Mountains in France—where a magnificently rendered hand, bleeding but not maimed, is held up not as a threat, but as a supplication for recognition. It is to this reaching out for recognition of a self's uniqueness that Kohut's concept of empathy for infantile grandiosity is so applicable. If the grandiosity can be understood as a demand for human recognition, then it need not trigger the conviction that such demands must be stopped at all costs, whatever basic needs they involve. If a human environment, responsive to the self-needs of another person does, as we believe, activate ego growth, then the sensitive acceptance of grandiose needs can open up the underlying wellsprings of creativity.

5

Idealization

If thou must love me, let it be for naught
Except for love's sake only. Do not say,
"I love her for her smile—her look—her way . . .
For these things in themselves, Beloved, may
Be changed . . .
But love me for love's sake, that evermore
Thou mayst love on, through love's eternity.

Elizabeth Barrett Browning

Love, it has been suggested (Bergmann, 1980), includes both idealization and a sense of infinite time. When love falters, the idealization intrinsic to it has been replaced with criticism. And as Elizabeth Barrett Browning and Martin Bergmann both imply, there is clearly a fear, at an adult level, of the failure of idealization when love fails.

Yet both Elizabeth Barrett Browning and Bergmann are talking about "object love," i.e., the love Freud (1914) delineated as being directed toward another person who is experienced as *different* from the self. This interpretation assumes that separation-individuation (Mahler et al., 1975), namely the acceptance of the natural difference between one's self and another, has occurred. Such awareness of differentiation, as we all know, can often make the participants feel that the relationship is almost impossible. And it is certainly true that sharp differences, perhaps involving a denial of the basic needs of the nuclear self for one or both participants in a relationship, can make its viability seriously questionable. Nevertheless, the greater the preoccupation with the differences in a relationship, the more likely it is that one or both individuals have not achieved differentiation and that their expectations of love still basically involve the fulfillment of their unmet infantile mirroring and idealizing needs.

As we noted in Chapter 1, the little child needs to idealize the parent, especially as he senses that his grandiose self cannot reliably master the world. Based on the selfobject transference reaction of adult patients, and corroborating Kohut, we proposed in Chapter 1 a longing for a conviction that the selfobject will be there when needed, that his or her strength and caring can be counted on when the child feels helpless or in pain. We also wonder whether the perfection of life in the womb—the nine months of reliable service in regard to temperature, nutrition, elimination, and, presumably, noiselessness—leaves the baby expecting a continuation of responsiveness, especially in an environment where he or she is called upon to breathe, take food in, eliminate, and do all sorts of other things that he or she never had to do in the womb. It could also be that a good symbiosis (Mahler et al., 1975) may make an infant especially hopeful that life can continue to be a paradise.

But more than service for basic needs is involved here. The child who desperately wants to know, "Will you be there when I need you? Can I count on your strength and your caring when I feel in despair and helpless?" is providing him- or herself with an ideal figure that may be based on intrauterine and/or extra-uterine experiences with a good parenting person—someone who will not fall apart under the stresses of life, whether for the child or for him- or herself. Such a figure who will be attuned to the child's emerging manifestations of his nuclear self—for example, whether he likes to run and play vigorous games, or paint or play with a musical instrument, or try to work with tools or write a story. An idealized parent will be interested, will try to find out what the child likes and help him or her to begin to do it. Self psychology also teaches us that the parent who conspicuously fails in his business aspirations and even turns to his young son for encouragement and advice, as in Kohut's example of Mr. A. (1971), is unfortunately making it very difficult for the son to internalize such a father as a superego to be looked up to, admired, and further emulated.

BOTH MOTHERS AND FATHERS CAN BE IDEALIZED

There does not seem to be much of a sexist difference in regard to superego development. Perhaps the nature of the superego really devolves on the most assertive parent. We should stress that idealization here may include pathological identifications with either parent so that the process of idealization itself can be subsumed to serve unconscious infantile needs. It can include identification with the father who, given his own psychopathic tendencies, may encourage them in his children. It can also include identification with a masochistic mother who can never say no to the most outrageous demands of either her husband or her children. This brings us to the issue of failed idealization which may involve pathological power operations by one or both parents. However, there may be a glimmer of hope remaining on the part of the child that someone will come along to offer a better, more growth-promoting thrust toward life.

CASE VIGNETTE

A supervisee presented the case* of Rosalie R., a 36-year-old Jewish woman, with blond hair, green eyes, and perhaps 10 pounds overweight. She had a 13-year-old son toward whom the patient was very angry. Rosalie saw the world as basically dangerous. Therefore, the supervisee believed, the patient always needed to be in control, as evidenced in her unrelenting efforts to get others to go along with her needs. She was a compulsive eater, presumably dealing with her unacceptable feelings in this

*A composite of cases contributed by Joanne Gates, M.S., and Fellow, American Institute for Psychotherapy and Psychoanalysis.

way. She expected perfection from herself and others, including
the therapist.

Supervisor: Did you sense that idealization might be a problem for
her transference with you in the very first session?

The supervisee, a sensitive woman, said that she had picked
up, early on, that Rosalie was quite intelligent, knew her way
around her world, but that her traumatic childhood had driven
her to believe she could rely only on herself.

Supervisor: Could such self-sufficiency be a defense against an
unfulfilled need to idealize someone in her childhood?
Supervisee: Well, you've picked up, as I picked up in the very first
session, that this woman had been somehow tragically deprived as a child. I felt then that I would have to be very
careful about seeming to want to control her or make her
dependent upon me, that it would only be in a relatively
undemanding atmosphere that she might be able to idealize
me.
Supervisor: Please tell me about her background.

The supervisee then went on to tell that Rosalie, the older of
two children, with a brother two years younger, had felt both her
parents were incapable of idealization. Her obese father was abusive and rageful, and many times the patient did not know what
angered him. He was the erratic breadwinner for the family, often
involved in shady business deals but also promising to make a
lot of money. Yet Rosalie craved his attention, perhaps because
she realized how weak and childlike her mother was. Her
mother's fear of her father and her inability to protect Rosalie
were recalled in a poignant memory of a time when her mother,
who was never supposed to go out by herself, asserted herself
and went to her friend's house with the two children. When they
came home, her father went into a rage. He took Rosalie's kitten,
which she dearly loved, and drowned it in a nearby stream. At
that point, Rosalie seemed to realize that her mother would not

protect her from her father's rage. But, the supervisee pointed out, there were more tragic developments to come.

Incest in Latency

Supervisor: That kind of experience could certainly arrest a child's ability to idealize either parent. Perhaps she also identified with the kitten who was killed. How old was she?

The supervisee said Rosalie was about five. Two years later, Rosalie's father began to approach her sexually while her mother played cards at a friend's house. This involved the father exposing himself and masturbating, while fondling her genitals. At the beginning of treatment, Rosalie's memories of this were very vague, but became more detailed as the treatment progressed. She recalled conflicting feelings—being very special, powerful, and powerless. Her father threatened her that something horrible would happen if she ever told her mother. Rosalie fantasized that either her mother would leave or would kill her or kill him.

Finally, after two years, at the age of nine, the patient told her mother. While her mother did not react violently, as her father had threatened, for Rosalie her mother's response was perhaps even more devastating. She did not fully believe Rosalie's story. Instead, Rosalie was sent to a "head" doctor to understand why she was telling such stories. She wasn't to tell anybody else about what she "accused" her father of doing or that she was seeing a "shrink." Thinking that she was being punished for doing something bad, Rosalie said she had felt awful and degraded. Above all, she felt she had no one to turn to who would believe her and try to understand her feelings and guard her from despair.

Further Disillusionments

Supervisor: How did her previous treatment affect her and how did she get to you?

The supervisee said she wanted to defer discussion about her first contacts with Rosalie until she had presented further disillusionments the patient had had. The "head" doctors she had seen from age nine until she married at age 20 had proved to be unhelpful, critical, and nonnourishing. For example, she always had to eat candy before and after each session, and she was a compulsive eater until she started treatment with the supervisee. However, her seemingly passive mother told her at age 14 that she was divorcing her father for her own reasons, never acknowledging that she believed Rosalie's story.

Rosalie became even more depressed when she realized that her mother could leave her father when *she* was ready to, but not for Rosalie's sake. They were also even poorer after leaving father, although her mother held down two jobs. Rosalie was put on antidepressants to relieve the depression that dominated her teenage years. Her high intelligence got her into a good high school where she read a lot as a means of escape. At 20, she married a man who seemed passive and safe, someone not given to explosive outbursts like her father. Soon she became "compulsively" involved with having sex with a woman friend she met in school. It seemed like an act of revenge against her passive, alcoholic husband. It was not clear how he found out about the other relationship, although early on she described her husband "as taking it and drinking all the time."

When she first heard about Rosalie's affair with her girlfriend, the supervisee wondered whether her husband had disillusioned her early on in the marriage or whether there was some strange compulsion to recreate her childhood situation where two people were being sexually abused, i.e., herself at the hands of her father, and her mother, who must have had a strange complex of feelings about her daughter replacing her, although she didn't acknowledge this at all. Moreover, the supervisee didn't want to explore issues that might further damage the patient's self-esteem or her capacity to idealize until the supervisee had a clearer view of how Rosalie was relating to the therapist.

The problem of what the sexual relationship with the girlfriend, Brenda, signified presented itself even more intensely when the therapist was informed in the first session, that 10 years later, when Rosalie's two-year-old son was left with Brenda as a baby-sitter, the latter sexually molested him. She later confessed it to Rosalie. This abuse involved fondling the child's penis. Although Rosalie never left her child with Brenda again, she continued the sexual relationship with Brenda for another 12 years.

The Limited Contract

Supervisor: And now you must really tell me just how you persuaded this immovable woman to come into treatment with you and stay in it for almost three years. Otherwise, I'll think you have a countertransference problem.

Supervisee: Well, perhaps it's a sort of repetition compulsion of expecting the worst, of being suspicious of the changes that have occurred and, of course, wondering about the validity of my approach to getting Rosalie into treatment. You see, in that first session I felt inundated by the difficult story of her life. I kept wondering what I could offer her that would persuade her to stay in treatment and work out her need to believe that she could find someone to help her, someone to trust and even look up to. Then, as I saw her sitting there in her coat as close to the door as she could get, I thought, "This lady is terrified of depending on me or on anyone after all the disappointments she's had. So the least threatening thing I can offer her is a time-limited approach."

So I said, "I realize you are a very busy woman." (She had just completed a degree in computer science and procured herself a promising job in a corporation.) "And I know you don't want to spend any more time in therapy at this point than necessary. So I'm suggesting a two-month contract for two sessions a week in which we'll work on two issues: first, how to understand your relationship with Brenda and its effects on your marriage; and second, how to deal with your son about the sexual issue, and hopefully, to help him make a better adjustment all around. At the end of the 16 sessions, we can evaluate where we are."

Rosalie, the supervisee recalled, moved her chair just a little bit closer to hers, although still safely near the door. She shook her head in disbelief. "You really mean . . . you'd give me a chance to decide after two months whether . . . I could just leave and not feel guilty?" The supervisee nodded.

"Well, it certainly doesn't sound like therapy so I'm willing to try it, though I don't trust you."

The Child and the Lost Bird

In discussing the first 16 sessions, the supervisee admitted that she had a countertransference issue, which she described as "incredible rescue plans about the son, Carl. The therapist saw Rosalie as a person who had been very hurt and abused growing up and who had unconsciously regressed back to infantile grandiosity in a determination never to be vulnerable and dependent again. This included never needing her son's love and thus being dependent on him. The supervisee also made a connection in her own mind between the pet kitten Rosalie's father had killed and her two-year-old son whom her lover had sexually abused, namely that Rosalie felt she could no longer risk loving something or someone that could be destroyed because it was too painful for her to endure.

So Rosalie defended herself against her love for and anxiety toward her son with denial and hostility. She described her child as a "wild animal." He was hyperactive, was scapegoated at school, and had no friends. She dragged the child like a damaged object from specialist to specialist and thought the world was saying to her, "Hey lady, what's the matter with that brat?"

The supervisee noted that Rosalie was convinced her son's problems reflected badly on her competence as a mother. This blow to her self-esteem triggered her grandiosity, which drove her in two ways: 1) She had to force the child to do better in the outside world and at home; and 2) she had to badger school teachers to get special treatment for Carl. Yet Rosalie could not consistently enforce limits, although the child was quite abusive to her. She looked down on the child as hopeless and did not directly try to help him, although seeking to fix the world up for him. The supervisee was particularly struck by her intolerance of Carl's fear of Brenda the girlfriend who had molested him. When the child said he hated Brenda and didn't want her in the house, Rosalie would say, "I don't tell you who your friends can be. So don't give me orders about it!"

The supervisee recognized Rosalie's narcissistic rage at Carl's effort to interfere with his mother's grandiosity. Yet, pushed by her need to "rescue the son" as a way to help Rosalie rescue herself, the supervisee thought that she might succeed in appealing to Rosalie's reasonable ego and thereby circumvent the revengeful grandiosity.

Feelings Count More Than Reason

In the context of appealing to Rosalie's reasonable ego which seemed to function so well in her work, the supervisee asked: "Well, considering what happened to Carl, is it so unreasonable that he wants to have this particular power over you?" The supervisee then wryly remembered how she felt as if she had stepped on a land mine and that the case was doomed.

Rosalie blazed back, "Well, what about *my* feelings? How dare this brat carry on the way he does, making me look like an idiot mother, and then have the nerve to expect I would deprive myself of my lover just because of something that happened so long ago and shouldn't matter any more anyway! I'm not even so sure he remembers the incidents with Brenda. He's just trying to manipulate me." So if this is all your new-fangled therapy approach amounts to, blaming me for Carl's being a mess, then I should leave right now and the hell with the contract!"

The supervisee realized she had to do something quickly to save the case. She also realized that in her concern for the child, she had not fully considered Rosalie's feelings of failure and unlovability—the very feelings she had felt as a child when her father tortured her in killing her kitten and in sexually abusing her, and her mother failed to protect her. Here the supervisee was doing the same thing, from Rosalie's standpoint. In trying to help relieve the mother/son struggle, the supervisee seemed to totally disregard Rosalie's feelings. So the supervisee took a deep breath and said:

"I realize now that when I asked that question about Carl, you must have felt I wasn't considering your feelings at all. And I guess it felt just like the times both your mother and father canceled out your feelings and did what they pleased!"

For a moment, Rosalie looked as if she were going to cry. But, obviously swallowing her feelings, she said grimly: "Well, you *are* the first person who has ever recognized that I can be hurt and despairing through no fault of my own, even though you did take Carl's side. But at least you admitted your mistake so I'll give you another chance. However, you've got to put my feelings first!"

Empathy and Idealization

Supervisor: Well, this is an excellent example of the important role empathy plays in the development of idealization which, as you know, Kohut found to be so crucial for the development of a cohesive self. And we see in Rosalie's case how quickly her vulnerable self-esteem fragments and she is overwhelmed by narcissistic rage. I imagine you've realized, too, that Rosalie just didn't seem to have anybody to look up to at all in her growing up.

It was not just a question of massive disillusionment in her father, first with his killing her kitten and then with the prolonged sexual abuse and warning her not to tell. He had never been an idealized figure for her in any way, except perhaps in a negative way of ordering her mother around. But she may have been disillusioned even in that respect, since he killed *her* kitten the day her mother disobeyed and went out to visit her friend. And the father seemed to be frightened of the consequences of telling the mother about the incest. It seems likely that Rosalie became contemptuous of his phony anger covering up fear, when her mother made Rosalie pay, rather than the father, by not believing her and by taking her to therapists. Of course, her mother seems to have been quite unempathic to Rosalie from early on and didn't present herself as a woman to be looked up to at all.

The supervisee nodded acquiesence and added that she had been wondering if it were possible for the therapist to be idealized and thus offer the patient the chance to resume arrested development, if both parents had been so disillusioning.

Supervisor: Well, this is still an open question, especially in view of Kohut's conceptual broadening of the bipolar self to the tripolar self (see Chapter 6; Kohut, 1984). He leaves the door open for idealized figures later in development, e.g., adolescence, and also in therapy. It also occurs to me that Rosalie's mother, in finally leaving the father and taking her two children with her, was giving Rosalie at age 14 quite an example of independence she wouldn't have expected of her seemingly passive, frightened mother. After all, her mother had to hold down two jobs and live in even greater poverty than with the father, in order to support herself and the two children without him.

There is also another idealizable possibility and that is, even though Rosalie condemns it understandably, the mother was trying to help her daughter by sending her to therapy from age nine. At the very least, she was holding out the possibility that whatever went wrong between her daughter and her husband, maybe it could be repaired for the daughter's sake. And who paid for all this therapy? Either the mother somehow had to manage it or she was able to take the initiative to find out how her daughter could get therapy without having to pay for it.

The Intimidating Patient

The supervisee agreed that these were possibilities she had to consider and perhaps cautiously introduce when the timing seemed just right. But she then went on to admit that Rosalie scared her, with a certain kind of intimidating look and a tendency to a pouncing attack. The dialogue continues:

Supervisee: Rosalie sometimes seems to move from feeling "who needs you" to wanting me as a selfobject and then she needs to control me as part of herself. If I say something that isn't perfectly attuned at that point, she becomes enraged at my lack of empathy. Sometimes it isn't clear whether she is furious with me as a failed part of herself who should have known what she needs, as in the grandiose transference; or whether I failed her as an idealized parent who could still read her mind and provide what she needs, but not quite as a part of herself.

Supervisor: This is a subtle point. I do think that with the massive regression to the grandiose self, there is a return to the very early months of life where the baby is not able to distinguish between her physical and psychological self and the selfobjects who care for her. As we know, if the caring is good, the baby has more and more capacity for optimal frustration, which leads to the internalization of all sorts of soothing and control mechanisms. And, as we know, the quite frequent occasions on which mother or father rise to care for the baby in a crisis state (e.g., a bodily pain or an accident) and soothe with their seemingly omniscient calm and strength, or help a child to have fun out of a threatening situation (e.g., a ball game), build either the expectation of an ideal supporter to be there when needed or an expectation that the child can become himself the ideal supporter.

Supervisee: It sounds like either way she needs me to soothe her in relation to what she's feeling. It will then be up to her to decide whether I'm a cooperative part of herself or an idealized selfobject.

Supervisor: Not quite. If you're just a part of herself, you're required to do what she wants and often it is to make the horrible experience not to have happened. If you're an idealized selfobject, you will be expected to be empathic because you have superior knowledge and you're not just an order-taker from her. For instance, she didn't want you to minimize her problems with Carl. She wanted you to let her know you realized how horrible they were for her as a reenactment of her early experiences of nobody caring about her feelings. So she wanted an empathic reaction to her horror, which is not necessarily soothing per se but becomes so ultimately as the child or adult realizes someone powerful understands his or her terrible predicament.

Supervisee: And conceivably could help.

The Power of Empathy

Supervisor: The expression of empathy, which Kohut came to realize, is mobilizing in itself. That someone else, and especially an idealizable person, can understand and appropriately resonate with the terrible experiences one has been through is to respect and validate them. The person who is suffering, child or adult, and is thus validated can then believe in the reality of his feelings and not have to be doubtful or apologetic about whether he is entitled to have such feelings.

The narcissistic rage that usually accompanies an invalidation of helplessness, horror, or terror—all feelings that fragment the cohesive self—often involves a wish to destroy the unempathic other, still conceived as an offending part of an omnipotent self. It is, perhaps, this wish to destroy the unempathic other that makes Rosalie's rage so scary. And, unless you realize all I have been saying, you may still underestimate the power of empathy in just trying to understand the awfulness of Rosalie's feelings when her father drowned her kitten and when he subjected her to sexual abuse. And the awfulness of her feelings was intensified with the realization that her mother did not believe her or understand how much she was suffering. Perhaps if her mother had only been empathic, even though she couldn't change anything, it might have helped.

The supervisee said she was beginning to glimpse the power of empathy. She realized that it probably was her empathy for her patient's not being able to accept a therapy situation, which could seem endless again, and her willingness to put the treatment on a limited contract basis that made it possible for Rosalie to even try it. The supervisee then said, "But I let her down when I became overly concerned with Carl and downplayed Rosalie's feelings. This was what had happened to her over and over in her childhood. No wonder she went into a rage!

Supervisor: If you can keep that "it's no wonder you are in a rage" feeling about whatever Rosalie is experiencing, for a long time, you may be able to do two seemingly impossible things: 1) You may be able to convince her that it's all right to be dependent, to need your empathy and that you can be relied upon to provide it; and 2) you may be able to convince her that she can dare to idealize you and look up to you as a person with important values you live by, values of caring about people, and that she may feel able to identify with these values and guide her life by them. I can't think of any more important ways in which you could help her.

Fear of Trusting

At a later supervisory session, the supervisee reported that she had tried hard to be empathic with the patient's rageful attacks, especially when they were focused on her and that this seemed to have brought about a diminution of Rosalie's rage and a gradual consideration of her fear of closeness. The supervisee said Rosalie realized that she couldn't get close to anyone because she couldn't put herself in the hands of another person who might do her in. This was clearly a three-way allusion, involving her parents and the supervisee who said, "I'm aware that in some way she's talking about me but I'm not touching this right now because she's going to back off."

This seemed to be a delicate point. If a patient like Rosalie, a battered child emotionally, is showing what Kohut (1971) called "a vulnerable tendril of idealization" (p. 221), it is very important to accept it, if at all possible. However, if a patient is showing much ambivalence, it is also important not to pressure the patient into a premature avowal. The supervisee, skillfully, did not call attention to the possibility of Rosalie's idealizing her, since that would have been premature. This was especially important because the patient was beginning to realize the difference between her need for attention and affection and her need for sex. The patient's promiscuous behavior in her adolescence involved looking for something she never quite got. Presumably this was why she married her husband at age 20.

Sex Equals Caring

Before Rosalie married, her sexual relationship with her husband-to-be was quite passionate and certainly more fulfilling than any sexual experience she had known. It was for this reason that she agreed to marry at age 20, against her mother's wishes and with her own doubts about her chosen mate's reliability in other areas. Her premonitions, unfortunately, were soon justified.

Although her husband at first continued to be the wonderfully caring lover in bed, he turned out to be very uncaring in most other aspects of life. He had great difficulty holding a job and providing a secure income. He had even more difficulty managing his space, as it were. He was extremely untidy, messy, and inconsiderate, leaving her no place to herself and making their home such a wreck she was embarrassed to have friends over. So their social life became very bleak. Perhaps the worst disappointment, though, was that partly as a result of heavy drinking, the husband showed no interest in what she might want or feel, including the efforts she had to make to provide an income for the family.

Grim Replays of the Patient's Childhood

All in all, apart from the "good sex," Rosalie experienced her marriage as a grim replay of her childhood, with no attention or affection but an abusive emphasis on sex. It was in this context that her sexual relationship with her woman friend became clearer to the supervisee.

Rosalie had longed for a close relationship with a caring woman, something her mother was never able to provide. It seemed likely that Rosalie had sexualized this need for a good selfobject and, accordingly, had not been surprised when Brenda disillusioned her by abusing her son. It was really a defense for Rosalie against needing or trusting anyone, as the therapist repeatedly realized. Also, Brenda's sexual attraction to Rosalie relieved Rosalie's anxiety that she could only be desirable to male failures like her husband and, by analogy, her father. Brenda also provided at least some relief from the dreary and unstimulating solitude of the messy house Rosalie's husband imposed on her. Finally, Rosalie's affair with this woman, behind her husband's back gave her a sense of power at least in revenging herself upon her husband, although she felt helpless in reaching him any other way. When this lover confessed that she had molested Rosalie's two-year-old son, what seemed like an incredible repetition of Rosalie's own childhood trauma immobilized her. She was once again debased and disillusioned by both her lover and her husband, as she had been by her parents, and was convinced that it had to be her fault.

Rosalie decided not to break up with her lover because, although Brenda had sexually abused her son, she was able to fulfill needs for attention and mirroring that were not being met by anyone else in Rosalie's life. This repeated Rosalie's experience that any attention to herself would always involve abuse. Also, she did not want to deprive herself of the physical relationship with her lover. Rosalie therefore regressed again to her narcissistic grandiosity, convincing herself she could handle everything, and proceeded to get college and graduate degrees while working as a secretary. With her degree in computer science she was then able to get herself a well-paying executive position. Meanwhile, her life at 39 was still like the emotional desert of childhood.

Where Is the Patient's Space?

The contract for the first 16 sessions came to an end while Rosalie was struggling with her terror of depending on the therapist and expecting to be disappointed once more. Rosalie had, however, revealed the emotional desert in which she was still living. The supervisee reported the quandary in which she found herself. If she encouraged the patient explicitly to make a 16-session contract, would Rosalie then see her as treacherous and as wanting to hang on to her, like the other therapists? But if the supervisee just let her go, leaving it strictly up to Rosalie, wouldn't this feel like the same indifference to her needs that she had experienced so much as a child and as an adult?

The supervisee's quandary was resolved by a sudden inspiration—perhaps an integration that therapists become able to make, based on their efforts to empathically understand a patient and on the unconscious processes that can produce an awareness of the patient's emotional needs at that point. Rosalie's description of how her husband's callous indifference and messiness made a wreck of her home and her compliance with having neither physical nor emotional space, although she was supporting the whole menage, led the supervisee to realize that the key issue in treatment might now be, "Where is your space?" Thus, when Rosalie rather defiantly announced that she was leaving treatment at the end of the contract and added, "I feel good in here, but maybe you're trying to lure me in," the supervisee felt relatively secure in saying to Rosalie, "I know. But *where* is your space?"

Rosalie did not answer the question then, but she returned for another 16-session contract after the supervisee's vacation. Rosalie announced that she wanted to work on her rights to space, time, and respect, indicating that she had heard and pondered the supervisee's question at the end of the first contract. Apparently, she experienced the very question as the therapist's acknowledgment that the latter believed Rosalie was entitled to her space and could demand it, rather than just hoping she would be given it if she did everything the powers that be wanted of her. It seemed clear to the supervisee that her acceptance of Rosalie's right to leave treatment at the end of the contract proved that the therapist believed Rosalie was entitled to her space in all relationships and could insist on it.

Cleaning Up the Mess

Rosalie not only believed she was entitled to her space through the therapist's acceptance of it, but she also acted on it vigorously.

For the first time, she threw herself into arranging her "space" the way she wanted it—with the same energy and determination she could show in her work to meet others' demands. She had confronted her husband with the choice of helping her reorganize and redecorate the house or leaving for good. That choice involved his exercising some control over his drinking and inactivity and actually trying to straighten out his mess—or being put out of Rosalie's life for good. If he could shape up and meet her demands on this count, she was prepared to reconsider divorcing him. If not, she was prepared to get rid of him and felt she could, on the basis of his continued drinking and lack of support.

Rosalie did not find the going easy. Her husband thought he could wear her down by procrastinating, as he often had in the past. He tried to make her feel sorry for him because of all the failures and disappointments he had had. He tried to undermine her conviction by being sexually seductive. But Rosalie's work with the therapist had convinced her sufficiently that she was entitled to her space, i.e., to having her needs considered. Therefore, she was determined not to be pushed off her course once more by other people's needs, no matter what they were or how pathetically they were presented. Rosalie pointed out that she had greatly overpaid her "dues" for this marriage, and if her husband were not willing to pay at least some of his, then he would be put out of the "club."

The Patient Gets Her Space

Rosalie's determination finally convinced and probably scared her husband. He began to help her instead of fighting her. After the cleanup, they began to spend more time together, buying furniture and redecorating so that Rosalie would be able to entertain business friends for the first time. In the course of this getting together, her husband showed signs of trying to give up drinking and to get himself a more creditable job than that of the unsuccessful traveling salesman he had been. Rosalie became suspicious. She would believe in his ability to make more thoroughgoing changes when she saw them. She was tired of broken promises. Nevertheless, she did appreciate what he had been able to do and she felt much less depressed and driven, now that she liked her space and could use it more socially.

The therapist was very encouraging in response to Rosalie's accounts of her achievements. The therapist was still striving to be empathic with Rosalie's feelings, but now she was focusing on sustaining Rosalie's sense of entitlement to her space.

Worries About Dependence

While Rosalie seemed pleased by the therapist's appreciation of her achievements, at the same time she more openly expressed her anxiety about the therapist's reliability. Could she depend on the therapist to be there for her? Would the therapist find a patient she liked better than Rosalie? Maybe the therapist would go into another profession. Maybe her fee would be raised so she couldn't afford treatment. Maybe the therapist would be hit by a bus.

As the therapist pointed out to her supervisor, there was quite a range of fears about daring to be dependent, from an apprehension that the therapist wouldn't be there for Rosalie emotionally or would prefer someone else, to death anxiety (for instance, the therapist would have an accident). At the supervisor's suggestion, the supervisee said, "It's natural that you would expect your hopes to be damaged and destroyed, because they so often were in your growing up."

This acceptance of both her fears of and longing for dependence led to a crucial acknowledgment that she wanted to stay in treatment, despite her anxieties about its reliability. It seemed to lead, the supervisee thought, to a more immediate access to her feelings. In contrast to her defensive, goal-directed attitude, which had helped her weather her difficult life, Rosalie now seemed able to relax more, to notice things around her like the therapist's office furniture and the trees outside the window.

Access to the Patient's Feelings for Her Son

In this crucial and precarious transition in treatment where the patient moves away from rigid defenses against feelings, especially feelings of longing and idealizing dependence, so that the grandiose self can function with a maximum of computer-like efficiency, it is essential that the therapist wait patiently to see where the denied and repressed affects may emerge, whether in relation to the self or to other people.

In Rosalie's case, while some feelings of tentative hope had arisen with her husband, she was still, understandably, skeptical. In relation to her son, Rosalie was confronted with painfully conflicting feelings about her son as herself and as the child for whom she was responsible. For some time, before she was able to get access to her feelings, Rosalie had been able to express a lot of anger toward her son for his inadequacies, including his abusive reactions toward his mother, his poor performance in school and socially, and even his appearance. "He's so big!" Rosalie exclaimed, "If he's not careful, he'll end up as obese as my father." She was also thinking of sending the boy away to boarding school, so that he could be controlled, be given manners, and be made more independent.

A Defense Against Needing Her Son

The supervisee realized that Rosalie's fears of dependence, so clearly exemplified in her transference reactions toward the therapist, would naturally be involved in her relationship to her son. There is so much expectation on the part of the unfulfilled parent that the child will fulfill the parent's unrealized aspirations that what the child may want or be capable of can so easily be snuffed out like a candle flame. The child's reactions to the exclusion of his or her nuclear self, which probably went on from infancy, are, inevitably, passive submission or revolution.

In the case of Rosalie's son, Carl, given his sexual trauma at the hands of Rosalie's lover plus the tormenting relationship between his mother and father, it seems as if Carl went the way of revolution. His speech problem suggests a tragic somatic expression of his difficulties in communicating with either of them. Conceivably, this could have been intensified at the age of two when his mother continued to be friendly with Brenda, even though

Carl insisted that he didn't want his mother to be friends with her. That the child continued to make this a demand for a proof of his mother's love raises a question of how much the mother interpreted any failure on the child's part as a result of the sexual abuse and how much the mother projected onto her son her own automatic inhibitions of feeling, as a result of her own father's prolonged sexual abuse, that is, not once but for years.

A Dawning Acceptance of the Patient's Feelings

In the next round of sessions, still on the two-month contract plan, Rosalie took a major step. She had been thinking for some time of sending her son away to boarding school because of the seemingly irresolvable problems between them. It is important to remember that in the second round of sessions, she had already taken a stand with her husband on her need for space and had actually brought about impressive changes in the house and in the way she lived, including much more socializing.

In the context of thinking about sending her child to boarding school but also of becoming more aware of her dependence on the therapist, Rosalie suddenly decided to give up her lover. Characteristically, she did not discuss this with her therapist. Her mode of living was to take an action when she felt able to and then to consider the consequences afterwards. This seems to be an expression of grandiosity in that she presumably will be able to handle whatever happens.

The Importance of Rosalie's Son

It seemed to the therapist that in becoming aware of her need for the therapist, Rosalie also became aware of her need for her son and, conversely, of her son's need for her. This was a poignant realization of how much she had needed her own mother to be concerned for her feelings and to have protected her against her father, however she could have. There seemed to be a sudden perception that what Carl needed to overcome his self-esteem problems was a conviction that his mother could protect him against unmanageable feelings stemming from sexual overarousal at the age of two. The fact that his mother had continued to have a relationship with this woman made the situation so anxiety-arousing for the child that he had continued through the years to beg his mother to stop letting Brenda into the house.

Whatever the child's perceptions of all this—which we can only guess at—it seems clear that Carl was getting the same lack of attention to his emotional needs that Rosalie herself had experienced. So it was a major acceptance of her self as well as her son when Rosalie decided to give up her lover and told her child that she was no longer going to be friendly with Brenda. Rosalie also confirmed to Carl that when he was little Brenda had fondled his penis and that this was not acceptable behavior. Rosalie made it clear to Carl that he had done nothing wrong. Thus, Rosalie was validating her son's experience that this abuse occurred—it was not a fantasy and it had been a very disturbing event in her son's life as well as in that of Rosalie. The fact that Rosalie then gave up the lover is an impressive expression of her concern for her son.

The Idealized Therapist

A movement toward idealization of the therapist came out of Rosalie's feeling more free in relation to her feelings and her right to express them. Rosalie characteristically expressed her idealization in terms of applause from other people. She reported that her friends and family "all want to know who is the therapist."

Rosalie said she told them, "It doesn't matter who—she's the perfect one for me." She smiled as she said this and the therapist accepted the idealization and smiled back appreciatively. However, the therapist knew to some extent what lay ahead. That included the therapist's capacity to foresee the outcome of the patient's decisions in crucial concerns to herself.

Both the supervisor and the supervisee agreed that there had been important positive changes in Rosalie in relation to herself, her family, her work, and her friends. She had also begun to develop a sense of humor and a capacity to think somewhat philosophically, which indicated a growth toward a higher form of idealized narcissism, as Kohut (1966) proposed.

THE THERAPIST-PATIENT FLOW: SEARCHING FOR THE MISSED IDEAL

As in all case presentations, we get a flavor of what the patient is like, including her life experiences and the interactions with the therapist. As detailed and graphic as these may be, however, it is difficult to capture, in words, the process of the interaction between two persons engaged in mutual exploration over time, together with the therapist's and patient's experiences within themselves.

Language still has the limitation of being unable to accurately reflect the poetry within people—along with their pain. Similarly, in listening to a patient detail his or her inner/outer flow of experiences, we must pay attention to the omissions, since, like the white space on the Rorschach, this gives additional clues to the person's life experience. One such omission in the case of Rosalie seemed to involve the mother, undoubtedly leading to the patient's excessive self-reliance, with a concomitant mistrust of others.

If the natural caretaker, the mother, is not available to the child at the preoedipal level (ages 0-4) because of, say, physical or emotional absence, illness, or death, one consequence is that the child experiences a major disillusionment in the strength and reliability of the all-powerful qualities of the mothering person.

This is what Jacobson (1964) termed premature disillusionment in the idealized parent. Such disillusionment is often defended against by a sense of loss and shame, as if the child blames himself for not being cared about. It can often be a major blow to a child if mother is not where he wants her to be when he wants her to be there. Since this usually happens with the therapist over the one or two months' summer vacation, some of the same feelings are likely to emerge.

In dealing with early needs for an idealized selfobject, we see, in our daily practice, such demands translated into the need for the therapist's availability and all-powerfulness. While Rosalie allowed herself the possibility of moving in and out of treatment, in terms of several 16-session programs, she expected the therapist to be constantly there for her. This is the demand of a two year old and not, by contrast, that of a seven or eight year old who, through adequate idealizing and mirroring experiences, has developed a fairly stable sense of self. At the two-year-old level, the search is going to be for the idealized selfobject who will provide him with instant and constant meeting of his needs. He cannot understand why mother or father, as the case may be, will not always be there to respond to his wants, such as join him in his excitement about walking or, if he gets sick, to immediately make him well.

Thinking of the occasions on which a little child two years old or younger can get terribly disappointed and expect magic from the parents, we can realize this is a similar situation that the therapist is now being confronted with. It is not just a matter of failing the patient in terms of being the ideal therapist at a higher level, such as taking an interest in what the patient is interested in as a life pursuit. It is, crucially, not being able to measure up to the impossible omnipotent demands of the little child for the idealized selfobject.

SLEEP DISORDERS AND LACK OF SOOTHING

Regression to the idealized selfobject, which we may see in our patients, comes about because of a failure of the idealized superego, such as the abuse Rosalie suffered at her father's hands. The intensity of the need for a comforting father figure is not so likely to occur if the mother is sensitively soothing from birth. Sometimes early deprivation becomes visible in patients who complain of their sleep disorders.

Although we are familiar with the phrase, "He's sleeping like a baby," in actuality babies need a great deal of help in sleeping. Babies who are properly soothed, fed and fondled, and have the right temperature will probably fall asleep pretty easily. However, they can be extremely sensitive to noise, particularly the kind of baby who isn't given much help in falling asleep.

As clinicians, we have heard our patients say, "I'm embarrassed to mention this but I need the light on to fall asleep"; or "I sleep with a radio next to my pillow and keep it on all night because it helps me"; or "I'm dismayed that sometimes I wake up with my thumb in my mouth; I thought I left that behind 30 years ago!"

As we listen to these confessions, we can conjecture that such a person has not been helped to fall asleep when he was a month or two old.

How to Develop Self-Soothing

Mother or father or even a babysitter needs to come in and sing to the baby or tell him a story or stroke him. If this has been done in a consistent fashion, there may come a point where mother decides that maybe he doesn't need quite so much singing or storytelling. She may then leave the room, but before he is quite ready to fall asleep; this is termed optimal frustration (Kohut, 1984). In such a situation, the baby may identify with the soother. He may sing to himself, tell himself a story, play with the blanket, and so forth. This may represent the basic extrauterine process of transmuting internalization (Kohut, 1971), whereby the baby takes over the soothing and other nurturing processes of his care-givers. It applies to sleeping but could also apply, for example, to feeding if the mother is very sensitive to when the child wants to begin to hold the bottle himself. These minute actions, under-taken by the baby himself in his copying of mother, comprise "the basic fabric of the ego" (Kohut, 1971).

Ego Functions and Development

Although there has been some consideration and theorizing about the importance of ego functions, such as relating them to the crucial ability to distinguish reality from infantile longings, we are still not clear about the genesis of ego functions and how they are synchronized with healthy development. It is almost as if they appear magically at the "right" time in development even though we know, especially when an ego function like speech breaks down, that they involve a slow and complex growth.

We are now referring to functions that are central to basic human living and involved in being able to perceive, speak, feel, think, remember, exercise judgment, and care for oneself and others. Obviously, ego functions can involve grave conflicts when they fail to develop at the appropriate point on the developmental timetable (Spitz, 1959). Indeed, Basch (1984) points out that if a child does not have requisite communicative encouragement at the point in the first year when he starts to babble, he may never learn to talk at all (e.g., the "feral" children raised by animals). And if a patient hasn't been helped to sleep easily and soundly as a baby, his or her whole life can be dominated by the problem of avoiding insomnia. Drug addiction, compulsive drinking, and dangerous sexual practices may be the unhealthy solutions for sleep inadequacies, as well as for other self-failures where adequate internalization of an idealized parent has not occurred.

Transmuting Internalization

The patient can be helped to develop transmuting internalization, i.e., the ability to be his own self-soother when trauma threatens. This can start with the therapist's empathic acceptance of the patient's early problems in falling asleep, waking up in the dark, or needing the absent mother right away. The therapist also has to recognize the dangerous solutions mentioned above to which the patient may have been driven. The steadfast understanding of the patient's frightening early needs for soothing can foster the therapist's internalization as the benign idealized selfobject the patient never had. Some relief may ensue if the patient is helped to realize that his own infantile grandiosity or primitive superego (e.g., his mother) may demand that he fall asleep instantly. Narcissistic rage at himself when he cannot comply may only intensify his wakefulness. And he attacks himself both for bodily and mental failures, along with the inadequacy of the idealized parent who failed to teach him the basic essentials for enjoyable living.

The therapist will also eventually get blasted by narcissistic rage as he fails to help the patient control his insomnia immediately.

Just as the infant wanted instant soothing, the adult wants instant sleep. The therapist needs to be patient in accepting the criticisms of his inadequacies in bringing about faster relief. The therapist also needs to be resourceful in suggesting various activities that may help a patient fall asleep gradually, e.g., exercising, or reading nonfiction since fiction may overstimulate. Above all, the patient should be warned against berating himself for all his failures, including his failure to overcome insomnia.

In this way, the therapist is offering himself as a benign and therefore idealizable superego to replace the harsh, nonidealized superego who actually may have interfered with the patient's sleeping as a child (e.g., Rosalie's incestuous father), or who may have been so critical that the patient felt he had no right to rest because he was such a failure.

It is the opportunity and the ultimate challenge for the therapist to support the patient's developmental movement toward the highest level of internalization—the superego ideal. It is here that values, judgments, ideals, and standards coalesce. If the therapist has been internalized as the benign superego, the patient's standards for living will be framed with a caring, soothing, protective attitude toward himself or herself and others. Like Rosalie, the patient will eventually learn to relax and give himself or herself and others not only theoretical room to breathe but also room to inhale and exhale with joy and pride.

CREATIVITY AND IDEALIZATION

Kohut's dawning recognition of the crucial importance of a developing cohesive self for a stable sense of individual fulfillment focused originally on the self's capacities for creativity to be found in the inborn nuclear self. In this connection, Kohut stressed the idea of the transformation of infantile narcissism into higher forms of expression, encompassing human creativity in both the arts and sciences (Freud, 1914). As Kohut (1966) noted "a leading part of the psychological equipment of creative people has been shaped through idealization" (p. 260).

In a review of Kohut's last book, *How Does Analysis Cure* (1984), the senior author stressed that:

> Kohut never departed from the high value he put on ideal-
> ization, seeing it as the second chance for realization of the
> nuclear self after healthy ambition was thwarted by the fail-
> ure of the mirroring selfobject. (White, 1984, p. 6)

With the internalization of a good selfobject therapist, the power
of ideal values and of idealization is open to everyone, at any age,
through either self psychological treatment or a fortunate finding
of a good selfobject. This would seem to constitute a safety valve
not only for self psychology, but also for the human race.

6

A Third Chance for the Nuclear Self: A Tripolar Self Through a Twinship

Kohut (1984) suggested a third narcissistic (i.e., selfobject) transference, namely the twinship. This suggestion seemed to flow naturally from his earlier recognition of an archaic twinship need as a part of the mirroring transference. In his last book, Kohut specifically proposed that adding a twinship or alter ego transference to the mirroring and idealizing transferences suggests the possibility of three separate lines of selfobject development. This is a change from Kohut's originally including the twinship transference under the mirror transference. The essence of the twinship selfobject relationship is similarity in interests and talents, along with the sense of being understood by someone like oneself.

This chapter will explore the implications of a tripolar self, as compared with Kohut's earlier concept of the bipolar self (1977), utilizing the two selfobject transferences he found arising spontaneously as a result of an impaired nuclear self.

THE SUPRAORDINATE SELF

Let us first summarize Kohut's radical concepts of the supraordinate self and the nuclear self from which the former arises. The

103

self in a central position is a far cry from the self as a part of the mental apparatus, or even Hartmann's concept of self-representations as a complement to object-representations in ego psychology. Kohut's concept of the self is "a supraordinated configuration whose significance transcends that of the sum of its parts" (1977, p. 97). But how does the supraordinate self, under the best growth conditions, arise?

Kohut (1977) believed that at birth a baby has a rudimentary self of innate potentialities that are nourished or thwarted by the sustained and specific interactions of the child and his selfobjects whereby, over and over, the selfobjects especially respond to certain potentialities of the baby's nuclear self. For instance, a motoric baby likes to move about and will probably be an early walker. However, a child more prone to verbalizing may be an early talker. It is important for parents to respond to these natural inclinations of the baby rather than to try to enforce some parental preference.

As a cluster of responded-to potentialities, the nuclear self thus becomes the supraordinate self, that is, "the cohesive and enduring psychic configuration" (Kohut, 1977, p. 177). This developed self forms the central sector of the personality and provides the basis for our awareness of being an independent center of initiative and of our body and mind forming a unit in space and a continuum in time. The burgeoning nuclear self, in an environment of nurturing responsiveness, thus becomes the repository of the ambitions and ideals fostered by the child's selfobjects and gradually implemented by correlated talents and skills.

As Kohut originally conceptualized it, the bipolar self is the capstone of this structure of the supraordinate self. Tragic Man is offered two chances to realize the surviving potentialities of his core nuclear self, given the dangers of an unresponsive environment. The first chance is the establishment of nuclear ambitions through the consolidation of the early grandiose-exhibitionistic fantasies, mainly in the second, third, and fourth years of life and requiring the mother's mirroring acceptance to confirm the healthy exhibitionism as an indispensable foundation for ambition.

The second chance for the realization of the potentialities of the nuclear self is the acquisition of the bulk of the specific idealized goals, usually emerging in the fourth, fifth, and sixth years of life. Kohut (1977) also proposed a "tension arc" (p. 180) to describe the "abiding flow" of psychological activity between the two poles of the self, that is, a person's basic pursuits toward which he is driven by his ambitions and led by his ideals, an idea Kohut had proposed as early as 1966.

His concept of the "mirroring transference" is to be seen in the ambition pole of the bipolar self, while the "idealizing transference" is visible in the pole of ideals. Kohut believed that just as the maternal selfobject's encouraging mirroring is indispensable to the fostering of healthy ambition, so too the mother's or father's attuned holding and carrying allow "merger experience with the selfobject's idealized omnipotence" (1977, p. 179). Constituents of the self acquired later may be fostered by parents of either sex.

Kohut's final conception of a third selfobject need, a twinship need, is deeply rooted in a probably archaic need to feel "human," based on an "overall likeness in the capacity for good and evil, in emotionality, in gesture and voice" (1984, p. 200). Such indications of our basic alikeness are "signposts of the human world that we need" without our being aware of our need as long as such reassurances are available.

Kohut (1984) finally came to view the twinship transference as the development of a third chance for a cohesive nuclear self, arising from shared skills, talents, and experiences with a good selfobject, presumably after the mirroring and idealizing needs had gone unfulfilled. This twinship concept also raises the possibility that the capacity to find and "secure" mature selfobjects in life could include twinship relationships, as well as those supporting mirroring and idealization needs. Kohut, in addition, noted that a twinship could encompass homosexuality where each partner may be the other's twin or alter ego, as with the heterosexual needs for similar goals or interests and with some artists' needs for "a transference of creativity" (1984, p. 201).

Clearly, the limitations imposed by the concept of a bipolar self, confined to the needs for mirroring or idealization, are overcome with the possibility of a twinship selfobject experience stimulating the development of talents and skills to carry out whatever goals (for example, compensatory structures) a twinship can help to sustain. Kohut (1977) first introduced the concept of the compensatory structure as making up for a primary defect in the self rather than merely covering over the defect, as a defensive structure does in his view. The compensatory structure, however, develops on its own and brings about a functional rehabilitation of the self by making up for earlier selfobject failures.

The possibility of a twinship or alter ego selfobject transference in relation to the idea of the compensatory structure offers the self psychologist the opportunity to become the "less traumatic selfobject" (Kohut, 1977, p. 204) around which the patient will try to organize his or her efforts toward health.

THE JOY IN TWINSHIP

The young child's striving toward validation of the nuclear self, however it may be achieved, involves poignant experiences of failure by parents in the mirroring and idealization needs of the child. It is conceivable that someone could seek to validate the grandiose self without any human attachments. Hitler would be an example of such a possibility, carried forward by his nonhuman narcissistic demand for world domination. However, and more hopefully, memories of twinship possibilities are likely to arise in the patient's struggle for validation of the nuclear self. For instance, Kohut proposed that someone may gradually appear in the patient's memories from childhood who was different from the hypochondriacal or nonsustaining member of the family, and was strong and idealizable:

> Within the context of the transference, an outline will gradually come to light of a person for whom the patient's early existence and actions were a source of genuine joy; the significance of this person as a silent pressure, as an alter ego or twin next to whom the child felt alive (the little girl doing chores in the kitchen next to her mother or grandmother; the little boy working in the basement next to his father or grandfather) will gradually become clear. (1984, p. 204)

In his formulation of the twinship transference, Kohut cited the self-validation and consequent enjoyment of working alongside someone who is doing and enjoying a similar occupation. Such a situation was described by one of Kohut's adult patients who recalled a memory of when she was four, making bread with her grandmother in the kitchen.

Awareness of the importance of this selfobject twinship came to Kohut, not through his patient's memory of her enjoyment of being with her grandmother, but through the awful loneliness the girl suffered at six when her cold, unresponsive parents moved and thus took her away. The self-validating experiences she had with her grandmother were replaced by a genie in a bottle to whom she talked after their separation. She did not accept Kohut's transference interpretation that he was the genie in the bottle, in view of his just-announced long vacation plans. Rather, she insisted that her embarrassment over continuing these talks into her adult life made her very anxious about revealing this "pathology" to her analyst, Kohut. However, she was able to tell him that the captive in the bottle was a twin, just like herself, and yet someone "sufficiently like her to understand her and to be understood by her. . . . This patient's need . . . was for a silent presence. She would talk to the twin, but the twin did not have to respond to her . . . just being together with the twin in silent communion was often the most satisfactory state" (p. 196).

This interpretation of the positive effects of silence in being together made clear to Kohut the significance of the long silences that had occurred in the treatment, that is, they were not resistances but a beneficial twinship experience. Yet the patient had felt so anxious and ashamed of this need that she had never communicated it to Kohut until the particular announcement of his unusually long vacation.

CASE VIGNETTE #1

The senior author has also had some experiences with patients that appear to validate Kohut's concept of the twinship transference and possibly, therefore, the idea of a tripolar self. In one case, also involving a grandparent, a woman in her thirties, Marion M., came for treatment because of seemingly obsessive symptoms in regard to her professional work. She had a devaluing, antisexual mother with upper-class strivings, and a depressed professional father. When her father was assigned in World War II to a diplomatic post in the Far East, she was left in the care of her paternal grandparents, even though her mother was permitted to go along and conceivably could have taken the little girl with her. However, her parents decided the child's health was too delicate to risk bringing her with them. Marion thought she was four when she was left with her grandparents, whom she remembered as much more attuned to her needs than her parents were when they returned after the end of World War II. Particularly, she remembered a kind of twinship response from her grandmother in terms of welcoming her into the kitchen to observe and sometimes to participate in her cooking. She remembered her grandfather's dancing with her and, therefore, his love of music, which became an obsessive need for her but which she could not allow herself to fulfill.

The Loss of Twinship in Death

Unlike Kohut's patient, Marion lost her grandparents, not just through separation, but through death. When her parents returned to take her back, they also moved into the house the grandparents were living in. Although there was some rationalization of the grandparents' moving out as the grandfather's need not to have stairs to climb, it seemed clear that the patient experienced their exodus as a forced leaving instigated by the parents or, at least, as a preference expressed by the grandparents. In either case, as with Kohut's patient, Marion did not feel considered. The more tragic outcome with this patient was that both grandparents died in a relatively short time after the return of the parents, whom the patient experienced as intruders.

In Marion's memory and experience, there was not any allowance for mourning the grandparents. It is not clear whether this was a denial of the traumatic task of such mourning or whether it was an acceptance of still another unresponded-to loss—that of her parents when she was four. The sad fact is that she had neither been able to let herself enjoy her musical gifts in any fulfilling way nor allowed herself to use her considerable intellectual talents in positions that rewarded her for all the effort she put out. Typically, she would become a slave for an unappreciative boss and would never receive the recognition she deserved and wanted until too late, i.e., after she had resigned. Apparently her talents, which had been supported by her grandparents, had become at the very least an ambivalent issue and perhaps something she felt not entitled to use or enjoy, especially after their death. What we are pinpointing here is the traumatic loss of a twinship selfobject experience, complicated by the confrontation of the actual death of both twinship selfobjects.

This loss may account for the lack of trust in the transference to the therapist (the senior author), although this idea was never explicitly spelled out. It appears that there may have been the same kind of terror over the childhood disappearance of the twinship that surfaced in Kohut's case, so any transference discussion was still too traumatic. The therapist felt very much like the listening twin in the genie bottle of Kohut's patient. Nevertheless, there was a growth in the patient's self-esteem, a reduction in her masochistic submission to authority's demands, and an increased consideration of her own future in the light of her uncaring husband's demands. The slow evolvement of her own acceptance of her self-needs pointed to the importance of the tragic disruption of the twinship needs provided by her grandparents, accompanied by the sudden reappearance of her long-absent parents who may have been seen as carriers of doom.

Barriers to Trust

While the treatment succeeded in making Marion more questioning of her acceptance of a deprived lifestyle, including her submission to authoritarian employers and her fruitless flirtation with a lifestyle that energized her, the twinship loss of the grandparents after the initial trauma of losing her parents presented a barrier to trusting again another twinship selfobject. However, there were indications of movement toward a twinship transference, reflected in her taking a firmer attitude toward the unrealistic demands of her present employer and her considering a search for a more stimulating job position. The twinship transference here involved a support of what appeared to be a growth movement for the self, with a constant awareness that what the patient needed for an empathic support of her self was a delicate affirmation of a forward impulse, but not a push.

CASE VIGNETTE #2

In another almost foreclosed case of twinship with a grandfather, the patient, John, as a latency age boy could not fully idealize his maternal grandfather, because the latter submitted to browbeating by a sadistic wife. However, John, in what seemed to be a twinship reaction, felt accepted and sustained by the grandfather's warm response to the patient's budding literary interests. Since John's father had died before his birth and his mother became withdrawn and depressed, John especially needed to feel sustained by his grandfather in the absence of adequate mirroring or idealization from both parents.

Unfortunately, the grandfather started to produce his own writings and read them to John, thereby ostensibly abandoning what could have been a twinship relationship. However, in the course of treatment, John became a successful editor after years of searching for the profession that would "turn him on." Having failed as an author, advertising copywriter, and TV newscaster—all professions involving an exhibitionistic ambition he could not sustain because of insufficient mirroring from anyone else before his treatment—John became very involved as an editor, with the help of compensatory structures developed during his analysis.

The possibility for these compensatory structures arose during the thwarted twinship relationship with his grandfather. In a kind of reverse twinship, when the grandfather began to use the boy as an audience for his own secretly produced writings, John became the appreciator of his grandfather's writing, as he was later to do when he became an editor of other writers' productions.

In the treatment, John's retrieval of the experience of being for his creative but degraded grandfather "a person . . . whose early existence and actions were a source of genuine joy" (Kohut, 1984, p. 204) enabled John to develop this early affirmation of his nuclear self in the profession of being an editor, with the unfailing support of the therapist.

The therapist's understanding of such childhood experiences "becomes pivotally important when the analysand's transference begins to turn to the analyst qua that childhood selfobject which, although not sufficiently responsive, had still been the best one available" (Kohut, 1984, p. 204). It was the therapist's highlighting of the twinship sustenance that John had given his grandfather—in being a source of genuine joy to the disappointed old man—that seemed to reactivate the potentiality for his compensatory structure of self-strength. This helped to solve John's long-standing problem of choosing a satisfying profession.

Kohut (1977) originally defined a compensatory structure, as we indicated on p. 106 of this chapter, in terms of "a functional rehabilitation of the self" (p. 3) to compensate for a defect in one pole of the self by strengthening the other pole. Moving from his original concept of a bipolar self, Kohut (1984) raised the possibility of a third chance, a tripolar self. He suggested that the incapacity of the selfobjects to meet the needs of one component of the self will trigger a stronger effort to get adequate reactions to the growth needs of the two other components. Thus, a health-sustaining "sectorial continuum" in the self may yet be developed.

In the case of John, it gradually became clear that it was a responsive alter ego experience—a nursemaid who read to him and even taught him how to read a little before he went to school—through which the compensatory structure of becoming an appreciative, helpful alter ego to a person with similar interests needing encouragement first began to develop. The nursemaid was fired when John was six, at the instigation of his intimidating grandmother who complained that the nursemaid spoiled John with too much attention and didn't do enough real work. Her departure drove him back into his regressive, exhibitionistic demands for attention from his depressed mother who, unable to mirror him, collapsed with exhaustion, while his punitive grandmother ignored his existence. The failures of these primary self-objects with respect to the mirroring he needed made him very vulnerable later on, when he tried to use his writing ability to get attention for his own creativity and for performance abilities. Any setback or failure to win significant encouragement and applause for his endeavors would catapult him into a paralyzing depression. To force himself to resume his performances, he turned more and more to dangerous stimulants, including alcohol and drugs, which increasingly impaired the quality of his productivity.

The Patient's Dream

It was in the midst of one of these impasses that John reported a dream about trying to read a story he had written to his grandfather. In the dream, his grandfather interrupted him and started to read a story of his own. The dream ended with his grandmother coming in and scolding both of them. In his associations, John recalled his earlier experience with the empathic nursemaid, who not only read to him but even started him on the path to an early mastery of reading and of writing. He had performed well in school scholastically but his regressive exhibitionism and demands for attention had made him unpopular with both teachers and students, so he soon became a lonely introvert. The grandmother, scolding both him and his grandfather, not only reminded him of how she had deprived him of his alter ego, the nursemaid, but also led to his comment that she couldn't stand his grandfather enjoying anything. John had felt so sorry for the rejected old man that he had listened to him read his stories, partly to spite his grandmother but also to try to give his grandfather some of the sense of being cared about that he had received from the nursemaid. At first, John had felt angry when his grandfather interrupted the boy's reading of his own stories and wanted applause from his grandfather. But he saw how excited and enthusiastic his grandfather had become when John let his grandfather read his own productions, despite the grandmother's intrusions. So John had become the attentive audience for his grandfather that he, John, had always wanted but never succeeded in finding in any reliable way.

The therapist became aware that possibly an alter ego selfobject need had developed through the nursemaid's empathic attention to John's needs after his traumatic early deprivation. The nursemaid, then, might have helped to stimulate the development of a compensatory structure by becoming an alter ego selfobject to John, if only briefly.

A Compensating Structure Surfaces

This thought became more significant to the therapist when John gave the day residue of the dream, which was that the night before the dream he had helped his eight-year-old son with a story he had to do for fourth grade class the next day. John had enjoyed the fact that his son had turned to him, at least for his opinion, since John had not been much in the habit of helping his children with their schoolwork. His son had used the pretext of wanting to check out some information in the story, but John sensed that the boy had really wanted John's reaction and even suggestions about the story. Instead of feeling too put upon or that he somehow could not rise to the occasion, John suddenly felt that he wanted to read his son's story and to help him make it better if it needed to be improved. This is, of course, a true editor's attitude.

So John, going along with his newly surfacing compensatory structure, read the story, liked that his son could do so well instead of feeling competitive and put down, and had some ideas about how the story might be improved. John's ability to give his son his overall positive reaction and at the same time suggest certain changes indicated that his compensatory structure, arising from his nursemaid, his deprived grandfather and the therapist as the approving selfobject, was surfacing to give him a more fulfilling way to deal with his own self-creative needs.

The therapist looked for a transference connection between John's unexpected willingness not only to look at his son's composition but also, without being the big authority figure, to give him some helpful and not too difficult suggestions for change. The therapist realized that John was reacting to his son in the same way as the therapist had for a long time reacted to John's traumatic reaction to rejections of his writings or to less than enthusiastic responses to his television appearances. While trying empathically to tune in to his narcissistic rage at any lack of positive response—let alone outright criticism or disapproval—the therapist had quite often slipped in some suggestions for perhaps emphasizing one point rather than another, a technique that John had accepted and then used with his son. The ability to exercise an editorial function with his son, as the therapist had delicately done with John, suggested that some transmuting internalization of the therapist had taken place, namely, an activation of the alter ego selfobject relationship with the punished nursemaid, which preceded the complex twinship relationship with the grandfather.

A Twinship Compensatory Structure for the Nuclear Self

Nevertheless, the components of empathy, similar interests and talents, and the experience of responsive appreciativeness seemed to coalesce; the nursemaid, the grandfather, and the therapist blended into a twinship compensatory structure for the vitally needed development of the patient's nuclear self. This late-blooming structure pointed a way in which John could travel with relative comfort and still use the talents and skills of his literary creativity for which he had never received adequate mirroring.

Thus, the germinating twinship selfobject transference developing between John and the therapist had finally surfaced as a compensatory structure, enabling John to deal helpfully and satisfyingly with his son, as he would come to deal with many other seekers of his editorial wisdom.

The twinsip or alter ego selfobject need, which spontaneously arises in treatment as a selfobject transference wish, was seen by Kohut as involving deep human needs to share similar feelings and experiences. Kohut noted that "anyone who has been away from his usual surroundings for some time—in a foreign country, for example—will remember the strengthening feeling of again

being surrounded by other people who are like himself" (in Goldberg & Stepansky, eds., 1984, p. 203).

It was certainly a component of John's feeling of twinship with
his grandfather that they were both unfairly treated and that he,
John, could derive some satisfaction and even comfort from trying
to give his grandfather some of what he needed. Even though
this empathic mirroring that John gave to his grandfather was not
then available to John, he was able to give it to his grandfather
with an unconscious hope that he would, later on, be treated
empathically in the same way. Thus, an early experience of a
twinship selfobject conceivably can be a bridge between the separate line of development of healthy narcissism and of the more
familiar line of object relations leading to romantic love. In the
twinship or alter ego relationship or transference there is a caring
about what the other person feels and thinks, even though that
person may not be experienced at a deep level as having an independent center of initiative. However, such a relationship could
exist on a more caring and sharing basis than the narcissistic
mirror relationship or the idealizing one. Kohut stressed the human quality of the twinship selfobject need—to feel human among
human beings—and in this sense, these feelings may be a bridge
to object love.

7

Intergenerational Continuity Versus Punishing Guilt

The possibility of self-realization, through both individual achievement and sexual fulfillment, permeates self psychology. This possibility is also supported by our own clinical experience that strengthening the self-esteem of a patient expands ego functioning. Thus the potential exists for more gratifying self and object relations, including more loving relationships between parents and children, i.e., intergenerational continuity. But this bright prospect for humankind is darkened by the shadow of the Oedipus complex.

Freud saw the Oedipus complex as the biological fate of human beings, burdening sexual fulfillment with guilt and fear, and handing on a heritage of jealousy and revenge down through the generations. He also saw the establishment of the superego, the conscience of humankind, as the outcome of the oedipal struggle in which the child gives up his or her incestuous longings out of terror threatened by castration and death. Thus, the human conscience provided by the superego is dominated by fear of punishment and destruction, and the positive consequences of caring

This is a modified version of a chapter that appeared in A. Goldberg (Ed.), *Progress in Self Psychology, Vol. 1* (New York: The Guilford Press, 1985), which is a collection of the papers presented at the 6th Annual Conference on Self Psychology, held in Los Angeles in 1983. Permission has been granted by the Guilford Press to publish this version.

for one's parents, children, friends, or even one's self seems fragile at best.

Basic issues about the Oedipus complex are raised by self psychology's elimination of the aggressive and libidinal drives as innate instinctual forces demanding discharge, often without regard to the target, as in the case of the child's tantrum, a rapist on the loose, or the retaliatory bombing of a civilian population. And Kohut did not shrink from these problems.

After paying due recognition to Freud's discovery of infantile sexuality and of the subsequent development of the structural id, ego, and superego theory, Kohut raised a surprising issue. He first proposed it in *The Restoration of the Self* (1977) and then elaborated on it (1982) shortly before his death. This suggestion has two components. One is that the Oedipus complex, far from being the terrifying, self-destructive drama implied by *Oedipus Rex*, can be a *joyous* experience if parents are psychologically healthy enough to welcome the advent of their child's natural heterosexual desire, along with the competition this implies with the same-sex parent.

The other component is that the terrifying experiences of oedipal longing and oedipal rage reflect an unresponsive environment for the child from birth; that is, the child never felt much responded to in terms of the developmental needs of each phase. We are using the phrase, "never much responded to," because there had to be enough empathic responsiveness to help the child build a somewhat cohesive self to avoid a schizoid or psychotic regression. The oedipal phase does involve the longing for another person to share one's needs physically and psychologically, so it is a conscious desire for a fulfilling selfobject. Since the parent of the opposite sex usually is the sexually idealized person, this suggests that physical aspects of the child's developing sexuality take center stage.

Kohut did not disclaim any of the foregoing but rather saw that the child needs an empathic response from his or her parents for arriving at and contending with this crucial developmental stage. He suggested that the normal Oedipus complex could be

> . . . less violent, less anxious, less deeply narcissistically wounding than we have come to believe—that it is altogether more exhilarating and, to speak in the language of mental-apparatus Guilty Man, even more pleasurable. (1977, p. 247)

In what turned out to be Kohut's last message on self psychology, namely, his paper, "Introspection, Empathy and the Semicircle of Mental Health" (1982), he stressed that a joyful Oedipus complex could be the hallmark of mental health, not only in the child but also in parents. He said:

> . . . healthy man experiences, and with deepest joy, the next generation as an extension of his own self. It is the primacy of the support for the succeeding generation, therefore, which is normal and human, and not intergenerational strife and wishes to kill. . . . (1982, p. 404)

The parent who lacks a healthy, cohesive, and vigorous self reacts competitively and seductively when his or her five-year-old makes an exhilarating move toward a new level of assertiveness and affection. Such a flawed parental self, which cannot respond in empathic identification with the child's experience of a new assertive-affectionate self, provokes a disintegration of the child's developing self. In response to this unsupportive environment, the fragmenting self of the child leads to the familiar breakup products of hostility and lust attributed to the Oedipus complex.

Oedipus, the tragic hero of Freud's universal version of parent-child relations, was a "rejected child," Kohut (1982) stressed in his last paper. In contrast to this failure of loving parenting, he cited Homer's story of Odysseus, who saved his infant son's life at the risk of his own, thus manifesting intergenerational caring rather than the pathological fear and jealousy that, in the Oedipus story, destroy both generations.

The conclusion to be drawn here is that jealousy, fear, disapproval of sexual interest and competition, and a punitive attitude toward the *normal* manifestation of these needs and capacities in a child indicate a pathological parental attitude. Thus, when a therapist encounters in a patient anxiety over fear of sex, competition with his or her rivals, and ambivalence about having children of his or her own, is this automatically to be ascribed to the patient's hostile rivalry and fear of punishment arising from an innate Oedipus complex? Or should we examine the quality of the parental environment before deciding that it all arises from the patient's drives? These issues certainly came to the fore in the following case.

CASE VIGNETTE

Ronald, a 35-year-old lawyer, consulted the senior author about marital problems, emphasizing that he did not want a child, although his wife was eager to have one. The patient also seemed perfectionistic, obstinate, with inhibited affect and a tendency to argue, which soon emerged as self-destructive in conflicts with his employer. The therapist thought these characteristics pointed toward an obsessive defensive picture covering up an underlying oedipal conflict, since there seemed to be almost no indication of a self psychological problem, so far as the therapist could see.

Ronald's childhood history seemed to validate a classical oedipal problem. His Irish mother had died from a cerebral hemorrhage when he was four and his English father had died of cancer when he was 12. In addition to the awful deprivation involved in losing his mother at such an early age, this child was subjected to an unresponsive group of maternal relatives who derogated not only his mother (for dying!) but also his father for being inadequate in terms of financial support. Thus, from a self psychological standpoint, both poles of the bipolar self—the ambition pole through maternal mirroring and the idealistic pole through the father's values—would seem to have been traumatically undermined and, as indicated in the previous chapter, in need of compensatory structures through the internalization of a good selfobject.

However, the patient's transference reactions to the therapist, definitively demonstrated that his central difficulties were self psychological and not traditionally oedipal. This involved a transference exploration, where the therapist asked if Ronald had any feelings about her absence over a Christmas vacation. He retorted with a rageful response about why she would think he had any feelings about her absence and why she would intrude herself into an analysis that he was paying for. While this reaction suggested that the patient was possibly including the therapist in a narcissistic mirror transference as part of himself rather than as a separate person in an object-related transference, the therapist also wondered whether he was denying any interest in or need for her because of embarrassment or anxiety, as one might expect with a traditional oedipal problem.

A Mirror Transference

The therapist decided not to press any further the issue of the familiar object-related transference feelings and instead to consider that Ronald's denial and resentment indicated a possible narcissistic transference. Given such a transference, the patient could reject the therapist's importance to him as a separate person and expect that she would be a responsive audience to him with "a gleam" in her maternal eye (Kohut, 1971), approving his early and later achievements, which his ill and prematurely deceased mother was never able to do.

Obviously, the patient's ability to experience positive mirroring as a reliable response from a mothering person depends on earlier experiences with that person where responsive attunement was provided to his anxiety over physical or emotional needs. Conceivably, the patient's mother, early on, was not able to be as attuned as he needed her to be. Or perhaps she had been fairly attuned and then, with the onset of her brain disorder, had ominously changed into an unresponding mother at the very time when he needed her for positive mirroring to support his proud phallic ambition, including his admiration for his body and his bold reaching out to the environment. Here the therapist was thinking in terms of Kohut's concept of intergenerational welcoming of the child's sexuality and rivalry and the pathological consequences of the parental inability to provide the welcome.

Since the therapist's question about whether the patient had any feelings about her absence had obviously aroused resentment, the therapist decided to express some empathy in case the patient had experienced her intervention as quite insensitive to what he was feeling, that is, as a failure in mirroring. So she said: "Perhaps my question about myself seemed intrusive and unattuned to your feelings about your marital and business problems."

The Patient Feels Listened To

Ronald sighed: "Well, I'm glad you're beginning *to listen to me* and hear how upset I've been feeling about my business going downhill since I started treatment and about my wife being so depressed. The only ideas you've ever given me about handling my troubles is to tell me I'm punishing myself for guilt over my parents' death. Even if this were so, I don't know what I can do about it."

The senior author, as therapist, felt Ronald's resentful remarks could be understood as an expectable response, expressing a negative therapeutic reaction* and perhaps even a validation of the therapist's earlier interpretations, for example, that he was unconsciously impelled to fail in his business and his marriage because he felt he did not deserve to live and be happy since his parents were dead. Above all, the patient might feel that his resentful emotions toward them conceivably could have killed them. The therapist wondered if Ronald's bringing up her previous interpretations spontaneously, perhaps as a defense against the negative therapeutic reaction, was actually a validation of it. Or was it an unusual expression of helplessness in response to her tentative effort at empathy?

Empathy Toward Helplessness

Recalling that Freud had said the negative therapeutic reaction "constitutes one of the most serious resistances" (S. Freud, 1923),

---

*See Chapter 8, p. 150 for a discussion of the negative therapeutic reaction.

the therapist decided that nothing would be irretrievably lost if she still focused on Kohut's empathic approach and the possibility that the patient was moving into a mirroring transference with her. The affect of helplessness, touched off by her effort at empathy, seemed to be a worthwhile self-deficit to explore, along with the spontaneous anger at the therapist's originally intruding herself into the scene—anger so characteristic of a frustrated mirror transference.

The therapist began to empathize consistently with the blows to the patient's self-esteem inflicted by his business troubles, and to focus on how difficult it must be for him to endure these, especially in view of his longstanding hopes for a quick and smashing success. She realized that in self psychology the need for mirroring directly involves not only the failure of the mothering person to support the child's healthy ambition, but also the defensive regression to the infantile grandiose self (see Chapter 4), who feels he has to do it all himself since the parents have failed him.

To the therapist's surprise, Ronald began to respond with real affect, indicating that he had received little empathy or interest during his childhood from his insensitive, overworked relatives, who had no time or understanding to give either to his painful loss of both parents or to his adolescent ambitious strivings. The latter, the therapist gradually came to realize, seemed to serve as a compensatory structure against an early self-deficit arising from both a paucity of mirroring and an inadequate idealization.

Frightening Ambitions

The patient's ambitions needed to be sustained, yet divested of infantile grandiose expectations that already seemed troublesome. Ronald began to admit how frightened he was of succeeding with his own law firm and that he was terrified of having children because he didn't think he would be able to spend enough time with them or to make enough money to give them a good life. In line with the concept of intergenerational continuity, he was not afraid that he would lose out with his children (that is, not be able to compete with his son), but rather that he could not care for them adequately, just as his father had failed him.

Ronald's conviction that he needed to give so much to his as-yet unborn child to spare the child the deprivations he himself had suffered could certainly have been interpreted as a reaction formation against his own anger at not having been given what he wanted from his father (that is, a big penis, his mother, and a father he could look up to rather than mourn). As the therapist speculated over these oedipal possibilities, she also thought of Kohut's view of the "second chance," namely, the idealizing aspect of the bipolar self with respect to the internalization of guiding values from one or both parents.

In the case of Ronald, one of these values seemed to involve the goal of being both a loving and a powerful parent who could help a child to get on the "right track" and also to believe he could be successful. This seemed to be an interesting and fertile fusion of both aspects of the original bipolar self—his healthy ambition and guiding ideals (see Chapter 6). That Ronald might have received some phase-appropriate mirroring from his mother before she became terminally ill raised a hopeful but also puzzling question about the fate of his infantile grandiosity when confronted with her death.

The therapist felt that some of Ronald's survivor guilt might be rooted in his narcissistic rage against himself when he could not prevent his mother's death and the presumably perplexing changes in her that preceded the fatal cerebral hemorrhage. It has been well documented that the child holds himself responsible for the reactions of his or her parents (A. Freud, 1962; Spitz, 1965; Kohut, 1977; Mahler et al., 1975; Miller, 1983; Weiner & White, 1982). Ronald's solution to his childhood traumas, it seemed, was to be the all-powerful parent giving to his child, so that the child could never find a flaw in the parental grandiosity arising from the failure of either mother or father. In this way, Ronald's putative children would never be at risk for the self-destructive shame and guilt that drove Ronald.

The therapist tried to draw together some of these thoughts in the following interpretation to Ronald: "If you could make any child of yours as happy as possible, then you would never have to experience the awful feelings of the parent who fails the child or the child who feels he should be able to make his sick parents well and happy."

Ronald then had a most unusual dream—what Kohut called a "self-state dream" (1971, 1977)—(to be discussed more fully in Chapter 8). The dream was about some explorers who were trying to trace the source of the Amazon River and suddenly found themselves in a lost world where supposedly extinct dinosaurs lived. The explorers were both joyously excited at their find and frightened of the dinosaurs.

It seemed to the therapist that this dream was a confirmation of her finally having found the attuned approach to Ronald's problems. The dream showed her orthodox but off-target approach to the Amazon's source. The lost world, however, is the real, relevant focus of the lost self, with the dinosaurs representing Ronald's ebullient but frightening grandiose self.

The therapist recognized the fear of the grandiose self and of the concomitant narcissistic rage against the self for failure (see Chapter 4) emerging in the confirming dinosaur dream. Ronald's associations to the dinosaur focused on the explorers' fear of the monsters rather than their joy in discovering their "real find"—that a supposed extinct species was still flourishing. When the therapist asked Ronald what was frightening about the dinosaurs, he said: "They seem like evolution gone wrong. They needed so much to be all-powerful that they grew their own armor, and then it almost immobilized them. Yet I saw a picture recently showing a dinosaur mother sort of crooning over a baby dinosaur. So it seems as though there's some evidence they weren't 100% destructive monsters."

The Need to Be All-Powerful

The therapist pointed out that there was some joy on the part of the explorers in the dream over finding the lost species alive. She then suggested that perhaps this discovery represented the patient's hope that she would be interested in some hidden aspect of himself that he felt was like a dinosaur—perhaps the need to be indomitable.

Ronald was silent for a few minutes and then said, "Well, the idea of being like a dinosaur is pretty repellent. Yet when you put it in terms of needing to be indomitable, it seems more acceptable. I'm beginning to see there were a lot of experiences in my life that would make me want to feel all-powerful even though I feared this would drive people away from me."

The Caring Dinosaur

The therapist intervened at this point, saying: "You also put a caring aspect of the dinosaur into the dream where the little one is being crooned over by the adult. It seems to show that you need to be all-powerful, partly because you need to take perfect care of any child you may have."

Ronald smiled warmly, perhaps for the first time in the analysis, and said, "But of course! That's why I want to be successful and rich. Then, any child of mine would never have to suffer. I don't see why you can sense this and yet my wife just doesn't understand it at all."

This open acknowledgment of the therapist's understanding his need to be all-powerful in order to provide perfect care and protection for his child was a welcome recognition that she was gradually becoming an attuned selfobject for him—one that he clearly never had. Ronald's reference to his wife raised the question of whether the therapist, as an empathic selfobject, should openly side with him against what he experienced as the obtuseness of his wife. His marital discord had been the alleged reason for his starting treatment. Was his reference to his wife now, at the point of his first acknowledgment of a selfobject transference, a test of the therapist's empathy?

The Therapist and the Wife's Reactions

The senior author as therapist realized that she had never explored how Ronald's wife had reacted to his desire to postpone having children until he was rich, because the therapist had assumed at the outset that this was a phallic-exhibitionistic defense against his underlying oedipal problem involving fear and guilt over having a child. Whatever his wife's reactions had been, the therapist had felt, from the traditional oedipal stance, that they were irrelevant to his unconscious conflict. Now she wondered if, given his underlying grandiosity, he had expected his wife as a part of his grandiose self to "know" why he had to get rich in order to have children. So the therapist took the risk of asking Ronald how his wife had reacted to his reasons for needing a lot of money before he had children. He said, a little surprised, "But why should I tell her? She should have known!"

The Fear of Narcissistic Rage

The extent of Ronald's fixation on his underlying grandiosity and his need for attuned mirroring by his wife thus became apparent in this revelation, not of his inability to communicate with his wife, but of his angry, hurt refusal to do so. It suggested an anxiety about expressing either his angry or his hurt feelings to anyone close to him, for fear any incomprehension would arouse his narcissistic rage as a defense against feeling utterly helpless in getting empathy or adequate mirroring from another.

Such narcissistic rage, of course, had burst forth in the transference when the therapist had raised the "unspeakable" question of whether Ronald had any feelings about her absence on vacation. To have such feelings, of course, would be to acknowledge the helplessness that accompanied an unmet need and a fear of the narcissistic rage turned against the self for not being able to fulfill such a need, especially by controlling the needed person as a part of one's grandiose self.

The Therapist Should Have Known

The issue of the transferential selfobject—particularly consideration of the patient's achieving internalization of the therapist as the empathic, mirroring selfobject he never had—involved the therapist in trying to discover the patient's feelings not only about herself but also about his own past which, like his wife, the therapist "should have known already." In addition, the therapist had to walk the tightrope of accepting Ronald's infantile grandiosity without encouraging its acting out to a point where his reckless need to prove himself all-powerful could end in actual disaster or misfortune.

After the dinosaur dream and its revealing associations, including Ronald's need for mind reading and mirroring by a potential selfobject, the therapist decided to move slowly in further supporting his acknowledged grandiosity, while striving to maintain an overall positive tuning in on both his ambition and his need for empathic mirroring. The result was that he began to gather himself together, closed out his own practice, and was soon able to land a good position with a well-established law firm.

Authority Figures and Self-Esteem

Gradually, Ronald began to work on his conflicts with authority in the context of blows to his self-esteem that he suffered when he failed to get 100% agreement from everyone about his ideas. When the therapist raised this problem delicately, slowly, and very tactfully in this perspective, Ronald was able to consider his unconscious grandiose need for absolute control (the dinosaur) which also involved his exhibitionistic conflict and the wish to command total admiration from his audience.

The unconscious grandiose configurations that underlay this need to command total understanding and appreciation from others revealed an inadequate mirroring experience with Ronald's mother. Seemingly, she was not able to separate herself enough from her own narcissistic, dominating mother to encourage healthy exhibitionism and self-esteem in her young son. On the contrary, it seemed that before her cerebral hemorrhage, she had turned to Ronald as if he were her parental selfobject, thus intensifying his fixation on his grandiose self and his consequent narcissistic rage against himself for not being able to save his mother from her tragic illness and death (Weiner & White, 1982).

Certainly, Ronald's desire to be a perfect parent stemmed partly from this sense of tragic failure and partly from his own feeling of developmental neglect, including his mother's inability to give him adequate mirroring, rather than expecting him to be the omnipotent parent (Miller, 1981).

Paternal Grandiosity

In addition to his mother's grandiose expectations of him, Ronald's father had shown somewhat grandiose independence after his wife's death by trying to maintain a home for his son, with the help of occasional girlfriends, and by fending off the suspect generosity of the mother's demeaning relatives. Conceivably, the father's somewhat strenuous efforts at self-sufficiency, including running a small hardware shop while trying to raise his son, could have inspired that son toward unflagging achievement of his own goal to become a successful, wealthy parent.

It was not clear whether Ronald blamed his father's unexpected death on the latter's hyperactive attempts to be self-sufficient. Certainly, the father's sudden death seemed to make more difficult the realization of Ronald's second need of the bipolar self, namely the chance to develop guiding values through the idealization of a parent after the failure of maternal mirroring. The postmortem criticism of his father, especially by his mother's relatives, further undermined Ronald's chances to idealize the father. It became particularly difficult to believe that his father had planned for him, when Ronald was confronted with having to depend upon resentful relatives and to work his way through college and law school because his father was financially inept. Ronald also revealed his anger at the father's girlfriends, condemning his father for his "infidelity" to Ronald's dead mother.

Releasing the Energies Locked in the Grandiose Self

Under these pressures from adverse life circumstances and developmental needs, Ronald's early fixation on his grandiose self obviously became intensified. Its pressure, therefore, was not relieved by the gradual release of narcissistic energy needed for the development of a reliable cohesive self. Ronald was left, as his father apparently had been before him, with only his perfectionistic, controlling, rageful but very needy grandiose self. And it was not until his analysis began to focus on his self-needs, including the awareness and acceptance of this primitive, omnipotent self, that the energies imprisoned in it could become available for his mature goals.

In recalling the shock of finding out that his father had cancer and the subsequent memories of feeling so ineffectual and hopeless in relation to his father's death—memories that brought back similar feelings about his mother's early death—Ronald became aware of a need to protect himself from ever feeling so utterly helpless again. This need, he was able to recognize in treatment, took the form of becoming a self-sufficient wealthy professional man, a goal partly influenced by a relative on his mother's side who was rich and contemptuous of Ronald's father. The therapist's exploration of Ronald's anger at this relative led to fuller expression and documentation of how alone, criticized, and even ridiculed he felt by his mother's relatives for his aspirations to go to college, become a lawyer, and be successful.

A Failure of Attunement

Ronald's grandiose expectations of his wife—and the therapist—that they should have known what his feelings were became much clearer when he and the therapist could talk about his deep feelings of isolation and rejection in his adolescence at the hands of his resentful relatives who supported this penniless orphan as an unpleasant "duty."

It would have been natural for a 12-year-old boy to have hoped that his grandmother, aunts, uncles, and cousins would have realized how shocked, frightened, and heartbroken he was at his father's unexpected death from cancer. This disappointment at their insensitivity was an aspect of his regression to his grandiose self that we can certainly understand in terms of Kohut's concept of aggression as a disintegration product in reaction to an unresponsive environment (see Chapter 2). From this standpoint, Ronald would have hoped, despite his natural distrust, that his relatives belatedly would have understood his hurt, his loss, his bewilderment, and especially his efforts to pull himself together to become a success and even repay them for their support.

However, the failure of Ronald's relatives to empathize with him, their ridicule of his "being too big for his britches," and their refusal to loan him money for even a relatively inexpensive state university only kindled the fires of narcissistic rage that drove his grandiosity. Nevertheless, it seems possible that the focus of Ronald's grandiose need to succeed took such a respectable and achievable form (i.e., to become a rich lawyer) as a kind of idealized reflection of his father's need to care for him by running an independent small business.

A Perfectionistic but Loving Goal

However, given Ronald's tragic early life, his high intelligence, and his aggressive grandiosity, he could very easily have turned to less laudable ways of "making it." Why he did not seems to be an indication that the concept of intergenerational continuity is rich in its potentials. Whatever mirroring, care, and idealizable values Ronald received from his sick, prematurely dying mother, from his father's cancer-defeated struggle to support him, and even from his grudging but still shelter-providing relatives, he brought out of this a perfectionistic goal to have children who would never want for anything. This is not an aggressive wish for revenge on all those who disappointed him. It could be seen as a wish to surpass them, in a kind of loving competition, to show that children should be taken care of. There is no destructive impulse here.

Internalization of the Therapist

As Ronald felt more reliably understood by the therapist as an empathic selfobject and as he became more realistically self-confident through transmuting internalization of her, he spontaneously began to consider having a child right away, before he made a real fortune. So, shortly before the treatment terminated, he became a delighted, proud father. It seemed a reliable indication that he had worked through much of his narcissistic grandiosity and that in the process he had internalized the therapist as a responsive and trustworthy selfobject. As a result, he had arrived at a cohesive sense of self and a differentiated level of object relations for which, as a symbolic change, he was able to thank the therapist warmly at the conclusion of the treatment.

That Ronald could develop from an isolated, hostile, joyless, success-driven person to a warm, responsive, joyful, and loving father in the course of a self psychologically oriented analysis was an impressive demonstration of the effectiveness of Kohut's concepts, particularly with reference to the possibility of the recovery of intergenerational continuity.

THE IMPACT OF THE SOCIAL ENVIRONMENT

The role of the responsive environment in fostering the potentialities of the individual self with its developmental hurdles to take, including oedipal sexuality and competitiveness, is also stretched by Kohut from the individual parent-child situation to the impact of alterations in the social environment upon people in general. The discovery of the selfobject transferences and of the plight of Tragic Man, "seeking to express the pattern of his nuclear self" (1977, p. 133) versus Guilty Man's aggression-ridden Oedipus complex, points to the effect of the changing social and cultural environment upon the children born into it.

Kohut, for instance, cites the emptiness and understimulation of the contemporary child brought up in a small family, with both parents working full time, no live-in help, and an implicit look-after-yourself attitude from the relatively indifferent environment. The contemporary child, feeling so unresponded to and thrown back on his or her insufficiently mirrored nuclear self, is likely to become the patient in treatment today, overly prone to self-fragmentation and experiencing the so-called neutral analyst as coldly indifferent to the patient's immobilizing empty depression.

By contrast, the patient Freud considered to be analyzable was one who grew up in an overstimulating environment in a large, often overinvolved family with servants who could and did seduce the children. The sexually tinged overinvolvement of parents, siblings, and servants, Kohut surmised, made the Oedipus complex *seem* to be a universal phenomenon rather than a predictable reaction to an overheated environment. From this standpoint, the minimal responsiveness of the rigidly neutral Freudian analyst could have been experienced as a welcome relief by the overly aroused patient to whom Freud first started listening.

Kohut made the point that the changing "psychotropic" factors—that is, the nature of the social environment confronting humankind—can account in part for the different kind of responsiveness a person may need from a potentially good selfobject in order to develop and sustain a cohesive self. He implied that analytic neutrality per se is not likely to lead to the internalization of the analyst as the appropriately responsive selfobject the patient needed but did not get. By the same token, the concept of an intergenerational attitude of "you're free to live your own life and don't ask me for my reactions" may point to an overemphasis on the parent and child being super-independent of each other. Parental acceptance of a child's ambitions—e.g., to be a dancer even though this may seem totally impractical—would be in the direction of mutual awareness of the other's needs despite their intersubjective reality. At the same time, the child, as he or she moves into adulthood, hopefully will be able to empathize somewhat with his or her parents' changing needs as age may alter goals and tastes. So the concept of intergenerational continuity, including an oedipal complex that is normally joyful, could be akin not to analytic neutrality or parallel play, but rather to a constant empathic friend who is always to be relied on for interest and understanding without seeking to control.

8

Traumatic States: Too Much, Too Little, or the Wrong Responsiveness

The patient, Martin L., a 29-year-old man not yet able to achieve recognition for his musical ability, told his male therapist that he was only able to overcome his insomnia with sadistic sexual fantasies about women. The therapist, having heard the patient's complaints before about *unrelieved* insomnia and using a self psychological approach, said: "But letting yourself have these fantasies helped you to overcome your insomnia."

The patient ragefully replied: "But I shouldn't have to resort to such appalling fantasies to be able to sleep! After all this treatment, why can't you help me to just fall asleep?"

Taken at face value, Martin's response seems justified. However, the patient's history would tell us that his lifelong insomnia had been at least partly due to his exposure to his mother's screaming fights with his father and that the emergence into consciousness of his sadistic grandiose fantasies about women (i.e., his mother) was a recent consequence of the treatment that now enabled him to sleep well for the first time. So his rage at his therapist over having the sadistic fantasies would seem to be an ungrateful reaction, especially in view of the fact that his chronic

133

insomnia had dominated both his professional and his social life.

The therapist, struggling to be empathic, had responded to Martin's rage as follows: "Of course, you would rather not have had all these angry feelings about your uncaring mother who wouldn't let you sleep." Martin yelled back, "Well, thanks for the eye-opener! It's great to know my darling mother made a sadist out of me!" The patient marched out, letting the door slam behind him, and did not show up for the next two sessions. When he returned, he started the session off with angry sarcasm. "I'm sure you'll be relieved to know that my insomnia is back along with the gory fantasies. So what can you do for me now, Mr. Shrink?"

Realizing that Martin was still in the highly charged, traumatic state of overstimulation, which the therapist's interpretation two sessions before had triggered, the therapist said quietly, "It's sometimes very difficult to get the right empathic response from someone quite significant to you, even though you've always wanted it. When you get it, it may feel like more than you can handle, so naturally you're trying to tone down the excitement."

Martin began to calm down, and his state of psychic imbalance became less intense. He smiled and with some embarrassment said, "You hit the target again, Doc, but now I guess I can manage it better."

This episode illustrates the onset, climax, and gradual abatement of a traumatic state involving the intense stimulation of longed-for acknowledgment of the abuses that a patient's self has been subjected to, which threatened his belief in his very right to exist, let alone be cared about by an empathic selfobject. If the therapist is able, often after considerable time, to help the patient resolve the traumatic state, he or she will be rewarded by transmuting internalization as a longed-for selfobject to foster the development of healthy self-structure. Indeed, it is the very lack of such structure that sometimes precipitates sexual acting out that may be dangerous to the patient's realistic situation.

CASE VIGNETTE: HOW COULD I HAVE DONE IT?

A particular danger involved in the onset of traumatic states is that of the person acting out, often with actual or potential perilous consequences. In the following case vignette, a male physician patient, Alan G., would feel compelled after a violent verbal interchange with his depressed wife to visit a men's room in the subway and find a sexual partner. The scene of the sexual activity was sometimes the men's room and sometimes the other man's apartment. Either situation could be highly dangerous for the physician. In the men's room he risked exposure, sometimes even picking up a detective who would arrest him, with a consequent threat to his professional reputation and his marriage. When he went to a stranger's apartment, he was sometimes assaulted or threatened with blackmail.

The female therapist at first focused on the dangerous reality consequences of this acting out, whatever unconscious motivations it involved. By seeking to be empathic with the fragmented self-feelings that were driving this patient, the therapist hoped to serve as the good selfobject which, obviously, this patient had not found in his wife or his parents. She thought that by appealing to whatever self-concern Alan had left, she could be experienced by him as nonpunitive and noncritical.

The therapist also felt that without more substantiating evidence, she could not interpret the dangerous homosexual acting out as a need for the development of more self-structure through the selfobject transference with her. What she did not realize, however, was that her focus on Alan's self-destructive tendencies made him feel criticized by her, as if he were an out-of-control child. What he needed was an acknowledgment by the therapist that she realized he must have had an overriding reason for his compulsive actions but that she wondered if he could tell her what this reason might be.

The Patient Feels Unprotected from Danger

Finally, after a particularly frightening encounter with a sadistic man whose apartment was filled with machetes and other lethal weapons, Alan informed the therapist at his next session that he was thinking of terminating. The treatment, he said, was not giving him the protection he needed to guard himself from his own frightening impulses. "Whether you realize it or not," he snarled, "I was lucky to get out of that man's clutches last night, without literally being carved up!"

The therapist, taken aback by his rage, said, perhaps somewhat defensively, "But I do realize the danger you put yourself in after you fight with your wife! What I don't understand is why you do it!"

Alan sighed heavily, almost as if he had finally neared an objective and said, "Well, why haven't you ever asked me why I think I do it, even though I know it's very dangerous?"

Although the therapist regarded herself as a self psychologist, she realized that, based on her earlier traditional training, she had been unconsciously holding back from putting any "suggestive pressure" on Alan to explain why he thought he was doing such dangerous things. She feared, for example, that he might think she was being critical of the homosexual nature of the self-destructive actions and that his ambivalence over his bisexuality might have intensified his "resistance." She also realized that she was still thinking in terms of "defense as resistance" rather than regarding a defense as a way to halt an unendurable experience of self-fragmentation (Kohut, 1984). So the therapist finally said, with some evident humility, "I know I should have asked this before, but why do you think you do it?"

Alan replied thoughtfully, "I feel better, just by hearing you ask why, as if you believed there must be a sense-making reason for what appears like insane behavior. That belief alone, I think, is partly why I am compelled to endanger myself. My wife does not believe that I am a human being any more, if I ever was to her. I just can't seem to bring her out of her depression. When she's in it, she treats me as if I were a doormat, without any feelings or needs. She makes me feel as helpless as my damned, depressed mother did, always turning her back on me and taking to her bed whenever I needed even her acknowledgment that I was alive! That's why I go to men's rooms to pick up guys. If I can do it there, it's as if I can do it anywhere!"

He paused, and the therapist, now intent on his every word, said, "Do what?"

Alan laughed bitterly and added, "I guess I wanted to make sure you were really listening and not just speculating. What I want to do—what I need to do—is arouse somebody enough, not only to look at me, to listen to me, to need my physical attentions, but even to abuse me if I withhold myself in any way! Total wanting and demanding is what I have to have to go on living. Can you understand? I could get my cold-as-ice father to beat me by deliberately defying him. But no matter what I did, I couldn't get her to pay any attention to me, whatsoever. Maybe that's why I became a doctor. Her headaches were always more important than me!"

The therapist replied, "And my preoccupation with what I thought were your alleged resistances to treatment, shown in your dangerous behavior, were more important to stop first before I tried to understand what you were expressing."

Alan laughed and said, "Well, it's no wonder I kept trying to clutch at someone like my father. At least he would beat up on me, even though he never tried to find out why I was such an impossible kid. You were beating up on me, too, in trying to get me to save myself even before I knew why I wanted to destroy myself. You seemed to be saying, more exactly, "Why should I need all this attention?" You were like my father as well as my mother."

The therapist sighed with relief that the transference now seemed to be more available than ever, but regretted that her own inhibited curiosity and empathy had driven the patient to such dangerous and painful lengths. She said, "I wish I could have heard and seen what you were expressing to me sooner."

Alan sighed, too, and then smiled: "The important thing is you finally did hear and see. No one ever could do that for me before." From that day on, the patient became more able and willing to explore further and deal with the needs of his traumatic state, i.e., the recognition of the existence of his separate self and needs even in life-threatening situations. The homosexual aspects of his dangerous efforts at self-validation appeared to involve a twinship need (see Chapter 6) i.e., a sexualization of a need for someone to share some of his interests and enthusiasms, especially since he was an only child.

These interests and enthusiasms included his curiosity about the human condition and his reactive empathy in wishing to better it that was to help him undergo the rigors of becoming a good physician. As Alan gradually accepted the woman therapist as the good, interested selfobject thaht he had never had, he began to develop a more cohesive self which could seek out a responsively loving woman who shared some of his interests—another physician.

Despite the difficulty in separating from his chronically depressed wife—a replica of his unresponding, unmirroring mother (Kohut, 1979), Alan was able to divorce her and to marry the woman physician, who proved to be a good selfobject, reflecting the resonance to his self-needs that he had first found with the therapist in the resolution of his traumatic state.

THE PERSEVERATIVE FAUX PAS

The faux pas represents, perhaps, humankind's universal acknowledgment of the violent blow to a person's self-esteem when he or she either makes a mistake or is subjected to an unexpected humiliation on an important occasion. The mistake is always construed to be one's own fault with concomitant rage against oneself; but the humiliation often involves the grandiose self, giving rise to infantile narcissistic rage. In either case, there is often a repetitive working over of the shame and rage aroused by such mistakes or humiliations (imagined, as much as real). Dealing with these blows to self-esteem involves the endurance of a prolonged traumatic state.

It is essential that the therapist recognize the intense painfulness of these situations that require the same attention and empathic acceptance on the part of a good selfobject that a major catastrophe demands. As Kohut (1971) noted:

> . . . a rejection occurred, suddenly and unexpectedly, just at the moment when the patient was most vulnerable to it, i.e., at the very moment when he had expected to shine and was anticipating acclaim in his fantasies. (pp. 230-231)

The suicidal wish to destroy oneself in order to do away with the humiliating moment and the narcissistic rage that what has happened cannot be undone involves a protracted working through and calls for the therapist's utmost patience and empathy.

Kohut noted that the shame following a slip of the tongue may equal that of other faux pas (e.g., talking too much about oneself in an inappropriate social situation) and that part of the shame arises over not feeling in control of one's own actions. Of course, a person takes for granted that he is in undisputed charge of himself; if not, he would be considered "out of his mind"—an insupportable narcissistic blow.

Freud urged that slips of the tongue should always be explored as direct messages from the unconscious (S. Freud, 1901). From this standpoint, the transferential or genetic implications of slips of the tongue are focused upon rather than the blows to one's self-esteem incurred in making them. Yet an empathic understanding of the self-fragmentation that ensues after painful slips of the tongue may do much to relieve the self-torture involved in a constant reliving of the catastrophic experience. A male supervisee brought the following example.

CASE VIGNETTE: DOWN THE RECEIVING LINE

Mary A., an attractive professional single woman in her early thirties, perseverated over a "receiving line" incident. She had taken her lover to the wedding of a close woman friend who was marrying a very prestigious and well-to-do man. Mary had consciously felt very happy for her friend who had been through a series of unhappy and even frightening love affairs before finding her new husband. At the same time, Mary was also aware of envious twinges that her own lover was not as clearly desirable as her friend's husband nor had he yet shown Mary that he wanted to marry her. Given her age, Mary was beginning to worry about whether to stay with her lover or look for a man more clearly interested in marriage.

As she went down the receiving line at the wedding, some of these painful and conflicting feelings flitted through her mind.

She was also impressed by the elegance of the wedding reception and by how lovely her friend looked, standing beside her handsome, distinguished husband. Approaching the bride, Mary suddenly found herself groping frantically for her lover's name to introduce him since the bride did not know him. The name, John Smith, rushed to Mary's mind and she stammered it out, only to remember that his name was really John Morrow, which she hastily added. She hoped that the bride would think that his name included Morrow and was not just John Smith. The bride, either rising to the occasion or under the stress of it, gave no noticeable reaction to the slip and smiled benignly as the couple passed by.

Mary related this experience to her therapist at her next session, two days after the wedding. Even though her lover had not seemed to overhear her slip of the tongue and the bride had taken no obvious notice, Mary reported that she was lying awake at night brooding about it and could not concentrate on her work as a public relations executive. She burst into tears as she described her embarrassment over the faux pas. "I felt so ashamed that I wanted to die when I realized what I had said," she sobbed.

Somewhat puzzled about the depth of her humiliation and her consequent self-derogation, the therapist asked, "But what could upset you so about this? So far, there's no evidence that either your boyfriend or your friend, the bride, heard your slip about John Smith. And if they did, neither of them apparently attached enough importance to it to mention it to you, even in fun."

Mary replied, with cold fury in her voice, "I might have known you wouldn't understand. Especially since you're a man. Let's forget about the whole thing. I don't want to discuss it any more! I feel like leaving this very minute!"

The therapist was caught off guard by her rage. He had immediately perceived what he viewed to be oedipal complications in the whole situation. It was natural that Mary would envy her friend's winning a handsome, distinguished husband while Mary was "stuck" with a less impressive lover who was't even offering to marry her. What with anger over the unfairness of the situation where, as with her father, the really desirable man was not available to her, the therapist thought that narcissistic rage at her own helplessness as well as at her ineptitude in making the slip of the tongue would inevitably overwhelm her. In addition, the paralyzing anxiety that she would lose not only her boyfriend for insulting him but also her friend, the bride, for both her stupidity and her jealousy could make her feel incapable of discussing the faux pas. But it was also no wonder, the therapist concluded, that she became enraged at his failure to realize its importance to her. Once again, as so often in the past, she had experienced him as unempathic when he minimized the assault upon her self-cohesion arising from what appeared to be a trivial mistake.

The therapist moved to overcome the psychic disjuncture between himself and Mary by saying, "I realize now that I sadly underestimated the impact of this faux pas on how you feel about yourself. That you could let your feelings even temporarily overcome the poise you expect of yourself had to be terrifying. I should have understood that that self-distrust was much more frightening than any reaction your friends might have had to what you said."

Mary sighed deeply and said, still frowning, "Well, at least you tuned in this time to why I was so thrown by this dumb thing I said. So you do listen to what I say sometimes and even seem to remember it. And I'm relieved you didn't try the old ploy that I didn't get my daddy, so no other man will do. I worry about my friend, though. If this marriage doesn't work out, where will she ever find a man like that again? I could say that my calling my boyfriend John Smith tells where I'm at."

Puzzled, the therapist risked an inquiry, hoping it wouldn't derail what seemed like a healing of the psychic disjuncture and an opening up of a new approach to the state of Mary's self. He said, "I'd like to hear more about where you think you're at in regard to calling him John Smith."

Mary replied (a little exasperated), "Well, I should think it would be obvious to *you*. You're the great synthesizer and explicator of my unconscious! So what does the name, John Smith, connote to you?"

The therapist grabbed at a fleeting association and said, "Well, wasn't it Captain John Smith who was saved from scalping by the

Indian princess, Pocahontas? In that case, John Smith's life depended upon the love of a powerful woman."

Mary (impressed), "Well, that idea only validates what I was about to say. I was thinking that the name, John Smith, symbolizes a very ordinary man, kind of a nobody. But for me, a nobody represents safety. If I lose interest in him or even if he loses interest in me, so what? It's not an irreparable loss because I can easily find another John Smith to replace him. But to lose a man like my friend is marrying, well, that would be curtains for me, and I think for her, too. You probably could never replace someone like that. And I, knowing myself, wouldn't even try. So there's the terrible squeeze of falling in love. If you find what you've always been looking for, you're sure to lose it. So why look?"

The therapist realized that Mary was possibly alluding to fears she had about accepting him as a good selfobject, as someone who tried to respond to or at least acknowledge all her neglected needs from childhood. She feared that at some point he would fail her and let her down as everyone else had so far and that she would turn away from him, too.

But then the search for the good selfobject would become impossible, in Mary's view, because she was sure she would never find in anyone else the kind of empathy she had received from the therapist. He realized that Mary's faux pas had led to a major problem involving her cohesive self and her fear of loss through dependence. And he knew that only through continued treatment could her self become strong enough to risk the anxieties of depending on other good selfobjects she could find outside therapy as her nuclear self flowered into a cohesive self. He said quietly, "I'm beginning to know how big a problem this is for you."

Mary sighed and said, "Well, at least you do see it now and even seem to understand it a little. And maybe that could make a difference."

SELF-STATE DREAMS

Traumatic states, as we have seen, involve unmanageable overstimulation which triggers fragmentation of the nuclear self, often to a frightening degree. The blows to the cohesion of the self, touched off by faux pas, often appear to be an overreaction to expectable human mistakes and miscalculations.

However, embedded in the overreaction and the endless working over of a faux pas may be a traumatic state that had remained concealed until the occurrence of the faux pas. In such cases, the therapist's empathic and unflagging efforts to try to comprehend and to help the patient comprehend the true significance of his or her experiences of trauma in these connections is of the utmost importance in fostering the transmuting internalization of the therapist as the good selfobject the patient never had.

Similarly, what Kohut described as "self-state" dreams can attempt, through verbalizable dream imagery, to control such traumatic states as the dread of overstimulation, or of self-disintegration, e.g., psychosis." Thus, Kohut added, self-state dreams "attempt to deal with the psychological danger by covering frightening nameless processes with namable visual imagery" (1977, p. 109).

Paul Tolpin (1983) pointed out that, in addition to the self-state dreams revealing either traumatic or exhuberant states of the self, there can be "dreams about the self in relation to its selfobjects" (p. 258). Tolpin stressed that these dreams rarely can be understood from their manifest content. Current associations, day residue, and a comprehension of the patient's genetics, dynamics, character, defensive tendencies and especially the transference, empathically grasped together, can shed light on the dream's meaning, both in regard to the present and to the patient's childhood.

CASE VIGNETTE

Two dreams from a female patient of the senior author will now be presented to show how an early traumatic state may manifest itself. The lack of a "corrective developmental dialogue" (Marian Tolpin, 1983, p. 369) with her parents had left the patient as a child with crucial deficits in self-consolidation. Dreams can then reflect changes in this traumatic state once a therapist begins to become the needed selfobject for the still self-maimed adult.

The patient, Martha, was a 35-year-old professional woman who was unhappy in her marriage to a husband 10 years her senior, uncertain about her choice of professional career, and prone to crippling depressions which greatly interfered with her considerable creative potential. She came into treatment, ostensibly to get direction in her love life and in her career. As it turned out, her self was in a very vulnerable state.

Her first self-state dream was an atypical "tidal wave" dream, which she recalled from an uncertain point in her childhood. It was atypical in that she was lying alone on the bottom of the ocean while the tidal wave went over her. Somehow, with magical grandiosity, she felt she could keep the water from either wetting her or drowning her. Yet she was very aware of the precariousness of her situation.

Her associations to her childhood confirmed the shakiness of her self-state. She was the only daughter of a popular female singer who had had some success in Broadway musicals but never quite made it as a well-known star. Her career, however, made it necessary for her to leave Martha at eight months of age with her maternal grandparents and her two younger sisters—Martha's aunts. Her father, also a singer, had broken up with her mother when Martha was about three months old and had taken off with another woman. So Martha was a fatherless only child, deposited in the care of her hardworking grandparents and aunts who ran a family restaurant.

Her mother, Louise, came home to visit Martha every summer when New York show business slumped. It seemed likely, in view of the state of Martha's self, that she became attached to her grandmother as a stable, if somewhat insensitive maternal self-object, only to have her controlling, seductive mother "take over" the parenting every summer. In addition, Martha's two aunts, one a temperamental bereft twin, and the other, a talented but frightened slave, competed with each other for the child's attention as well as with Louise and the grandmother.

Martha's grandfather was a loner and an unreliable provider. However, he was very responsive and encouraging in helping her learn to do things. But he was violent if opposed by either his wife or his daughters. Martha grew up convinced, on the basis of her experience with her original selfobjects, that she always had to be "up for grabs" by anyone who wanted her enough to fight for her. Her performances did not count, so that her yearnings for reliable mirroring, for values she truly believed in, for accomplishments consonant with her talents simply did not matter in the human marketplace. If she were not to be abandoned forever, with the unavoidable fear arising from her mother's leaving her at eight months with her grandparents and the subsequent haggling over who should command her love, then she had to be attuned to whatever the victorious haggler demanded of her.

The Fragile Nuclear Self

There could be no expectation that Martha's fragile nuclear self could make any demands in conflict with the conquering but unempathic selfobject. Given her high intelligence and abundance of capacities and talents, Martha had little obvious difficulty in adjusting to the winner who wanted her, whether in a love or a work situation. The price of her super adjustment was to be found in the first tidal wave dream. She could only fend off total inundation of her nuclear self by calling upon her grandiose self fantasies that no one, "nothing" could ever touch her, let alone do her in. The only power that could hold the ocean back was God. Martha, raised as an Irish Catholic, was familiar with the Bible stories of Moses holding the Red Sea back while he led the Jews out of Egypt to the promised land.

Martha's unconscious grandiosity was put to the test, finally, in relation to her work. She came into treatment in a panic as to how to resolve her mounting hatred for her work as a political lobbyist for corporate interests and her increasing resentment of her husband's goals and values as a successful corporate executive. While this struggle over what she basically opposed had been going on for some years, the growing conflict over the use of nuclear energy, with its environmental dangers, had made her aware of how much she would like to be working for the abolition or at least sharp limitation of nuclear power rather than for the expansion of it. Her husband's corporation favored the all-out use of nuclear power, including the use of nuclear weapons in war, if necessary. While Martha had tried, characteristically, to keep her most deeply felt opinions on these political issues detached from her professional performance and from her husband's awareness, she had found it more and more difficult to respond to him sexually with any more passion than a dutiful acquiescence. To further complicate her life, she had found herself increasingly attracted to Jim, a man several years younger than herself, who was deeply involved as an activist against the nuclear power coalition.

Indeed, she had taken, for her, the most perilous steps of revealing her true feelings about the terrors involved in the expansion of industrial nuclear power, let alone her fears of nuclear war. Especially, she admired Jim's total dedication to the values he believed in, whatever they cost him.

The therapist, confronted with what appeared to be both a professional and a marital crisis in Martha's life, sensed that a much deeper crisis of the nuclear self was involved, although certainly if Martha were to follow her feelings and her values at that point, it would involve a total reorganization of her life. When the therapist asked Martha what she herself would like to do, Martha seemed stunned.

"But that's the point!" she gasped. "Nobody has ever asked me what I really want to do." Everybody, even Jim, assumed that she would agree with or go along with what the other wanted. This very assumption turned her off, even from people she truly admired. She desperately wanted someone to say, "Well what do *you* really want?" The therapist was the first person she could recall ever asking that question. In the next session, Martha gave the therapist a gift, the redreaming of her early self-state dream of being at the bottom of the ocean under a tidal wave.

Rescuing the Nuclear Self

In this second self-state dream, the tidal wave was observable at a distance, way out in the middle of the ocean. Martha, as she was at that emotional point in treatment, was dashing into the ocean fully clothed to rescue a little girl who was playing about in the water, oblivious to the tidal wave. Behind Martha was a younger man, trying to catch up to her in order to help her save the child. Except for the tidal wave in the distance, the ocean was calm and the weather was beautiful.

At first, Martha seemed rather baffled by the dream. She associated to the young man who was trying to help her rescue the child as reminding her of Jim, the younger activist to whom she was romantically attracted, "except that the man in the dream had blond hair and Jim has dark hair," Martha mused. Then she smiled and said, "But, of course! You (the therapist) have blond hair! And I felt so good about yesterday's session! You seemed actually concerned about what I wanted and what I feel able to do right now. Even Jim pushes me in the direction he wants to take." Her voice faltered and she sounded depressed.

The therapist wondered if the little girl in the dream represented Martha's self at some point of developmental arrest (Stolorow & Lachmann, 1980) and if Martha's experience of the therapist's empathic concern with what Martha wanted at the previous session (i.e., concern with the vulnerable state of her self) had opened up the possibility of the therapist beginning to be internalized as a good selfobject. The therapist recognized that the tidal wave in the dream, still threatening but at a distance, symbolized the connection between this new self-state dream and the recurring childhood dream Martha had first brought into treatment.

The dream still revealed an inevitable distrust of the potential good selfobject and the early conviction that Martha could only trust herself and therefore had to be omnipotent in order to be safe in a tidal wave world. This was symbolized, the therapist thought, by the fact that Martha was dashing into the ocean to save the little girl, and even the potential good selfobject—the combination of Jim and the therapist, indicated by the blond hair—was lagging behind Martha's grandiose self striving to save the child. Still, the therapist thought, there was a potential empathic helper in the dream in the figure of Jim, and the threat of engulfing overstimulation and self-fragmentation, symbolized by the tidal wave, was at a distance as compared with its over-powering presence in the recurring dream of Martha at the bottom of the ocean. How old was the child, the therapist wondered? Perhaps that would give some clue to whatever point of developmental arrest might be indicated by the child in need of rescuing.

These thoughts had flickered through the therapist's mind as she had listened to Martha's initial associations to the dream, winding up with the connection Martha had made with her experience of the therapist as a potential good selfobject in the session the day before. The therapist said, "I'm wondering about the little girl whom you're rescuing in the dream. How old do you think she was?"

Martha's face brightened fleetingly at the question and she said, "She probably was about seven." Then she added, with a shocked expression on her face, "Oh my God! That was the summer my mother took us all to Atlantic City! And I almost drowned in the Atlantic. That's what the tidal wave was! It felt like a tidal wave. I was so scared . . . I went under, I thought I was going to drown. Oh my God, how could they have let that happen to me?" She started to sob soundlessly at first, then with more and more of a gasping sound. "They really didn't care. I was just a bone for them to haggle over. They could only think about themselves, never about me! I guess I wanted to die anyway, I felt so alone. . . ."

The therapist was shocked by the realization that the first self-state tidal dream represented not only the patient's repressed grandiose self-sufficiency arising out of unempathic caretaking but also a real brush with death arising out of that same indifferent environment. The therapist said softly, "How awful for you! Were you knocked over by a wave?"

Martha nodded, drew a deep breath, and said fairly calmly, even with a touch of humor, "I was a summer cottage kid. We used to go to a little lake about 20 miles away from my home town. I loved the water and I was the only one in my whole family who could swim a little. I got puffed up about that and when my mother took us to the ocean at Atlantic City, I thought it was just a big lake. She let me just run in, didn't warn me about the waves, and quickly got involved with a new friend she'd picked up on the beach.

The therapist said, with amazement at such neglect, "She let you run into the Atlantic Ocean all by yourself and didn't even watch you?"

Martha nodded. The therapist then asked, still a little disbelieving, "But what about your grandparents and your aunts? Where were they?"

Martha laughed a bit cynically, "Well, my grandmother was always into the food department so she was busily unpacking the lunch. And my aunts were either following my mother around or picking up strangers on the beach, too. Don't get me wrong. I don't mean picking up men, although sometimes it was a man. But mostly it was other women to hold forth with."

The therapist became more clearly aware that Martha failed to get either minimum safeguarding from danger or adequate mirroring for her achievements like swimming in the ocean. So she said, "I would have thought all of them would have wanted to watch you swimming in the ocean, since they couldn't swim, even if they didn't have sense enough to know it was dangerous."

Martha shrugged and said, "Well, there was always a lot of talk about my accomplishments but when it came to really being there with me and for me, it never quite came off. Other people, friends, and strangers always came before me. When I got attention that day was when my body was tossed up by the sea onto the stones on the beach. My head landed on a rock and started to bleed but I had so much salt water up my nose and in my throat that I couldn't talk, let alone scream. But a nice lifeguard came running over to me, saw the blood on my head, picked me up, and asked where my parents were; and I pointed in the direction of my mother. He carried me over to her, got her to stop talking long enough to listen to his question, 'Is this your little girl?' She took one look at me, screamed 'My baby, what have you done to yourself?' and tried to grab me away from the lifeguard. He held on to me and said, 'We'd better take her to the locker rooms. There's a nurse there who can bandage her head.' He got me to the nurse, despite my mother's screams and sobs about what had I done to myself and why wasn't I more careful and she would never let me swim again."

Martha sighed deeply, then continued, "I didn't need any stitches for my head, but I guess I wished they'd stitch up my mother's mouth! She played the scene for all it was worth and got all the attention and nobody ever did get around to asking me how it happened. But I wasn't allowed to go in swimming for the rest of the summer because I was so 'thoughtless.' "

The therapist recognized that the tidal wave image represented both a terrifying physical trauma and an unforgettable experience of maternal unattunement. She said, softly, "It was all so awful for you. How did you get thrown up on the beach?" Martha said grimly, "Well, I was used to wading into lake water, then ducking myself and starting to swim. The ocean waves were too fast for me. One of them just picked me and threw me back on the beach. But that's such a terrifying experience of nature's raw power! When that big wave hit me, I felt I was killed. I think I passed out until I hit the rock on the beach. But I never went in the ocean again."

The therapist added, "And naturally you have never wanted to get into a situation again, either physical or a psychological one, where you can't protect yourself against all contingencies, including needing someone who doesn't really care about you."

Martha nodded her head thoughtfully: "That's why I worry about Jim. Does he really want me to have what I want? I don't want him to turn out like my husband."

"And naturally, you don't feel you can count on me fully yet to help you understand what you want," the therapist added.

Martha smiled wistfully and said, "Well, I realize I'm likely to be more cautious than a really secure patient would be. But I think we've really started to go in wading together. And for me, that's taking a big chance!"

THE NEGATIVE THERAPEUTIC REACTION

Because the negative therapeutic reaction has been regarded as the most difficult deadlock with a patient that a therapist can encounter, it seems appropriate to include it in this chapter since such a situation often produces a mounting traumatic state in the therapist.

Freud (1918) appeared to have been driven for the first time by such a state to set a termination date for a patient, namely the Wolf Man, who not only was apathetic about actively working in analysis but also negatively reacted with exacerbated symptoms whenever Freud seemed to clear something up. At first, setting the termination date appeared to overcome the Wolf Man's fixation on his illness, thus providing Freud with all the material he needed to understand the patient's infantile neurosis. However, as we may remember, the Wolf Man returned to Vienna, an impoverished and poorly functioning man after the Russian Revolution, and required further treatment not only by Freud but also by Ruth Mack Brunswick.

"Mourning and Melancholia" (1917), with its picture of the self-denigration and self-deprivation of the melancholic, led the way to Freud's ultimate delineation of the negative therapeutic reaction in "The Ego and the Id" (1923), where he noted that some patients' conditions became worse when the analyst noted their progress in the treatment. He confessed that one can begin by considering patients' reactions as defiance or as an attempt to prove their superiority to the analyst. But later the analyst may become convinced that praise or appreciation may actually undermine the treatment. Patients display what is called a "negative therapeutic reaction," which "reveals itself as the most powerful of all obstacles to recovery, more powerful than the familiar ones of narcissistic inaccessibility, a negative attitude towards the physician, and clinging to the gain from illness" (Freud, 1961, p. 49). Freud concluded that the analyst is dealing with the patient's sense of guilt, which requires the punishment of suffering. But as far as the patient is concerned, "he does not feel guilty, he feels ill. . . . He holds fast to the . . . explanation that treatment by analysis is not the right remedy for his case" (Freud, 1961, pp. 49-50).

Brandschaft, in "The Negativism of the Negative Therapeutic Reaction and the Psychology of the Self" (1983), noted that Freud concluded and stressed in his treatment that it is the repressed, unconscious impulses that are at the root of the patient's guilt, even when the patient's guilt is conscious, as in obsessional neurosis and masochism. Brandschaft later concluded that it is often the analyst's insistence that the patient must be guilty, i.e., feel "bad" about something that arouses a feeling of hopelessness leading to the negative therapeutic reaction and even to the regressive production of borderline symptoms (Brandschaft & Stolorow, 1984).

In addition to unconscious guilt, other approaches to the negative therapeutic reaction are reviewed by Brandschaft, including Abraham's (1919) focus on narcissistic resistances, such as an inclination to feel "humiliated by every fact that is established in their psychoanalysis"; Riviere's (1936) ideas about unconscious depression, mania, and the need for omnipotent control of the analyst; Olinick's (1964) fear of primary identification with a love object entailing loss of the self; and Asch's (1976) use of Mahler's developmental approach involving fear of separation from a possessive mother. Brandschaft (1983) also cites a later (1933, *New Introductory Lectures)* comment by Freud on his reflections on the negative therapeutic reactions giving rise to the whole metapsychology of psychoanalysis:

> Our first purpose, of course, was to understand the disorders of the human mind, because a remarkable experience had shown that here understanding and cure almost coincide, that a traversable road leads from one to the other. (p. 145)

Foreshadowing self psychology, Brandschaft suggests that Freud's statement implies that "negative therapeutic reactions do not arise from intrapsychic sources strictly within the patient as 'a need to fail,' but from a failure of understanding of the interaction between patient and analyst" (p. 337).

The recognition that depression at approaching termination was not inevitably an indication of persisting unconscious guilt but rather failure on the therapist's part to "recognize the narcissistic disorders as primary and the defective self as the core" (p. 347) led Brandschaft to realize that "the goals I sought in each case were incompatible with the goals the patient was pursuing" (p. 347). When his goals were incongruous with those of the patient, he concluded he had to abandon such goals and "stop insisting that in their opposition they were defeating both themselves and me" (p. 348). He cites a woman patient of his as saying, well into her analysis, "The first thing I had to get across to you was how important what you thought of me was . . . I couldn't disagree with you because I was afraid of worse consequences—that you would think I was resisting when I wanted so much to cooperate. So I tried to see and use and apply what you said" (p. 348). But she had felt, in many interpretations, that the analyst was being again like the father she had looked to for support in developing reliable self-esteem and he often said: 'Take her back to the store and get another one!' "

Upon starting her treatment, this woman patient, Caroline (Brandschaft & Stolorow, 1984b) had shown borderline characteristics and paranoid distrust, which had arisen in the "intersubjective field consisting of her vulnerable, fragmentation-prone self and a failing archaic selfobject (her husband)" (p. 355). These characteristics remained and were often intensified "in the new intersubjective field of the psychoanalytic situation" (ibid.), when her self-fragmentation was unwittingly triggered by the analyst's unreliable responsiveness and faulty interpretative stance. Replicated in both her marriage and in her analysis were "the specific traumatogenic failures of her original selfobject" (ibid). Caroline had tried to deal with these failures by becoming a selfobject for her mother and later, her analyst, pushing herself to do what she thought was demanded. When the analyst gradually became able to comprehend with empathy Caroline's archaic subjective states, she was able to establish with him the specific selfobject ties she required. Then her "borderline" features dropped away.

The negative therapeutic reaction and/or the regressive borderline phenomenon, from a self psychological standpoint, appears to arise from the failure of the therapist to empathically understand a patient's specific selfobject needs. This kind of intersubjective field involving "a precarious, vulnerable self and a failing archaic selfobject" (Brandschaft and Stolorow, 1984b, p. 356) is dramatically described by Kohut (1984) in the case of a male patient who had come for treatment after several "failures" with previous analysts. As the negative therapeutic reaction developed, Kohut was subjected to searing attacks. He kept the patient in an ultimately successful treatment by discovering that he had to learn "to see things exclusively in his [the patient's] way and not at all in *my* way" (p. 182). By achieving almost total immersion in the patient's feelings, Kohut was able to reverse Freud's gloomy prophecy of inevitable failure in these cases.

Empathy, it appears, is the key to treating effectively the traumatic states outlined in this chapter. Whether it is an anxiety-arousing overstimulation from a therapist's response so empathic that the patient feels flooded and resorts to regressive ways to prevent self-fragmentation or whether it is the apparent wall of opposition to any selfobject approaches by the therapist (the negative therapeutic reaction), the therapist must seek, through experience-near empathy, to imagine how the patient must feel on the basis of his known history, and therefore what he must need at this moment in time from the therapist. Only in this way does the therapist stand a good chance of becoming the longed-for good selfobject even in cases of seemingly severe pathology.

9

Special Populations

As we have indicated throughout this book, self psychology offers those suffering from developmental arrests—perhaps even borderline and psychotic patients—more effective psychotherapeutic help than ever before. We suggest that self psychology also helps difficult-to-treat patients arrive at a better state of being. Obviously, in this chapter we cannot possibly consider all of these special groups of patients, so we have chosen two—the child abuser and the older adult.

We believe, on the basis of our experience and observation, that if psychotherapists were to be queried about their interest in working with either of these two special populations, probably an overwhelming majority would say: "I would do it if I absolutely had to, but I'd rather not. They are so difficult to work with! Is there really a possibility for lasting change? I like to work with people where a change for the better or even a 'recovery' is more probable."

We will now examine how a self psychology treatment approach can lead to constructive change in such patients and concomitant feelings of effectiveness in the therapist.

TREATING THE CHILD ABUSER

The extent of physical child abuse in this country is horrendous and still relatively unknown. The figures are uncertain, dependent

155

as they are on reports from doctors and hospitals treating obviously abused children. Such reports often lack reliable verifi-
cation from the parents, who tend to blame other causes, or the
child himself, rather than admit that they either hurt the child or
did not provide quick relief soon enough, e.g., a broken bone
resulting from an accident which was not adequately treated in
time.

Even from an empathic self psychology standpoint, one of the
most difficult patients to treat, in terms of the therapist's own
reactions, may be a child abuser, especially a parent. What the
therapist is confronting in abusing parents is their narcissistic rage
over their inablility to *make* their child react as if he or she were
part of the parent's self and really knew what was wanted. Even
though this may sound rather trite by now, a parent's sadism is
erupting from the same sense of helplessness that the baby is
showing: how to get the other or the world to do what is demanded. Presumably, helplessness is equated with a collapse of
self-esteem, a falling apart of the self so that desperate measures
seem essential to restore it. Those desperate measures, unfortunately, are too often grabbed at through child abuse. From a self
psychological perspective, therefore, the therapist is called upon
to be empathically responsive to the victimization and deep hurt
experienced by the abusing person, almost as if the abuser had
been as battered as his or her child.

CASE VIGNETTE

The following case* illustrates how aggression toward a child
can be decreased by the therapist tuning in to the pain of the
parent.

Abusive Mothers Not Truly Mirrored

Susan A. started treatment with a colleague, who has extensive
experience in working with neglectful and abusive mothers. Using

*Case contributed by Jane Wilkins, D.S.W. Candidate.

a self psychology approach, the therapist had become aware that mothers abusing children were most often women who had not received approval and pleasure in the mirror of their own parents' eyes. They therefore looked to their own children to provide them, belatedly, with this desperately needed recognition and admiration.

In presenting this case at the senior author's bi-weekly Seminar on Self Psychology, the therapist stressed that so long as a child provided the appreciation needed by the mother, self-esteem could be maintained. When the applause failed, the mother's narcissistic rage erupted along with her inner experience of a disrupted, i.e., fragmenting, self. Then the mother-child relation often deteriorated into grim child abuse. Given this early deprivation on the part of the mother as a child herself and the probable failure of her children to be reliably responsive, the therapist had found that the demand for this affirmation would usually be transferred to the therapist.

Susan was an attractive, single parent who was 27 years old. Her complaint and reason for coming into treatment was her difficulty in managing her eight-year-old son. She described his behavior as "negativistic and defiant. He just won't listen to me. Everything becomes a power struggle and I wonder who's in control. I am also devastated by his school work. He just doesn't live up to his potential, and I don't know what to do about it."

Susan went on to tell the therapist that she just won't sign her son's homework papers when "they're not up to par." She stressed that "he's got to do better. It's infuriating!"

Fragile Self-Worth Leads to Abuse

In treatment, it became apparent to the therapist that Susan needed constant admiration from her eight-year-old son as a way of supporting her fragile sense of self-worth. When she was thwarted or felt humiliated, she could not control herself, and this resulted in physical attacks upon her son.

In describing one such incident to the therapist, Susan said her current boyfriend was in her apartment, and she had just told her young son to take his bath. He responded negatively and bad-mouthed her. She felt belittled and humiliated in front of her boyfriend. Without thinking, she flung herself on her son and began beating him. Shaken and frightened, she later reported that she had not been aware of how brutally she had been hitting him.

The bruises on his cheeks and body showed unmistakably that he had been attacked, so Susan kept him home from school. She didn't want others to know what she had done. This episode led to a dim awareness, expressed by her in session, that her own sense of a deflated self had led to the attack.

A traditional approach in therapy might have led the therapist to view this patient's continuous battles with her son as a result of her "childish dependency" needs. However, well-grounded in self psychology, the therapist recognized that her patient's needs for empathic understanding were paramount; she therefore directed many of her remarks to meeting that very need. For example, the therapist told Susan that she realized how much Susan needed to be respected and obeyed by her son and that not feeling appropriately acknowledged by him left her feeling vulnerable, helpless and, consequently, outraged. The therapist also raised the possibility that this bath struggle could have felt like a dreadful repetition from the past, which could explain the intensity of her response to her son.

A Need for Empathic Echoing

The therapist told us how she perceived Susan: "I understood that her outbursts were not out of frustration but out of her own need to be echoed empathically. Only in being responded to by feeling understood could she believe herself to be acceptable, valid as a person, and not beyond the pale of humanity." She went on to say that the patient could not tell the therapist about the abuse of her son at first, because she felt it was so disgraceful.

The therapist said, "It wasn't until I proved my empathy that she could believe I saw her as a worthwhile human being, that I was able to listen to this and, far from rejecting her, show concern about her humiliation and desperation." What was basic in this therapist's approach and of the utmost therapeutic value lay in her understanding of her patient's unmet needs for mirroring and affirmation and not moralistically rejecting the immature and unacceptable forms through which these were expressed.

Expressions of Aggression as Needs for Self-Enhancing Reflections

The therapist's stance was to get across to the patient that she understood the difficulty she was having in acknowledging unacceptable aspects of herself. The therapist stressed that when the patient was with the therapist she felt a continuity about herself and, by contrast, she experienced devastating disappointment when she felt a breach, i.e., a failure in her continuity, which she did not expect to be understood at all.

Rather than dealing with Susan's defenses against intrapsychic conflict, the therapist focused on the gaps in the development of Susan's psychic structure which had blocked the development of a reliably cohesive self. Interpretations also did not focus on Susan's angry responses as indicative of her inability to synthesize good and bad internal object-representations. The therapist believed, on the basis of her experience with self psychology, that such interpretations do not consider what the real issues are or the damage to the patient's self-esteem by such confrontations. The true significance, it was felt, involved not a struggle for object love but rather, as the therapist pointed out, a need for "self-enhancing reflection: to be looked at, approvingly and admiringly, and, with this self-confirmation, to be able to go on with further firming and development of the core of her being."

The following condensed passages from the therapist's presentation at the Seminar illustrate the unfolding of Susan's self-object needs as they manifested themselves in treatment:

> Skeptical about therapy, the patient did not at first talk about thoughts and experiences. Susan was particularly reluctant to discuss creative experiences, such as attempts at writing, fearing this would bring ridicule. However, she seemed obviously pleased at the therapist's interest in these when they

did appear. Never having felt valued for these pursuits, she at first felt surprise at this interest and exclaimed: "No one has ever listened to me before this way." Soon after, she brought a journal she was keeping to the therapy session. The therapist reflected her appreciation of this beautifully put together journal. The patient basked in that reaction. In evoking the therapist's recognition and affirmation, a significant shift occurred in the way in which the therapist was being experienced by this patient. A revived need for the mirroring function of self-enhancement was being fulfilled!

Susan's anticipation of criticism and disapproval provided additional compelling evidence, from a self psychological point of view, of her urgent need for a more comforting and responsive selfobject. Taking up the patient's expectations toward the therapist yielded important memories of her early childhood in which she had sought relief from damaging and humiliating encounters with her mother. This led her to concentrate her efforts on what would please or delight and not upset her mother.

Empathic responses, little known in Susan's former repertoire, were given to help her empathize with the lonely little girl she must have been rather than the tough, self-sufficient one her mother had told her she was. Unmirrored most of the time as a child, she had sought constant activity to ward off feelings of deadness and fragmentation. Through the therapist's approach and sensitivity to Susan, the patient's proneness to fragmented self-states, rage, and primitive sexualized responses as a way to establish self-restoration diminished. Susan eventually gained sufficient confidence in herself so that her dependence on her child as a narcissistic extension of herself was greatly reduced, as well as her need to physically abuse her son.

The therapist emphasized that this self psychology approach seemed to promise more constructive and enduring outcomes than an emphasis on child neglect and the maladaptive, inappropriate patterns of interaction inherent therein. She felt that stressing the latter often failed to recognize that the selfobject needs of the parent are *valid* and not unresolved "dependency" fixations from childhood.

This approach allows the therapist to actually function as a part of the patient's psyche, not by buttressing ego functions and so-called reality testing, but rather by participating in the patient's psychological reality. Understanding a context in which intense, pervasive selfobject needs are revived in the service of shoring up a crumbling sense of self may foster greater tolerance of such primitive narcissistic attitudes and deepen a therapist's appreciation of the severity of the primary disturbance. This may, in turn, lead to more therapists being able and willing to work with parents accused of abuse where, as we have stressed, empathy rather than a morality stance can be most effective.

This ability on the part of therapists to work with a population considered very difficult and to be avoided may be yet another plus for self psychology, as well as helping therapists in their continuous search for newer, more creative ways in which to experience themselves.

TREATMENT OF THE OLDER ADULT

The fact that the aging human brain has unrealized potentialities for growth in a truly enriching environment was headlined in the *Science Times* recently (*The New York Times*, July 30, 1985). This exciting ability of the aging brain to "forge new connections to other cells" (p. C-1), even to the extent of compensating for early deficiencies through enriched later learning, underlines the widening vistas for the older adult, already offered by self psychology (see Introduction).

In stark contrast to this heartening discovery are the dismal statistics showing how untapped are the existing resources for supplying psychological services for the elderly. At the same time, the suicide rate for those over 65 accounts for at least 25% of the total population. Sadly enough, the admission rate to mental hospitals is disproportionately high for the elderly, while their use of outpatient services is very low (Sargent, 1982).

As with child-abusing parents, it seems to us that a more traditional psychotherapeutic approach in treating older people has often intensified their sense of helplessness and guilt so far as being able to make their lives more fulfilling. In addition, the actual experiences reported to us by some elderly patients who wouldn't give up the search for a more gratifying life have convinced us that there is a deep-seated, if unconscious, reluctance among many therapists to treat older people. Until now, there have been few self psychologists in our field working with any age group, including the older one. Perhaps this is due to therapists' own archaic grandiosity in their need to be all-powerful and, using the scalpel approach, to completely exorcise all "neurosis"! Sitting opposite a patient in his or her sixties, seventies, or eighties with a history and layering of complexities might be an affront to be avoided by such therapists, i.e., the inability to accept limitations and work within the confines of a quality-of-life framework rather than quantity of years to be lived. Translated into self psychological terms, it is our concept of the grandiose self in the therapist, with its accompanying narcissistic rage at every disappointment, that may be the barrier to treating the older adult. Is it any wonder then that, based upon numerous self-reported vignettes, the older adult seeks medical treatment where "instant cure" in the form of a drug is offered, as against a more time-consuming, process-oriented approach, such as psychotherapy?

CASE VIGNETTE #1

Leaving aside all of the reservations about the possibility of effectively treating the older person, let us look at an actual case. The patient, Amy G., is an 83-year-old woman living in the community. She had been hospitalized briefly 20 years previously for depression. She had been a widow for the past eight years, and was now seeking psychotherapy to relieve her reactivated depression. Quite simply she wanted to "feel better and happier than I am now." It was not easy for this patient, as with so many older adults, to ask for help, as shown in the following interchange.

Patient: I feel so ashamed and embarrassed at having to ask for assistance. I just hate it.

Therapist (seeking to empathize with her): I can understand how hard it is for someone as independent as yourself to ask for any help at all. But maybe we could think about what's missing in your life now and see what might be done.

Patient: It seems like nothing—so small and insignificant. I don't even know if I should talk about it.

Therapist: It must be important to you, otherwise it wouldn't be there inside of you, depressing you. You know, everything you feel and think can be relevant to your continuing well-being.

Note that the therapist deliberately avoided traditional interpretations that would center on resistance, anger at the therapist, or a reaction formation to stress, feeling insignificant as a denial of the need to be grandly exhibitionistic. Clearly, the therapist was using a self psychology approach.

Patient: I can't seem to manage my life in the way I'd like. For instance, when a bus I am waiting for arrives, I have to ask the driver, while everyone is looking at me, to please drive up closer to the curb so that I can get up on the steps. Even when he does, and most of them do, I am huffing and puffing by the time I've gotten into the bus. By then, some people around me are offering me seats and everyone is staring at the old lady.

Therapist (attuned to the self psychological approach of the grandiose self, its rage at any imperfection and limitation of self): Well, I can see how you might resent others' offering you help because you have always felt you should be able to handle anything by yourself.

Patient (seeming pleased and surprised): Yes, well, I guess I have always felt I should depend only upon myself. However, I know that for many years I did what I thought everyone else wanted me to do—first my older sisters and parents and then later, George, my husband.

Here, instead of focusing on either the concrete, reality-based issue of the need for this elderly woman to help herself in situations that present real difficulties, or the defense against this need, the therapist was considering the deeper unconscious demands of the grandiose self, which tolerates no imperfections, including those intrinsic to aging. The therapist's purpose is always to build a more cohesive self at any age. It was anticipated that through this building and the internalization of the therapist, the patient would not only develop additional needed structures for more successful living, but also, hopefully receive the mirroring she had never received from her always-busy, seemingly indifferent parents and, later, her demanding spouse.

When it was discovered, in later sessions, that Amy wrote not only high quality poetry but also some lively plays, she was encouraged to bring them in and read them, which she did during some sessions. It was also at this point that she spoke of the desire to publish and joined a writing class at one of the senior centers to which she belonged, where she was often touted as one of its most outstanding writer/poets. The therapist, acting as the self-object who encouraged healthy ambition and exhibitionism, noted the marked decrease of material related to disability and limitation, and the increase of ideas connected with ambition. For example, "I'd love to write a book. I think I will!" Amy's depression lifted as she was able to tap her writing ability in a sustained way, knowing that she had an appreciative audience.

We are here considering ambition perhaps even of a surfacing grandiose self at age 83. But why not? Even in our seemingly age-stratified society where youth is revered, there are surprising acknowledgments of what age has to offer in terms of Nobel Prize winners, presidents of major governments (including our own), and a near worship of aging artists, e.g., Picasso, Chagall, along with Eleanor Roosevelt and feminist leaders. Nevertheless, in our world, the older person, and the aging woman in particular, is often dethroned, desexed and debarred in no uncertain terms.

It is true that older persons do not seek psychotherapy because there's too little encouragement to change after about age 60. On the other hand, there seems to be less and less respect for the seductive rocking chair and tranquilizing medications. And it has been our experience that the later years may offer possibilities for various forms of creativity: in the arts, sciences, and politics; or, in the discovery of new selfobjects after earlier losses or disappointments. The development of a "new," more cohesive self tends to occur with an increase in stable self-esteem arising from attuned selfobjects, starting with the therapist and extending to other compatible people. In addition, as we have indicated, the discovery of unsuspected talents can widen the world for older people as well as for youth. Let us illustrate with another case the possible achievement of finding a new selfobject.

CASE VIGNETTE #2

Jim B. came for treatment at age 84. This represented a triumph of perseverance, since several agencies had already rejected him because of his age. Jim's presenting symptoms were feelings of hopelessness and depression, which he related to his wife's death three years earlier after 51 years of marriage. Upon waking, he would feel he did not deserve to live through the day and would compulsively go out to relieve his despair. Another symptom, which he traced back to age four, was a compulsive need to get away from knives, belts, and ties for fear he would be driven to hurt himself. For instance, he wore suspenders and a bow tie (if a tie was indicated). As for knives, he would manage to turn any point away from him.

His treatment goal was to "feel better." He led a lonely life, sharing an apartment with another aged man who spent little time there. Working part-time as a messenger, Jim appeared for work hours ahead of time simply because he was lonely.

Jim's closest relative was a nephew who had referred him for treatment. His marriage had been childless and had had a symbiotic coloration. He and his wife had operated various retail stores until she became an invalid with Parkinson's disease. For 15 years before her death, he had nursed her untiringly.

Jim's twin brother and two older brothers had died some years ago. Born in rural Poland, the patient was four when his father had left for the United States to make more money and a home for his family. He eventually brought the family to the United

States 11 years later. Jim recalled the sad mornings when he, his mother, and his brothers would look out to sea, and his mother would berate his father for leaving them. This memory led to the therapist's hypothesis that the patient ambivalently experienced his father's leaving both as a desertion and as the outcome of a pathologically resolved oedipal competition. The failure of his father as an idealized selfobject, i.e., someone through whom Jim could strengthen his bipolar self, was focused upon by the therapist in connection with an adolescent memory of his father's uncaring and unwelcoming attitude. This memory involved his father's refusing to buy Jim an ice cream cone upon the latter's arrival in America at age 15. The therapist linked this rejection to the earlier abandonment at age four.

The initial focus of the treatment was an effort to relieve Jim's hopelessness and sense of unworthiness in two ways: 1) to undo the self-aggression, recognizing that this was the end product of a pathological father-son relationship and not due to an innate drive (Kohut, 1982); and 2) to increase Jim's self-esteem by the use of an empathic approach that would allow for the internalization of the therapist as a good selfobject (Kohut & Wolf, 1978). The therapist thus sought to help Jim understand his ambivalence toward his mother, father, and wife, all of whom he felt had deserted him. The therapist reminded Jim that one can be angry at the hardship imposed by a loved person without necessarily totally withdrawing love. His seemingly positive oedipal transference was accepted without interpretation, and his enthusiastic reaction of: "If I could find a woman like you, I'd marry her" was used to encourage his interest in available women. After three years of treatment, the patient at 87 did succeed in marrying a widow four years younger.

Jim's second marriage was achieved after many sessions in which he expressed apprehension about his sexual capability. Gradually, his fear of closeness and of disappointing his prospective wife were reduced through his verbalization of his feelings and the empathic interpretations of the therapist that his fears of being rejected were natural. Earlier, the therapist and the patient together had decided that he need not tell his wife-to-be of his phobic fears about knives, belts, and ties. He was relieved that only he and the therapist would ever know his "piece of craziness." After his remarriage, Jim and his wife came to one session together, ostensibly so the wife could meet "the doctor who helped me." This appreciation was accepted positively by the therapist. Termination was discussed soon after and mutually agreed upon.

What were some of the ways in which self psychology was applied in the above case? In addition to empathizing with the patient's difficult life, the therapist was able to offer hope in the form of some modified, attainable goal, which would help relieve his lonely life and thereby attenuate his lifelong psychic pain. This was done by using the selfobject transference to strengthen the patient's cohesive self, which was reflected in the fact that he was able to change his life.

Self psychological approaches were consciously employed as a means of building upon long-standing adaptive defenses. The therapist focused on Jim's chances of finding another love relationship by gambling on his capacity to endure frustration and disappointment (as shown in his coping with his first wife's long illness and his difficult roommate). The therapist also accepted his constructive albeit compulsive activity in dealing with his phobias, e.g., avoidance of knives, belts, and ties, and his need to seek company, e.g., getting to work early to avoid depression. While the therapist was aware of some of the unconscious conflicts implied in the phobias and in his rather masculine second wife, the here-and-now orientation was emphasized. Similarly, Jim's libidinal oedipal transference reactions to the therapist were handled as indications that the patient could hope for and seek a new marital relationship. This overall approach was deemed appropriate to the reality that, for this patient, time was not as "unlimited" in the concrete sense as for a younger person, and some satisfactions in continuing to live were pressing needs. A reduction in symptoms and an increased capacity for zestful living became the goals, which were achieved.

THE GROUP AND THE OLDER ADULT

It is sometimes difficult to remember that the advanced-age patient sitting before us, in individual or group settings, was once a child. But obviously he or she was, and consequently the complex patterns that now appear have taken many years to form. Where traditional theory focuses on development in terms of concepts such as id, ego, and superego, self psychology speaks little about these hypothetical structures. However, in relation to the oedipus complex, it is proposed (see Chapter 7) that the latter can be a joyful experience in a nonpathological environment (Kohut, 1984).

As therapists, we are aware that the human mind encompasses a complex group of images and memory traces, i.e., self- and object-representations, which originally represented mother, father, brother, sister, enemies, friends, and so forth. All are to be eventually perceived, in the natural process of growth, as distinct from the self. Where there is a lack of a firm self, indicating a developmental arrest (Stolorow & Lachmann, 1980, p. 5), there is a need to feel and to experience others as similar to or part of the self. While the "group self" may be clinically expressed in group cohesion, it also offers a continued possibility for further structural changes with respect to individuation. In growth-fostering conditions, group therapy can stimulate and encourage such individual differentiation as the group itself goes from stage to stage, over a period of time.

Initiating the Older Adult into the Group

Before introducing the older patient into the group, whether that group is age-homogeneous or age-heterogeneous, the therapist works with the patient in preparatory individual sessions, the objective being to establish a "firm selfobject transference" (Harwood, 1983). Once this is accomplished, joining the group can supply the patient with a wealth of potential selfobjects: the group's individual members, the group as an entity unto itself, and the therapist. If all goes well, the patient gains the group's acceptance and understanding and draws from its strength, while recognizing the group's separateness and the uniqueness of each individual member. In the group, the patient can receive empathic understanding, insight into the genetic roots of his or her problems, and empathy for other people in return.

*The Group as Multiple Selfobjects**

Martin Z. was the new member entering a group, which had been ongoing for one-and-a-half years. He had been referred to the group by his physician who thought that it would be helpful to him. Martin was 69 years old and had recently suffered a mild heart attack. He was married and living with his wife of 40 years plus their single daughter, aged 37. A self-employed insurance salesman, Martin now worked on a part-time basis.

The psychotherapy group was composed of seven people, five women and two men, with Martin altering the composition to three men. All were over 60 and living independently. They were responsive to Martin and appeared to accept him easily.

In the group, Martin spent a lot of time talking about his past accomplishments, which included his having seen active duty in World War II and his being very involved in the veterans' organization of his choice. He also placed great emphasis on his having been a most capable businessman, though he said that bad luck had stopped him from "really striking it rich." Martin's focus of disappointments centered on his wife and daughter not recognizing his past accomplishments and "seeing me as a failure." He especially pointed out that were it not for the fact that he was supporting his grown daughter who had difficulty in keeping jobs, he would be financially more secure. It appeared to the group and the leader that he would willingly help his daughter if the family were more appreciative of him and the stresses he was experiencing.

Since the group had been exposed to the self psychological approach of the leader, both they and the leader offered empathic

*Case vignette contributed by William Weiner, ACSW.

responses. Martin's need to be appreciated was often stated, and appreciation and applause were given to him. Group members would admire his World War II feats and listen intently as he related some of his daring exploits. Comments such as, "I would never be able to do anything as courageous as that" and "You must have been scared but still you knew you had a job to do and did it," were often heard. Martin appeared most welcoming of and heartened by this admiration. When he went into greater detail about his activities during the war, the leader, unlike his unappreciative family, allowed for and encouraged this life-review process, feeling that an integration of past experiences was a necessary and healthy aspect of one's aging (Butler, 1977).

While applauding his accomplishments and giving full credence to them, the group also recognized Martin's need for dependency and his disappointment that he could not rely on his family to respond to him in the way in which he would like. The group encouraged him to be more direct in expressing his needs, without being defensive about them. When he complained about his ability to continue working and his fear of having another heart attack if he were to continue any kind of strenuous schedule, the group said: "Tell Joanna and Sallie (wife and daughter) that you're not 21 anymore and need some time off. Don't be afraid to tell them. Get what you want. You have to take care of yourself. You're entitled."

Though Kohut does not address the question of group therapy in detail, he does state that group pressure may diminish individuality and that the therapist must safeguard the evolving nuclear self. The therapist accomplishes this by ensuring that all patients are encouraged to discover and to march to "the beat of their own drummer" (cited in Harwood, 1983, p. 33).

With the eventual development of a firm, cohesive self, other benefits accrue. In addition to the important realization that hope is possible at any age, the older patient sees the possibility for the development of altruism and the resumed growth of a cohesive self that has finally received empathy. The older patient can also gain the understanding and acknowledgment that he is not alone in needing affirmation of the grandiose self and merger with an idealized parent imago. Through all these benefits runs the strong thread or lifeline of the therapeutic experience as a reworking or redirecting of derailed development in healthier, more rewarding directions.

Termination

Termination can be considered when the new, more cohesive self has unfolded and the group idealized parent imago has been internalized. This newly formed cohesive self, secure in its base of self-esteem, can now use itself as its own thermostat in regulating self-esteem and holding onto its ideals while attempting to implement its ambitions. Since the group and the therapist have now become a part of the person terminating, they are no longer needed as suppliers and reinforcers of self-esteem. Rather, they remain embedded within the terminating member as both a part of his or her new psychic structure, while also appreciated for each of their own individual qualities. As described in our brief case of Martin Z., it is anticipated that at point of termination, he will feel more secure in his own talents and skills, be able to ask most directly for what it is he needs from others, and take pleasure in his burgeoning cohesive self.

LATER LIFE: AN AGE FOR TRANSFORMATION

The developing awareness that the aged can continue to work and thrive in an enriching environment (see p. 161) has already been demonstrated by the impressive activities of many older people, whether such thinkers and writers as George Bernard Shaw and Sigmund Freud, or musicians like Vladimir Horowitz, Artur Rubinstein, and Igor Stravinsky. Two years ago, an 80-year-old feminine champion of world peace, Alvah Myrdal, was the co-winner of the Nobel Peace Prize. And Martha Graham's continuing recognition by the press reminds us that this tradition-breaking dancer kept dancing until 75 and is still, at 90, an impressive choreographer. Indeed, the founder of self psychology himself, Heinz Kohut, made his most memorable and seminal contributions to self psychology as a new theory of human development, in his sixties, before his untimely death at 68.

In connection with all these seemingly indefatigable, creative people, we can certainly ask whether their crucial experiences in infancy and childhood favored the creative self-development that is still blooming in old age. From the standpoint of self psychology, we would have to assume that all of them had adequate mirroring from their mothers' gleaming eyes which fostered a healthy ambition to realize their talents. Or, if their mothers were not available for this kind of good selfobject support, then perhaps a father, an uncle, a grandparent, even an older sibling provided an ideal to look up to, an ideal by which these people were led. So even if maternal mirroring failed them, they were able to have a second chance to realize their nuclear selves through the idealizing potential of the bipolar self.

Growth, expansion, creativity, and the exhilaration of life are part of a process that runs throughout life. For those practicing self psychology, clinical vignettes illustrating this process make it concrete and specific. For example, one 81-year-old female patient, bursting with life but who is house-bound for much of the day with a senile husband, said enthusiastically: "I won't think of a nursing home for him. I love him too much and can take care of him. But I am thinking of having an affair. I don't mind giving up some time to someone I have loved for 48 years but I do mind giving up all of my sexuality." Whereas with another patient at another stage in life, the therapist might have questioned potential acting out, with this patient all the therapist said was: "Great. How good that you can still feel so alive and want to stay with your life-force, despite your impossible situation."

Self psychology most decidedly provides the framework for choices reinforcing life. And life at 10, 20, or 80 is something to be appreciated! For it is that which connects the 10-year-old to the 20-year-old to the 80-year-old.

> Grandmother, you gave me the wealth of detail. You taught me to love grass and moss, ants and butterflies. . . . You gave me my first trees and my first sunset, mushroom hunts and the bliss of long walks. (Almedingen, 1984, p. 23)

As the number of cases formerly regarded as almost hopeless have responded successfully to treatment with self psychology, so the importance of stable esteem in a person's ability to develop and enjoy a good life is demonstrated. There is also increasing interest in the potentialities of a self psychological treatment approach to alcoholism and other addictions. As the theory and practice of self psychology expand, there is every hope that other special populations, such as criminals, will become more responsive to treatment. The term "special population" may then take on a challenging meaning rather than that of a group for whom there is no hope.

10

The Joy of Psychotherapy

In preceding chapters, we have explored some of the major concepts of self psychology and attempted to show their relevance to the art/science of psychoanalysis and psychotherapy. In this chapter, we will discuss joy and even humor, one of Kohut's higher forms of narcissism (Kohut, 1966). For joy and humor—like effervescent bubbles inside of us and hopefully inside our patients eventually—do make our art/science so satisfying that they compensate for all the anxiety, self-doubt, and narcissistic blows that we, as therapists, undertake to bear in the complex, painful process of bringing a nuclear self to birth.

WHAT DOES THE THERAPIST *DO*?

"I don't know what you *do*, but whatever it is—you're so damn good at it." This comment was made by a patient to his therapist after a few months of treatment. The therapist had been using self psychological concepts and noticed that her patients "felt good" after a relatively short period of time, compared to her former use of other, more traditional approaches. Indeed, what *does* the therapist *do* in being concerned with the patient's self state?

While many occupations have hard-and-fast parameters of behavior, the field of psychotherapy has "flexibility." More pre-

174

cisely, it has ambiguity. This ambiguity does not necessarily arise from the therapist's life experience or goals. It comes to us, and perhaps unexpectedly, in the profession we have chosen. Let us look at this hypothetical but not improbable vignette. We wake up in the morning for the day, whatever that may involve, and proceed to our office, which may be far from our home or nearby. Some therapists may only move from room to room, making sure appropriate doors are closed, beds made, and intrusions kept to a minimum. The day could be bright and sunny, cold and rainy, hot and humid, snowy and blustery—but the therapist shows up. We say to ourselves: "Ready or not, here I come."

The allotted time comes for the patient to arrive. We wait and it is now a few minutes after the scheduled time, but no patient. We wait and we wait. In our imagination, we may be doing the following:

Therapist (on the phone to the patient): Listen, I'm here waiting for you but you haven't come. I'd like to know if you're going to show up at all, be a little late, a lot late, or medium-type late. If you're a little late, I could run down for some overdue food shopping. If you're medium-type late, I could go for a quick morning walk. And if you're really going to be all-the-way late, I could grab a fast game of racquet ball at the gym down the block. The point is: I'd really like to know so I can decide what to do.

Though we may *think* the above, we usually *do not* make the call. We wait throughout the entire 45- or 50-minute period, sometimes wondering if we could have missed the bell or the knock. Do we call at the end of a no-show session to find out if something is wrong, if the patient is ill? Do we wait until that evening to inquire why he missed his appointment and whether he wants a make-up session? Do we wait until the next session in order to see what comes up? Would our introducing it, either by a telephone call or in the next session, show the patient that we felt concerned about the absence, or would it be experienced as a reprimand? There is little doubt that we, as therapists, would choose a particular psychotherapeutic option as our way of dealing with this common situation. But there are few rules about handling this "late" or "missed" session problem that are adhered to by all of us.

The possibilities for dealing with this scenario are vast, as many and varied as we therapists are as a group. We lack a standardization, a plan of action that can be put into effect unfailingly, given a little human error here and there. We are our own data bank! We *do* as we are! This "doing" is largely determined by ourselves as people, given the range in age, background, years of training, personal style, choice of therapeutic approach and natural style. However, we do need to consider, with respect to the intersubjective issue (see Chapter 8 on Traumatic States), whether our style and assumptions may collide dangerously with our patients' self needs.

TO BE HUMAN

The self psychologist, like his colleagues using other approaches, hopefully thinks of himself or herself as human rather than a kind of curing machine. To be human is, to the authors' minds, to be in touch with the inner experience of our humanity, our warmth, our essential cohesiveness, and our joy. Yet, these are intangibles that we are hard pressed to clarify, much as the vaunted neutrality of the therapist, which is being regarded more and more as nonhuman.

In the classic science fiction thriller, *The Invasion of the Body Snatchers,* people are co-opted by their duplicates who resemble them in all ways, including owning their memory banks, facial characteristics, and habits, but who lack "humanness." One of the first characters to notice this in her uncle attempts to describe the loss to the major protagonist in the film. She explains that "Uncle George seems like Uncle George—only he isn't. He says all the right things, does all the right things, but something is missing. He doesn't look at me the way Uncle George did. He doesn't see me. He's not Uncle George." The "new" people in the film are devoid of humanness because of their lack of affect.

In their proselytization, they state that life is too full of pain, misery, problems, conflicts, and that their way is a better one. When asked about love and joy, they reply that these feelings also can be done away with, since they create their own problems, too.

In viewing this movie, reminiscent of others (such as *The Step-ford Wives* about a group of women who performed in robot-like ways), we think of the lack of experienced joy in the lives of some of our patients. Yet, for us to be effective and to help bring about some positive change in them, we need to be able to stimulate the capacity for joy with which all of us are born. We need, above all, to be in touch with our own "bubble," relish it, savor it, hug it, and preserve it for ourselves when the demands of our work seem too much.

But how do we help our patients feel that sense of aliveness which is experienced as joy? We have, throughout this book, shown how difficult it is for many patients to feel that they are entitled to any joy in life. Sometimes this grim conviction arises, as we shall see in this chapter, from a life-narrowing physical disability which forecloses many of the normal sources of joyful satisfaction for the patient. Again, a person may be afflicted with a deeply-held conviction that he is not free to enjoy anything because his parents made him feel that he was supposed to suffer like them—in other words, his joy always feels like an affront to a loved one. Finally, there are patients who feel doomed to lose whatever love or joy they may attain because fate is "out to get them."

It is not easy to answer specifically our original question of how we help our patients welcome joy. Above all, we start out by trying to be empathic to their feelings of fear, hopelessness, and doom, and that joy can never exist for them. As we have tried to show in various cases presented in this book, the very awareness that a patient has of the therapist's empathy with him or her is a movement toward a feeling of self-worth which is the foundation stone of joy. We do not want to give this impression that in safeguarding our own bubble of joy we ever try to impose it on a patient grappling with hopelessness. Perhaps there is nothing

more unempathic to a patient mired in misery than to be told that
he surely is going to feel better the day after tomorrow. What that
patient desperately needs and what we try to provide is the delicate attunement with his actual feelings *now*, in so far as we can,
but which perhaps he never experienced before. It is this reliable
provision of a therapeutic ambience that lays the foundation for
the growth of a nuclear self that feels unquestionably entitled to
joy.

RETAINING OUR JOY

How do we retain our own joy when patients cancel without
phoning or sob for 45 minutes, claiming that they don't feel helped
after three years and life is miserable, or when our work hours
seem endless? We therapists are able to retain the spark of joy
because we wish to help others experience joy. If this were not
so, we could not stay in our chosen field! Perhaps, too, as Alice
Miller (1981) says, therapists have to have experienced their own
psychological slavery as children in order to reexperience themselves with joy. Whatever the complex answers to this question,
we certainly need to retain the bubble inside ourselves, so that
we can help our patient during his or her time with us; we also
need to let it expand as we leave our office and return to our
private lives. This may include a capacity to venture into un-
charted areas of creativity which we may have wistfully bypassed
in our youth. Or it may involve our becoming social or political
activists.

However we may enlarge our lives, either through new selfobjects and/or higher forms of narcissism, somehow we maintain
the capacity to listen to problems all day long and enjoy ourselves,
as we choose, at the day's end. The therapist, with a genuine
capacity for joy, hopefully can transmit that feeling to his or her
patient as the therapist is internalized as a good selfobject. Even
with deep depression, the patient often experiences at least the
therapist's concern for him and a hope for a regenerative future.

In cases where there appears to be a transitory empathic failure
or an adamant negative therapeutic reaction, we can think of this

as a problem of countertransference or of intersubjectivity (see Chapter 8). Whatever the particular difficulty, somehow our patient felt we did not understand his feelings in the way in which he felt he needed to be understood. Our empathy and our explaining—two of our most vital instruments, as Kohut (1984) stressed (see also Chapter 4)—missed the mark, either in specific instances or in the overall approach. When the patient tells us this, what do we *feel* at that moment? Is our feeling then reflected in how we relate to the patient or do we feel one thing and say another, based on our training, our understanding of our training, our natural style, and our orientation to our work?

AFFECTS AS THE CENTER OF THE SELF

In the complexities and stresses of trying to know where we are affectively with a patient (e.g., have we disillusioned the patient by being inaccessible over the weekend or have we failed the patient, as a reliable, perfectly functioning part of himself, by not somehow keeping him from coming down with the flu), there is, of course, a larger consideration. It is implied in the foregoing discussion of how we ultimately help a patient to enjoy some potentialities of life, no matter how frustrated the patient may feel when the therapist or other selfobject is not available on call.

The idea that selfobject functions may relate "fundamentally to the integration of affect" has been presented by Socarides and Stolorow (1984–1985). They see affects as "organizers of self-experience throughout development, if met with the requisite affirming, accepting, differentiating, synthesizing and containing responses from caregivers." Socarides and Stolorow point out that if a child's affective needs are not adequately responded to, he becomes prone to self-fragmentation because his feelings, being disregarded, are not included in his self-experience. In addition to stressing that Kohut discovered the importance of mirroring the child's exhibitionistic experiences involving feelings of pride and excitement along with early merging with idealized parental strength, providing a calming of a child's distresses, the authors

note that Kohut proposed that normally empathic parents can react with joy and pride to a child's oedipal sexuality and competition. Acceptance of the child's normal oedipal feelings is seen as ensuring an oedipal experience that will *not* be pathological.

Basch (1984) also sees flexible parental responsiveness to the child's burgeoning affects as crucial in the development of a cohesive self and of the capacity for object love. He stresses that the human infant is *human* from the start, that the baby is hungry for stimulation, shows a clear preference for human communication and responds with a full range of affect, *if* given the opportunity. "Motherhood," Basch concludes, "does not become a viable part of the self concept in the act of giving birth, or through hormonal stimulation, but through the ongoing selfobject transactions between a mother and her baby. The same can be said of any significant relationship, including of course that between psychoanalyst and analysand" (1984, p. 36).

AFFECTS AS INNER CONNECTEDNESS

Clynes (1980) suggests that emotional expression for all of us is experienced as a "form of inner connectedness" (p. 298). But this connectedness may shift and move backward or forward, as Kohut (1984) points out, embodying "the shift in an essentially persisting self-selfobject relationship from one level to another" (p. 188). He suggests that a seeming forward move, where a child moves toward a bird or squirrel as spring comes to the park, may be an "empathic resonance of shared joy," an assertive act compared with physical holding or, having taken the step, the child may look anxiously back at mother to reassure himself she is there if he needs her for holding. In either case, hopefully, the mother will perceive her child's joy or tremulous anxiety if she is a reliably responsive selfobject. And so we, as psychotherapists, must continually strive to be attuned to the expected but also to the unexpected shifts in our patients' feelings so that they can come to trust that their feelings will be noticed and connected with, as they never were in childhood.

CASE VIGNETTE

Is it not possible that in our seeking to provide a healing process for our patients, we too are being healed? Let us illustrate this possibility with a case history told to us by a colleague.

From the Life of a Psychotherapist:
*The Shadow of the Cat Goddess**

Dr. Purcell went to the door of her first-floor apartment and summoned the doorman: "Joseph, in 10 minutes or so, I expect a patient who may be physically handicapped. Will you please help her up the three steps to my door?" She went back into her office to wait. Her uneasiness made her disapprove of herself. Perhaps she shouldn't work with this patient, a severely crippled woman. Gross disability embarrassed her. Oddly enough, Kohut's theories on infantile grandiosity had always reminded her of her own hunches about greediness, envy, heroism, even grandiosity in the sick. But why? Did she still believe, whatever the controversial research, that a person could become ill and deformed rather than express his or her unacceptable demands? Or was it that the deformed, finding themselves blatantly sticking out like sore thumbs, were then able to bring out wishes for exhibitionism, for reparation, for retribution? And how could a therapist help such a patient to accept reality maturely?

Kathy Fellini was announced on the intercom. The front door opened and the slow, punctuating iron footsteps got closer and closer as they crossed the hallway.

"I'm in here, Miss Fellini."

Kathy appeared at the office threshold, a small thin woman of almost 40. She supported herself on steel crutches attached to her semi-withered forearms.

"I'll need a relatively hard, high chair and a footstool."

"I'm sure my couch will do, and here, take my footstool; I don't really need it."

---

*Case contributed by Juana Culhane, C.S.W.

Kathy settled herself slowly but with aplomb; no awkwardness, no impatience, no apologies.

The two women faced each other. There was a silence for a minute or two.

Kathy stared at Dr. Purcell as if looking beyond her and said: "Aren't you going to ask me how I became so crippled?"

Dr. Purcell recalled her musing about the psychological aspects of deformity and was struck by the patient's swift focus on it. What did this indicate? She said, "I certainly want to hear about it."

Kathy seemed to become a little less defensive, but added cautiously, "I don't need to tell you, but you should know so you don't have to keep wondering about it."

Dr. Purcell nodded empathically and said, "So what happened?"

Kathy continued in the same pompous tone. "In my late teens I got a severe, fast-moving case of juvenile rheumatoid arthritis, an inflammatory disease that destroys all forms of tissue."

Dr. Purcell nodded slightly, frowning, as if in pain.

"I still get flair-ups of rheumatoid arthritis from time to time, in one system or other. It doesn't attack just the joints. There's no cure either."

"I know," murmured Dr. Purcell.

"But I recently had a dream that disturbs me and that's why I'm here. I dreamt I was holding my cat in my arms as though she was a baby and she was sick. However, she's been dead almost a year."

Dr. Purcell was about to say, "How strange," then caught herself, thinking it might not be strange to Kathy and simply nodded.

"I was in Egypt recently, on a Nile cruise," Kathy continued. "I have always been fascinated by Bast, the cat goddess, by all her amulets and statuettes; I needed to visit her in her home. I feel one with Bast. She loved music and dancing and protected everyone from all evil. Her father was the Sun-God. I knew my cat had not really died at all. That's why I never got another cat; my cat was still around. But then, as I said, I dreamt that she was sick, maybe dying. Why am I dreaming this? She's really a part of me. She mustn't die!"

Dr. Purcell recalled Kohut's focus on infantile omnipotent fantasies, including bringing the dead back to life to overcome terrible loss. She cautiously asked, "You feel she's part of you?"

"Well, not really, except that I'm keeping her alive. She is like my very own creation. Don't you understand?"

Dr. Purcell sensed a need for some attunement here which could help Kathy to continue treatment or drive her away. She said cautiously, "You mean through the strength of your mind? Do you actually see or hear your cat?"

"I do see and hear her sometimes, in a waking-dream sort of way—the way I see my father who died almost 20 years ago." Kathy paused as if a little embarrassed. Then she sighed and went on: "I saw him smiling down at me in my crib, with a gold tooth gleaming."

Dr. Purcell looked relieved at the possibility that Kathy was not talking about an hallucination and asked: "It's a memory then?"

"Yes, but I remember it often. And one time his disembodied head floated over me, empty eye-sockets, with a lascivious smile. It wasn't a dream. It was an image, a real presence. He's not dead either, not really. He died on the same date of the month as my birthday. He lives through my existence. I once even dreamt that I gave birth to him. I was so frightened at having to take care of such a grand baby! Not too long ago I forgot to save him a seat at a picnic table and he became very upset."

Dr. Purcell's earlier anxiety about the possible diagnosis for Kathy returned. The dreams and memories seemed perilously close to deeper pathology than Dr. Purcell had expected. She chose to defer any exploration of this anxiety-arousing material until a later session. So she said, "Well, I think it's most important to consider your feelings about all this, but today I do need to get some additional basic information."

Kathy sighed and said with resignation, "All right, but I do have to get back to all this because that's why I'm here."

Dr. Purcell thought a good deal about Kathy. Obviously, she had been able to function quite well, having received a Doctorate in Education in Rehabilitative Medicine. She had been working for some time with severely crippled children, in a small, private hospital. After her father died, an aunt and uncle had been financially supportive in regard to her education. However, they had moved to Florida, leaving Kathy to look after herself. She and her mother had never been able to live together.

In subsequent sessions, Dr. Purcell began to explore the possible connections between Kathy's dream about her sick cat and her resurrection fantasies about her dead father. In connection with the dream about giving birth to her father, Kathy began to talk enthusiastically about him: "He was so marvelous, glorious, erudite, and sensitive! But he was terribly deprived and misunderstood. While I adored him, I had to work hard at being worthy of him, to give him the proper recognition."

Dr. Purcell decided not to bring up the image of the possibly oedipal lascivious smile at this time and asked instead, "How was he so deprived?"

Kathy seemed to relax a little, as if Dr. Purcell's question implied that her tragic life had made some sense. She said, "Well, first, he was a bright little boy, very happy with the people he thought were his real parents, but who actually were foster parents. One day, when he was five, this witch appears who says she's his *real* mother, and drags him off from Italy to America where she has pressured his father to remarry her. The shock was said to be so great that he lost all of his hair, and it never again grew back except the way it grows on babies, wispy-like.

"His mother," Kathy's tone grew harsh, "expected him to love her instantly and to understand why she had given him up when he was born. When he couldn't love her, she turned against him and, as he recalled, never approved of anything he did. His father had no time for him, since he was always working or with his friends. The father felt he had been blackmailed into returning to his marriage because of his son and took no interest in my father. So, at 14, my father ran away.

"As he used to tell me when I was little, he desperately needed to find someone who could appreciate his real value. He just *knew* he was special. To start seeing the world, he rode on trains as a hobo. To get an education, he read castaway books and talked to many, older runaways who were intellectuals, rebels, and rejects.

They used to eat by working in restaurants occasionally. He used to tell me how awful it was to be hungry and not know where to get food."

"Did he find anyone special who took him under their wing?" Dr. Purcell asked, wondering about the impact upon Kathy of this tragic, searching, neglected figure of her father as a kind of young genius.

"No, not really. He always had to look after himself. For instance, he taught himself to be a radio technician and he ended up in Egypt, working for an airline."

When Dr. Purcell heard that Kathy's father had his first success of a sort in Egypt, she wondered whether there was any connection here with Kathy's recent visit to Egypt and what sounded like a reunion with Bast, the cat goddess.

"Your father stayed in Egypt for awhile?" Dr. Purcell asked Kathy.

Kathy smiled sadly. "Yes, he stayed long enough to find my mother who seemed like the perfect woman since she admired him so much at first. She came from a small village, with hardly any education. I guess he thought he could form her into anything he needed."

Sensing this idea as a clue to what might be Kathy's terrifying masochistic somatization, Dr. Purcell leaned forward and asked earnestly, "What do you think of his wanting that?"

"Why not? He knew he was special, he knew what he needed. But she wasn't up to it; she failed him miserably. To this day she prides herself on remaining the same, just herself, untouched, untaught, unmolded."

Dr. Purcell wondered if Kathy had also found her mother so unresponsive that she had to turn to her father and even become his slave in order to feel loved at all. "Where is your mother now?" she asked.

"Oh, here in town, for the last 30 years or so, as healthy as can be. Even time has hardly left a mark on her," Kathy said contemptuously.

For sessions afterwards, Dr. Purcell was tempted to ask what Kathy thought of the difference between her untouched mother and the gruesome "sculpting" created by the disease. But Kathy seemed not to see the grotesque disparity. Perhaps it was best to wait. It was wiser to stay with why Kathy had come to her, with her own view of what was wrong.

"You said in the beginning that you felt one with Bast," Dr. Purcell said. "I don't understand what she has to do with the dream of your dying cat?"

"Well, of course, I'm not really one with her; did I say that?"

"Yes."

"No, I meant that I admired her because she is a protector against all harm. She's omnipresent. I feel she would never allow any cat to die."

"But your dream . . . "

"That's what I don't understand. I knew my cat had really died a year ago but then only bodily. She was still with me. I made her be with me. So why dream that she's dying? It frightens me!"

Dr. Purcell realized Kathy was struggling between her hold on reality and her omnipotent fantasies of controlling life and death through Bast.

"I don't know, it's as if she's going away. I feel alone and weak. What's happening to me? Oh, I also dreamt of many squirming cats on a bed and I was horrified at their screeching calls for food and attention."

Dr. Purcell wondered if the hungry cats represented not only Kathy's years of deprivation but also all those people who had demanded of her, including the deformed children she worked with. She asked, "You feel pressured by what you should do?"

"No, not really. I want to do what I must do."

Dr. Purcell wondered if that meant keeping her dead father alive. But after a period of tense silence, Dr. Purcell decided to explore elsewhere. She asked, "Besides the dreams, what has been happening to you lately?"

"Nothing much. I've been looking for a new job. The grant on my present work with disabled children is running out. I went to a large, well-known hospital for an interview, and I was left with a very bad feeling, one I can't explain."

Directly appealing to Kathy's omnipotence, Dr. Purcell said, "Try."

"Well, everyone looked at me as if I were asking for the moon," Kathy said, frowning at Dr. Purcell as if she were angry at having to recall this humiliating experience.

"What gave you that impression?" Dr. Purcell asked gently.

"They kept wondering how I could be prompt in the morning and how I could work without a lot of help. Generally, they wondered how reliable I was."

"What did you say?" Dr. Purcell asked, listening for echoes of Kathy's arrogant father.

Kathy shrugged, as if the answer should be obvious, and replied: "I said, of course I'd have to come in after the rush hour, as I do now in my present job, that I was used to working with an assistant to do what I couldn't do. Also, I'd need time off to see my physician, that is, my rheumatologist, or my occupational therapist to get an adjustment on my leg braces and/or my canes, or I'd need to see my physical therapist to help me with my exercises."

Dr. Purcell was somewhat surprised at the privileges Kathy demanded as an invalid, even before her prospective employers had had a chance to realize her competence. "What do you think they decided?" she risked.

"Oh, that I was somehow too presumptuous, too big for my breeches, nervy, and unlikeable."

"But your physical disability does require special consideration," Dr. Purcell said, trying not to join with Kathy's critics.

"I suppose so, but I have always generally pulled my own weight and done very well! I may have a disability but I'm not handicapped," Kathy said, with mounting hauteur. She almost snarled, "I'm not! I've risen above it all, above them too. I can show them up. Despite everything, I'm still on my feet. They owe me!"

Dr. Purcell was torn between confronting Kathy with the unreality of her expectations and the realization that Kathy's manipulative parents did "owe her." "I know how you feel," she said.

Kathy suddenly quieted down. She became silent. Then she began to weep, huddled in the corner of the couch, her now contracted elbows and frozen shoulders preventing her hands from reaching up to her eyes.

Dr. Purcell took some of the Kleenex from the box in front of Kathy. Leaning over, she gently wiped her face and then she returned to her own seat. Kathy had not resisted and Dr. Purcell felt more hopeful that Kathy could accept a little help, despite her omnipotence.

"Do you feel as if you're given a lot and that perhaps it's been too much?"

"I don't know what you mean," Kathy said, her weariness evident in her voice.

"Perhaps the Bast within you has given too much. Perhaps she's tired now."

In the following sessions, Dr. Purcell tried to clarify the image of Kathy's Bast.

"When did you first become attached to Bast?"

After five minutes of silence, Kathy sighed softly, "When I was growing up; those first years in Egypt, my father would take me to the Cairo Museum. Of course, I was fascinated by the mummies, the cobras, vultures, falcons, and crocodiles, but what caught my eye especially were the cats, all sitting so proudly, so naturally, their bodies self-contained and balanced, not even needing a headdress. It was then that I learned that they were all representations of the goddess, Bast, and that she fought evil and loved joyfulness. I had always loved cats anyway, and it was then and there that I decided to make Bast my godmother. I began to collect statues of cats. For me they were all Bast. I used to line them up and I would dance around them as I hummed a tune to myself."

Dr. Purcell smiled and said, "What did your parents think of all this?"

"My father loved it," Kathy said wistfully. "He would come into my room to watch me as soon as he heard my humming. My mother, even though she was Egyptian, thought it was all nonsense. By then, she just found me impossible, saying that I was too much for her, that she wished I'd slow down and do what she said. But she wasn't important. Even my father hardly spoke to her. He always came to me to really talk. He even told me how my mother didn't understand that he needed a lot of affection. Looking back, I realize he really meant attention, pampering, passion, and a sense of adventure. She just didn't know how to give it to him."

"So you made up your mind to be something special for him?"

"Yes. Of course, I couldn't really be a wife, but it was as if we could play at it, you know, play house."

"How did you play house?" Dr. Purcell asked softly.

"Well, I remember best the time when he moved here to New York, and he'd help me with my school papers; he had so much to say and I could get it across to people for him."

"What were the papers about?" Dr. Purcell asked, wondering if Kathy was anxious about the sexual implications of playing house.

"Oh, you know, history papers, papers on the Russian Revolution and how glorious it was, and art history papers about Mexican revolutionary painters like Rivera, Orozco and Siqueiros."

Dr. Purcell wondered whether such unconventional papers could have got Kathy into trouble. But she decided to focus on the sexual aspects of playing house. "Did you have any fun, playing house?"

"Well, once he sent me to camp. He had to convince the management that I was much more mature than 16 because it was a left-wing camp for people 21 and over. It was the kind of camp he'd always wanted to go to—lectures, discussions, walks in the country, classical music concerts, folk dancing, and simply being with a lot of intelligent people. You see, he was very timid. We never saw anyone. We never had family friends to dinner, and we never went to anyone's house.

Dr. Purcell realized then that Kathy had become disillusioned with her father and that, in order to deny this, she had to remember him as larger than life, as immortal. In failing to do this, she crippled herself as she had seen him crippled. But Dr. Purcell realized that she had to go slowly in this delicate, dangerous area.

Surprisingly, Kathy chuckled with pleasure as she remembered another incident.

"He sent me to a people's drama acting group. We had moved

to the city by then. Once I had to act out one of the Lincoln Brigade songs. I chose one, something like "Up and Down." I can't remember now. I had very long hair then, and I swung my head up into the air and down to the floor, my hair tying and untying itself around me. I was transformed and I loved it!"

"So, 'playing house' helped to open up a new, exciting world for you?" Dr. Purcell asked, thinking that Kathy's infantile omnipotence offset at least some of her disillusionment with her father.

"Oh, yes!" But then Kathy's mood changed. Her twisted hands trembled delicately, and she became silent. After about five minutes of pressuring quiet, Kathy said: "I guess you're wondering why I shut up. I suddenly remembered how it all came to an end."

Dr. Purcell said softly, "Please tell me about it."

Kathy looked past the therapist as she said lifelessly: "Once when I submitted an article to my high school newspaper, using the *Daily Worker* as a source, I was criticized in the auditorium, in front of the whole school. I was told to 'go back where I came from.' I was so destroyed, I ran home all the way, crept into my bed and stayed there, sick with something like the flu for a couple of weeks."

"How terrible for you!" Dr. Purcell said.

"Actually, it was nothing. It passed." As if to dismiss the therapist's empathy, Kathy laughed. "It was the same when I was at that camp. I was sick in bed for the whole first week, and then I was fine and loved it all for the second week!"

"Was it just the flu?" Dr. Purcell asked, wondering if it could have been the first warnings of juvenile rheumatoid arthritis.

"Well, something like it. I was dizzy, weak, and I kept throwing up." Kathy's tone was impatient, as if she didn't want to discuss this.

"How did your parents react to your illness?" Dr. Purcell asked, while wondering if she should persist.

"Oh, they never knew about the camp illness. The other time my mother took care of me, you know, after the school incident, and she seemed to enjoy it. My father became very busy. I couldn't blame him. I had become such a bore!'' Kathy now seemed overly casual as if to discourage the therapist's concern.

''Being sick was not part of your 'playing house'?'' Dr. Purcell ventured.

''Of course not! We weren't 'playing doctor'!'' retorted Kathy indignantly.

The therapist decided to take the risk of focusing on Kathy's deprivation. ''Wouldn't you have wanted to 'play doctor' with your father, sometimes, just a little? You know, to feel cared for, to be soothed?''

Kathy looked at Dr. Purcell with stricken eyes. She seemed about to say something angry, and then she began to sob, to wail. This time she didn't make the futile attempt to raise her hands to wipe away her tears. Dr. Purcell came over to her and again gently wiped Kathy's face.

''Not too long afterwards I became really ill, when I was 17. I stiffened up like a corpse and couldn't get out of bed. My father became so sad, so lonely. He seemed to have lost everything that he needed so badly. I mean, even the things I had done to sustain his interest in life. He became very remote, very depressed and one day, a year or so later, he had a sudden heart attack and died.''

Kathy started to sob as if she could never stop. Dr. Purcell stood over her, trying to stanch the tears.

''You wanted so badly to give him happiness, and you still feel you failed?'' the therapist asked, daring to bring it down to the present.

''Yes, I have failed him and my cat and Bast, my immortal godmother. I've failed them all and I deserve to suffer!'' Kathy screamed.

''But Kathy, what about you? Didn't you deserve happiness, too?'' The therapist took the great risk of focusing on Kathy's downgraded, abhorred self.

''I can only be happy if he's happy!'' Kathy sobbed hoarsely.

Dr. Purcell paused. Should she say what she believed had to be said? Finally, she looked Kathy in the eye and said clearly, ''Isn't it possible that despite whatever caused your illness, once it appeared, it was trying to tell you something?"

"What?"

"That you exist, that you are a distinct presence in space, with your own needs, feelings, and potentials."

Kathy turned away from Dr. Purcell with a ferocity suggesting fury. Drawing on this force, she struggled to her feet, and left without a word. Dr. Purcell felt she had lost her connection with Kathy's hated self.

Kathy did not return for her next two sessions, nor did she call. Dr. Purcell was about to telephone her when Kathy's rheumatologist called from a hospital. He said Kathy was extremely ill with an acute inflammation not only of her joints but of all her tissues, including those of her lungs, her heart, and her kidneys. She was totally immobilized.

Apparently, according to the doctor, some infection triggered her immune system into such an overkill reaction that her own physiological defense system was mistakenly warring against her.

The doctor thought that perhaps Dr. Purcell could help since Kathy seemed to be emotionally distressed and, oddly enough, it didn't seem to be about her illness. She was not responding to medication at all. In the state she was in, any one of the major organs affected could totally fail her, and Kathy could die.

Dr. Purcell knew that whatever had gone wrong was involved with why Kathy had come for help in the first place. Of course, why hadn't she, as a therapist, understood sooner! The dying cat was Kathy! Her dead cat and her dead father were calling her forth, to do something or die. But what? It was almost as if Kathy had failed them, not kept her part of the bargain. What bargain? That Kathy could be alive, and share Bast's supremeness and specialness, only if it included her father? She owed him, she had let him down, she had become ill and imperfect, and he had died. But he had left Bast in his stead. Bast had to be kept alive if Kathy were to live. Dr. Purcell had made a mistake. She should never have alluded to Kathy as an entity, as having a unique self. That was only pure potential. There was really no Kathy, only Bast.

The father had lured Kathy's self away from her very early. He needed this extension of himself to feel alive. Kathy was his mirror, proving that he existed. Kathy's mother had refused to sacrifice herself to him and had remained untouched. But why hadn't she tried to save her daughter? But, of course, she couldn't; Dr. Purcell realized that Kathy's mother had to be another version of her father's real mother who had used him, just as the father used Kathy!

But this did not take account of what Kathy had done with her unconscious longings to be both the perfect godmother, Bast, and the omnipotent father for her deprived father and deprived self. The crucial problem was the narcissistic rage she turned against herself, whenever she failed to be perfect. When her father died, her only recourse was to cripple her own body with rage at her failure to keep her father, her godmother Bast, and her cat self gloriously alive forever. It seemed likely that Dr. Purcell was now included in this rage and, typically, Kathy was punishing herself for Dr. Purcell's "mistake" in trying to save Kathy's rejected, real self.

Dr. Purcell decided to visit Kathy in the hospital. As she approached Kathy's room, she wondered if she was doing the right thing. This case had worried her, stirred up her own omnipotence. She saw that she had focused too soon on the oedipal sexual problem implied in "playing house" and that she had become obsessed with making Kathy aware of the psychosomatic origin of her illness. She also realized that Kathy, spurred by her own omnipotence, had become, through great painful effort, a trained professional caring for crippled children. She had attained what her father never achieved, despite all his wild dreams, even though she had to achieve it as a cripple herself—perhaps the price of inviting attention to herself. Maybe, Dr. Purcell thought, she could regain Kathy's confidence by pointing out how much Kathy (i.e., Bast) had achieved through her omnipotence, rather than stressing how deprived Kathy's self was.

Although Dr. Purcell walked in softly, Kathy opened her eyes, and without moving her head or body, she turned her eyes and looked fixedly at her visitor. There was no expression on her face.

Dr. Purcell pulled up a chair and sat next to the bed being careful not to bump it, conscious of the intense pain in Kathy's body.

"Hello, Kathy."

No answer. They sat staring at each other for several long minutes. Dr. Purcell then turned away and looked around the room; there were flowers, plants, cards. Kathy was not alone. People knew her, saw her as a person, remembered her, probably sympathized with her for having such a terrible disease, probably wondered how fate could be so cruel to such a brave soul. Was it truly brave to give oneself totally to another, and then to create another self in order to live, Dr. Purcell wondered again? But then she thought of all the crippled children Kathy had helped.

Kathy finally spoke: "You never accepted my Bast. You never saw her or liked her."

Dr. Purcell smiled. She opened her handbag and took out a small box. Inside were two wrapped objects. She carefully unwrapped one of the objects and revealed a deep green clay copy of an ancient Egyptian cat, sitting on its haunches.

Kathy did not say anything. She just stared at the cat. Dr. Purcell put it on the night-table.

Then she unwrapped the second object. It was a much smaller statue, in a faded turquoise, with earth deeply ingrained in the curves. It was Bast, seated on a throne, with her left hand holding an ankh, a cross with a looped top, which is the Egyptian symbol of life.

Kathy's eyes sparkled with pride and wonder.

"How beautiful!" she whispered as one of her frail hands, with stiff, twisted fingers, reached for it. Dr. Purcell moved Bast closer to her hand. Kathy's fingers slowly uncurled, wrapped themselves around the little figure, and grasped her in a firm embrace, as she said to Dr. Purcell, "You really believe in me, after all!"

Dr. Purcell's struggle to understand empathically her very different patient, who had been so hurt that even an almost perfect responsiveness on the therapist's part frightened and terrorized her, underlines the complex implications of the concept of intersubjectivity, as presented by Brandschaft and Stolorow (1984b).

This can involve, as Dr. Purcell discovered, having to help a patient like Kathy comprehend her long life struggle to validate what her tortured father, seeking stable ideals himself, had tried to give her in ways too confusing for a child to fully understand. Consequently, it became a special triumph for Dr. Purcell to realize that she played a major part in encouraging Kathy to continue her work with handicapped children with a new focus on helping them to discover joy in their own lives.

To find someone who enjoys life to the hilt may offer a patient the possibility of a new ideal to emulate. This is a role that we therapists can seek to fulfill, both to our own advantage as well as to that of our patients. The joy of participating in effective psychotherapy (doing or receiving) is ultimately the unique fulfillment of discovering and fostering a nuclear self, either in another person or even in ourselves. It is being present on the day of creation.

References

Abraham, K. (1919). A particular form of resistance against the psycho-analytic method. In *Selected Papers on Psychoanalysis*. New York: Basic Books, 1953.

Ader, R. *Psychoneuroimmunology*. New York: The Academic Press, 1981.

Alexander, F. *Psychoanalysis and Psychotherapy: Developments in Theory*. New York: Norton, 1956.

Almedingen, E.M. Gifts from my grandmother. In C. Streich (Ed.), *Grandparents' House*. New York: Greenwillow Books, 1984.

Anthony, E.J. The influence babies bring to bear on their upbringing. In J.D. Call, E. Galenson, & R.L. Tyson (Eds.), *Frontiers of International Psychiatry*. New York: Basic Books, 1984.

Asch, S. Varieties of negative therapeutic reaction and problems of technique. *Journal of the American Psychoanalytic Association*, 24, 383-407, 1976.

Atwood, G.E. & Stolorow, R. *Structures of Subjectivity*. Hillsdale, N.J.: The Analytic Press, 1984.

Basch, M.F. Theory formation in chapter VII: A critique. *Journal of the American Psychoanalytic Association*, 24, 61-100, 1976.

Basch, M.F. Selfobjects and selfobject transference: Theoretical implications. In P.E. Stepansky & G. Goldberg (Eds.), *Kohut's Legacy*. Hillsdale, N.J.: The Analytic Press, 1984.

Beebe, B. & Stern, D. Engagement and disengagement in early object experiences. In N. Freedman & S. Grand (Eds.), *Communicative Structures and Psychic Structures*. New York: Plenum Press, 1977.

Beebe, B. Mother-infant mutual influence and precursors of self and object representations. In J. Masling (Ed.), *Empirical Studies of Psychoanalytic Theories*, *Vol. II*. Hillsdale, N.J.: The Analytic Press, in press.

Benitez-Bloch, R. Including the active elderly in group psychotherapy. In B. MacLennan, S. Saul, & M.B. Weiner (Eds.), *Groups and the Elderly*. New York: International Universities Press, in press.

Bergmann, M. On the intrapsychic function of falling in love. *Psychoanalytic Quarterly*, 69, 56-77, 1980.

Binswanger, L. *Sigmund Freud: Reminiscences of a Friendship* (N. Gutterman trans). New York: Grune & Stratton, 1956.

Blanck, G. & Blanck, E. *Ego Psychology: Theory and Practice*. New York and London: Columbia University Press, 1974.

Brandschaft, B. The negativism of the negative therapeutic reaction and the psychology of the self. In A. Goldberg, (Ed.), *The Future of Psychoanalysis*. New York: International Universities Press, 1983.

Brandschaft, B. & Stolorow, R.D. A current perspective on difficult patients. In P.E. Stepansky & A. Goldberg (Eds.), *Kohut's Legacy*. Hillsdale, N.J.: The Analytic Press, 1984a.

Brandschaft, B. & Stolorow, R. Borderline concept: Pathological character or iatrogenic myth? In J. Lichtenberg, M. Burnstein, & D. Silver (Eds.), *Empathy II*. Hillsdale, N.J.: The Analytic Press, 1984b.

Browning, Barrett, E. If thou must love me. *The Standard Book of British and American Verse*. Garden City, N.Y.: The Garden City Publishing Company, 1932.

Butler, R.N. & Lewis, M.I. *Aging and Mental Health*. St. Louis, MO: C.V. Mosby, 1977.

Clynes, M. The communication of emotion: Theory of sentics. In R. Plutchik & H. Kellerman (Eds.), *Emotion: Theory, Research and Experience, Vol. I*. New York: The Academic Press, 1980.

Cousins, N. *Anatomy of an Illness*. New York: W.W. Norton, 1979.

Cousins, N. *The Healing Heart: Antidotes to Panic and Helplessness*. New York: W.W. Norton, 1983.

Doran, M. Van (Ed.). The egyptian book of the dead. In *An Anthology of World Poetry*. New York: Reynal and Hitchcock, 1936.

Erikson, E. The psychoanalytic concept of aggression. *International Journal of Psychoanalysis, 52*, 137-144, 1971.

Freud, A. Assessment of childhood disturbances. *The Psychoanalytic Study of the Child*. New York: International Universities Press, *17*, 149-158, 1962.

Freud, S. (1901). *The Psychology of Everyday Life*. London: Hogarth Press, 1960.

Freud, S. (1905). Three essays on the theory of sexuality. *Standard Edition*. London: Hogarth Press, *7*, 125-245, 1953.

Freud, S. (1911). Psycho-analytic notes on an autobiographical account of a case of paranoia. *Standard Edition*. London: Hogarth Press, *12*, 3-82, 1958.

Freud, S. (1912). Recommendations to physicians practicing psycho-analysis. *Standard Edition*. London: Hogarth Press, *12*, 111-120, 1958.

Freud, S. (1913). On the beginning of treatment. *Standard Edition*. London: Hogarth Press, *12*, 121-144, 1958.

Freud, S. (1914). On narcissism. *Standard Edition*. London: Hogarth Press, *14*, 69-102, 1957.

Freud, S. (1915). Mourning and melancholia. *Standard Edition*. London: Hogarth Press, *14*, 237-258, 1957.

Freud, S. (1918). From the history of an infantile neurosis. *Standard Edition*. London: Hogarth Press, *17*, 1-22, 1955.

Freud, S. (1921). Group psychology and the analysis of the ego. *Standard Edition*. London: Hogarth Press, *18*, 67-143, 1955.

Freud, S. (1923). Negative therapeutic reaction. *Standard Edition*. London: Hogarth Press, *19*, 49-50, 166, 1961.

Freud, S. (1923b). The ego and the id. *Standard Edition*. London: Hogarth Press, *19*, 3-66, 1961.

Freud, S. (1933). New introductory lectures. *Standard Edition*. London: Hogarth Press, *22*, 3-182, 1964.

Goldberg, A. Introduction. In A. Goldberg & H. Kohut (Eds.), *The Psychology of the Self: A Casebook*. New York: International Universities Press, 1978.

Goldberg, J. *Psychotherapeutic Treatment of Cancer Patients*. New York: The Free Press, 1981.

Goldstein, E.G. *Ego Psychology and Social Work Practice*. New York: The Free Press, 1984.

Gunther, M. Aggression, self psychology and health. In A. Goldberg (Ed.), *Advances in Self Psychology*. New York: International Universities Press, 1980.

Hammer, S. The mind as healer. *Science Digest, 92*, 46-100, 1984.

Hartmann, H. Comments on the psychoanalytic theory of the ego. In *Essays in Ego Psychology*. New York: International Universities Press, 1950.

Hartmann, H. The mutual influences in the development of ego and the id. *The Psychoanalytic Study of the Child, 7*, 9-30, 1952.

Hartmann, H. *Contributions to the Metapsychology of Schizophrenia*. New York: International Universities Press, 1964.

Hartmann, H., Kris, E., & Lowenstein, R.M. Notes on the theory of aggression. *The Psychoanalytic Study of the Child*. New York: International Universities Press, *3/4*, 9-36, 1949.

Harwood, I.H. The application of self psychology concepts to group psychotherapy. *International Journal Group Psychotherapy, 33*, 469-487, 1983.

Hedges, L.E. *Listening Perspectives in Psychotherapy*. New York: Jason Aronson, 1983.

Holt, R.R. A review of some of Freud's biological assumptions and their influence on his theories. In N.S. Greenfield & W.C. Lewis (Eds.), *Psychoanalysis and Current Biological Thought*. Madison, WI: University of Wisconsin Press, 1965.

Jacobson, E. Self and the object world. *The Psychoanalytic Study of the Child*. New York: International Universities Press, *9*, 75-127, 1954.

Jaynes, J. *The Origin of Consciousness in the Breakdown of the Bicameral Mind*. Boston: Houghton Mifflin, 1976.

Kafka, F. The metamorphosis. In N.N. Glatzer (Ed.), *The Complete Stories*. New York: Schocken Books, 1971.

Kahn, E. Heinz Kohut and Carl Rogers: A timely comparison. *American Psychologist, 40*, 893-904, 1985.

Kernberg, O. *Borderline Conditions and Pathological Narcissism*. New York: Jason Aronson, 1975.

Kohut, H. Introspection, empathy and psychoanalysis. *Journal of the American Psychoanalytic Association, 7*, 459-483, 1959.

Kohut, H. Forms and transformation of narcissism. *Journal of the American Psychoanalytic Association, 14*, 243-272, 1966.

Kohut, H. Narcissism as a resistance and as a driving force in psychoanalysis. In P. Ornstein (Ed.), *The Search for the Self, Vol. II*. New York: International Universities Press, 615-658, 1978.

Kohut, H. *The Analysis of the Self*. New York: International Universities Press, 1971.

Kohut, H. Thoughts on narcissism and narcissistic rage. *Psychoanalytic Study of the Child, 27,* 360-400, 1972.

Kohut, H. *The Restoration of the Self.* New York: International Universities Press, 1977.

Kohut, H. Remarks about the formation of the self. In P. Ornstein (Ed.), *The Search for the Self, Vol. II.* New York: International Universities Press, 1978a.

Kohut, H. Psychoanalysis in a troubled world. In P. Ornstein (Ed.), *The Search for the Self, Vol. II.* New York: International Universities Press, 1978b.

Kohut, H. The two analyses of Mr. Z. *International Journal of Psychoanalysis, 60,* 3-27, 1979.

Kohut, H. Introspection, empathy and the semicircle of mental health. *International Journal of Psychoanalysis, 63,* 395-407, 1982.

Kohut, H. *How Does Analysis Cure?* (A. Goldberg, ed., with P. Stepansky.) Chicago & London: University of Chicago Press, 1984.

Kohut, H. & Wolf, E. The disorders of the self and their treatment: An outline. *International Journal of Psychoanalysis, 59,* 413-425, 1978.

Kramer, P. On discovering one's identity: A case report. *Psychoanalytic Study of the Child.* New York: International Universities Press, 10, 47-74, 1955.

Kubie, L.S. Panel: The concept of psychic energy, reporter A.H. Modell. *Journal of the American Psychoanalytic Association, 11,* 605-611, 1963.

Laudenslager, M.L., Ryan, S.M., Drugan, R.C., Hucon, R.L., & Maier, S.F. Coping and immunosuppressions, inescapable but not escapable shock suppresses lymphocyte proliferation. *Science, 221,* 568-570, 1983.

Lichtenberg, J. Factors in the development of the sense of the object. *Journal of the American Psychoanalytic Association, 27,* 375-386, 1979.

Lichtenberg, J. An application of the self psychological viewpoint to psychoanalytic technique. In J. Lichtenberg & S. Kaplan (Eds.), *Reflections on Self Psychology.* Hillsdale, N.J.: The Analytic Press, 1983.

Mahler, M.S. On the first three phases of the separation-individuation process. *Journal of the American Psychoanalytic Association, 21,* 135-154, 1971.

Mahler, M.S. A study of the separation-individuation process and its possible applications to borderline phenomena in the psychoanalytic process. *The Selected Papers of Margaret S. Mahler, Vol. II.* New York: Jason Aronson, 1979.

Mahler, M.S., Pine, F., & Bergman, A. *The Psychological Birth of the Human Infant: Symbiosis and Individuation.* New York: Basic Books, 1975.

Miller, A. *The Drama of the Gifted Child.* New York: Basic Books, 1981.

Miller, A. *For Your Own Good.* New York: Farrar, Straus & Giroux, 1983.

Miller, A. *Thou Shalt Not Be Aware.* New York: Farrar, Straus & Giroux, 1984.

Modell, A.A. A narcissistic defense against affect and the illusion of self-sufficiency. *International Journal of Psychoanalysis, 56,* 275-282, 1975.

Olinick, S. The negative therapeutic reaction. *International Journal of Psychoanalysis, 45,* 540-548, 1964.

O'Neill, E. *Long Day's Journey Into Night.* New Haven and New London: Yale University Press, 1955.

Ornstein, A. Psychoanalytic psychotherapy: A contemporary perspective. In P. Stepansky & A. Goldberg (Eds.), *Kohut's Legacy.* Hillsdale, N.J.: The Analytic Press, 1984.

Ornstein, P. (Ed.) *The Search for the Self, Vol. I.* New York: International Universities Press, 1978a.

Ornstein, P. (Ed.) *The Search for the Self, Vol. II.* New York: International Universities Press, 1978b.

Ornstein, P. Self psychology and the concept of health. In *Advances in Self Psychology.* New York: International Universities Press, 1980.

Pelletier, K.R. *Mind as Healer, Mind as Slayer.* New York: Delta, 1977.

Peterfreund, E. Information, systems and psychoanalysis. *Psychological Issues Monograph, 25/26.* New York: International Universities Press, 1971.

Plutchik, R. & Kellerman, H. *Theories of Emotion, Vol. I.* New York: The Academic Press, 1980.

Riviere, J. A contribution to the analysis of the negative therapeutic reaction. *International Journal of Psychoanalysis, 17,* 304-320, 1936.

Rosenblatt, A.D. & Thickstun, J.T. A study of the concept of psychic energy. *International Journal of Psychoanalysis, 51,* 265-278, 1970.

Sander, L.W. Infant and caretaking environment: Investigation and conceptualization of adaptive behavior in a system of increasing complexity. In E.J. Anthony (Ed.), *Explorations in Child Psychiatry.* New York: Plenum Press, 1975.

Sargent, S.S. Therapy and self-actualization in the later years with nontraditional approaches. *Psychotherapy: Theory, Research and Practice, 19,* 522-531, 1982.

Simonton, C. & Simonton, S.M. *Getting Well Again.* Los Angeles: J.P. Tarcher, 1978.

Spitz, R. *No and Yes.* New York: International Universities Press, 1957.

Spitz, R. *The First Year of Life.* New York: International Universities Press, 1965.

Socarides, D.D. & Stolorow, R.D. Affects and selfobjects. *The Annual of Psychoanalysis,* 1984–1985, Vol. xii–xiii, pp. 105-119.

Spruiell, V. Three strands of narcissism. *Psychoanalytic Quarterly, 44,* 577-595.

Stern, D.N. *The First Relationship: Infant and Mother.* Cambridge, MA: Harvard University Press, 1977.

Stolorow, R. & Lachmann, F. *Psychoanalysis of Developmental Arrests: Theory and Treatment.* New York: International Universities Press, 1980.

Stolorow, R., Atwood, G., & Lachmann, F. Transference and countertransference in the analysis of developmental arrests. *Bulletin of the Menninger Clinic, 45,* 20-28, 1981.

Straus, E.W. The upright posture. *Psychiatric Quarterly, 26,* 529-561, 1952.

Tolpin, M. Corrective emotional experience: A self-psychological evaluation. In A. Goldberg (Ed.), *The Future of Psychoanalysis.* New York: International Universities Press, 1983.

Tolpin, M. *Controversies about Development, Givens and Experiences.* Paper presented at the Seventh Annual Self Psychology Conference, Toronto, Canada, 1984.

Tolpin, P. Corrective emotional experience: A self psychological reevaluation. In A. Goldberg (Ed.), *The Future of Psychoanalysis.* New York: International Universities Press, 1983.

Tolpin, P. Self psychology and the interpretation of dreams. In A. Goldberg (Ed.), *The Future of Psychoanalysis.* New York: International Universities Press, 1983.

Weiner, M.B., Teresi, J., & Streich, C. *Old People Are a Burden But Not My Parents.* Englewood, N.J.: Prentice Hall, 1983.

Weiner, M.B. Aging as ongoing adaptation to partial loss. In M. Tallmer (Ed.), *The Life-Threatened Elderly*. New York: Columbia University Press, 1984.

Weiner, M.B. & White, M.T. Depression as the search for the lost self. *Psychotherapy: Theory, Practice, and Research, 19*, 491-499, 1982.

Weiner, M.B. & Wilensky, H. A psychotherapeutic approach to emotional problems of the elderly. *Journal of Nursing Care, 11*, 9-10, 1978.

White, M.T. Self relations, object relations and pathological narcissism. *Psychoanalytic Review, 67*, 11-23, 1980.

White, M.T. Discussion of narcissistic transferences: Implications for the treatment of couples by Gertrude Schwartzman, M.S. *Dynamic Psychotherapy, 2*, 15-17, 1984.

Wolf, E.S. Empathy and countertransference. In A. Goldberg, (Ed.), *The Future of Psychoanalysis*. New York: International Universities Press, 1983a.

Wolf, E.S. Concluding statement. In A. Goldberg (Ed.), *The Future of Psychoanalysis*. New York: International Universities Press, 1983b.

Index

Abandonment, 14, 20
Abraham, K., 152
Abuse, child, xxiii, 155–161
Acting-out behavior, 127
  sexual, 134–138
Ader, R., xxvi
Adolescence, 85
Adults, older, *see* Older adults
Affect, 176
  as the center of the self, 179–180
  inner connectedness and, 180
Aged, *see* Older adults
Aggression, xx, xxvi, 117, 130
  constructive, 22–23
  as a disintegration product, 14–15
  modifiable through empathy, xxix–xxx
  nonresponsive environment and, xii
  as a reaction to a provocation, 19
  self-aggression, 166
  toward the mother, 64
Alcoholism, 173
Alexander, F., xxi, 42
Almedingen, E.M., 172
Alter ego, 103, 105–106, 111–115, *see also*
  Twinship selfobject relationship
Altruism, 170
Ambition, 8, 11, 13, 60–61
  bipolar self and, 119
  divested on grandiose expectations,
    122–124
  exhibitionism and, 104–105, 110
  grandiosity and, 57, 73
  older adult and, 164
Ambivalence, 88
Analytic neutrality, xxvi, 131–132, 176

Anger, *see* Narcissistic rage
Anthony, E.J., xx
Anthropology, xv
Anxiety, 22
Arrested development, 51–52, 85,
  147–148, 168
Asch, S., 152
Assertiveness, 23, 33
Attuned feedback, 5, *see also* Empathy
Atwood, G.E., 19
Authority, conflicts with, 127

Basch, M.F., xx, 23–24, 100, 180
Beebe, B., xx
Benign superego, 24
Bergmann, M., 75
Bicameral mind, xvi, xxx
Bipolar self, 13, 103–105, 123, 128, 166,
  172
  poles of the, 119
  tripolar self and, 85, 103, 107, 111
Bisexuality, 136
Blanck, E., 22
Blanck, G., 22
Body image, xxi
Borderline personality disorder, xvi
Borderline symptoms, 152–153
Brain, aging and, 161, 171
Brandschaft, B., xxv, 14, 151–154, 194
Brazelton, T.B., 36
Butler, R.N., 170

Cancer, xxvii–xxviii
Castration, 116
Cathexis, xvii–xviii

203

Child abuse, xxiii, 48, 155–161
  incest, 79–84, 87, 90, 95–96
Children, *see also* Infants; Parent-Child
    interaction
  abusive parents' need for recognition
      from, 157
  affective needs of, 179–180
  aggression and, xii
  ambivalence about having, 119,
      122–123, 126
  competition with the same-sex parent,
      117–119, 131
  corrective developmental dialogue and,
      xxi
  developing sexuality, 117–118
  to fulfill parent's expectations, 94
  as a narcissistic extension of the parent,
      160
  need to idealize the parent imago, 8–11,
      76, 97–98
  psychotropic environment and, xxii
  as responsible for parent's reactions,
      123
  social environment and, 131–132
Clynes, M., 180
Compensatory structure, 106, 110–111,
    113–115, 119, 122
Competition with the same-sex parent,
    117–119, 131
Consciousness, evolution of the, xvi
Control, 77–78, 86, 127, 132
  narcissistic rage and, 58–60
  over the body-mind self, 64
  of the therapist, 152
Control theory, 23
Corrective developmental dialogue, 143
Countertransference, 9, 13, 179, *see also*
    Transference
  empathy towards patients and, 40
  objectivity and, 35
  patient's touching gesture and, 55
  rescue fantasy and, 82
Cousins, N., xxvii
Creativity, 4, 11, 74
  idealization and, 101–102
  older adult and, 165, 172
  therapist's work and, 178
  transference of, 105
Criminals, 173
Cybernetics, 23

Death, 116
  anxiety, 93
  fear of, 58
  loss of twinship in, 108–109
  omnipotent fantasies and, 183, 186

Defenses, 82
  masochistic, 54
  self-sufficiency as, 78
  as a way to halt self-fragmentation, 136
Denial, 82, 94
  of mourning tasks, 108–109
  older adult and, 163
Dependency, 78, 81, 88, 142
  fear of, 29
  older adults and, 170
  on the therapist, 93–94
Depression, 37, 80, 112, 131, 136, 144
  masochism and, 60
  older adults and, 162, 164–165
  terminating therapy and, 152
Development
  arrested, 51–52, 85, 147–148, 168
  corrective developmental dialogue, 144
  ego functions and, 99–100
  grandiosity as a normal stage of, 61–62
  phallic stage, 62, 70
Diagnosis, empathy and, 46–47
Differentiation, 75–76
Disillusionment, 97
Disintegration feelings, 32
Dreams
  case example, 28–30, 112–113, 124–127,
      183
  self-state, 143–150
Drive theory, xix
Drug abuse, 100, 112

Ego, xvii
  alter ego, 105–106, 111–115
  cathexis, xvii–xviii
  development, 47
  healthy development and, 99
  infantile grandiose self and, 7–8
  the self and, xviii–xx
Ego psychology, xv
  impact on psychotherapeutic thinking,
      xxii
Elderly, *see* Older adults
Empathy, xi, xxiii–xxiv, xxv–xxx, 12
  child's developing sexuality and,
      117–119
  definition, 41
  diagnosis and, 46–47
  Freud's stance on, 39–41
  helplessness and, 121–122
  idealization and, 84–85, 87–88
  joy in life and, 177
  Kohut's description of, 58
  older adults and, 167, 169–170
  therapist's failure to use, 20, 22, 25,
      43–45, 179

Empathy (*continued*)
  therapist's lack of, 16
  to use or not to use, 36–38
  traumatic states and, 154
  treating child abusers and, 158–159, 161
Environment
  aggression and, xii
  internalization of a healthy self and,
    xx–xxi
  social, 131–132
  unresponsive, xxii, 14, 19, 24, 130
Erikson, E., 22, 36
Exhibitionism, 110, 112
  development of stable self-esteem and,
    61
  need for parents to mirror, 104–105, 179
  phallic stage of development and, 62, 70

Fantasies, 11
  grandiose-exhibitionistic, 104
  rescue, 28, 30–31, 82
  of resurrection, 183–184
  sadistic sexual, 133–134
Faux pas, 138–143
Feedback, attuned, 5, *see also* Empathy
Flight-or-fight reaction, xxix
Fragmentation of the self, 4–5, 52–53, 84,
    87, 131
  affective needs and, 179
  defenses as a way to halt, 136
  dream symbolism of, 148
  oedipus complex and, 118
  overstimulation and, 154
  traumatic states and, 143
Freud, A., 36, 123
Freud, S., xvi–xviii, xx, 6, 13, 23, 38–40,
    73, 75, 101, 116–118, 121, 132, 139,
    151, 154
Frustration
  optimal, 8, 86, 99
  tolerance, 36, 167

Goldberg, A., xxiii, xxv, 35, 115, 168
Goldberg, J., xxvi
Goldstein, E.G., xxii
Grandiose-exhibitionistic fantasies, 104
Grandiosity, xi, xxiv–xxv, xxix
  case example, 27–30, 32–33, 124–130,
    145
  censure of, 74
  creativity and, 4
  faux pas and, 138
  manifested in treatment, 6–8
  narcissistic rage and, 57–60
  older adult and, 163–164
  physical/mental invulnerability and, 66

regression to, 61, 82, 86, 90, 122, 129
  transference and, 86
Grandparents, 107–108, 110–113, 115
Gratification, 38–39
  definition, 41
Group therapy, 168–171
Guided imagery, xxviii
Guilt, 49, 123
  negative therapeutic reactions and,
    151–153
  sexual fulfillment and, 116
Gunther, M., 23

Hallucinations, xv
Hammer, S., xxviii
Handicapped, 181
Hartmann, H., xvii–xix, 22, 24, 36, 42, 104
Harwood, I.H., 168
Heart disease, xxvii
Hedges, L.E., 21
Helplessness, xxvii–xxviii, 27, 31, 71
  child abuse and, 156
  empathy toward, 49, 121–122
  need to protect oneself from, 129
Holt, R.R., 24
Homosexuality, 105, 135, 137
Hopelessness, 152
  older adult and, 165
Hostility, 82
  Oedipus complex and, 118–119
Humanistic psychology, xxvi
Humiliation, 138–140, 152, 157–158, 160
Hyperactivity, 82
Hypercathexis, xviii–xix
Hypochondria, 71
Hypothalamus, xxviii
Hysterical seductiveness, 26

Idealization, 119, 128, 130, 172
  creativity and, 101–102
  empathy and, 84–85, 87–88
  failed, 77
  of the parent, 8–11, 76–77, 86, 97–98,
    171
  of the therapist, 85–86, 88, 96, 98,
    100–102
  transference, 4, 103, 105
  trust and, 81–82
Idealized narcissism, 96
Identifications, pathological, 77
Illness, 66
  effects of empathic experiences on,
    xxvii–xxviii
  psychosomatic, 193
Immune system, xxvi–xxix, 192
  self-esteem and, xi

Incest, case example, 79–84, 87, 90, 95–96
Independence, 42, *see also* Dependency
Infantile grandiose self, *see* Grandiosity
Infants, 86, *see also* Children; Parent-child
    interaction
    affect and, 180
    development of self-soothing, 99–100
    development of the supraordinate self,
        104
    grandiosity and, 4
    primary narcissism and, 5–6
    seeking selfobject interaction, xx
    sleep and, 98
Inner connectedness, 180
Insomnia, 100–101, 133–134
Intergenerational continuity, xxix, 116,
    118, 130–132
Internalization, transmuting, 8, 99–101,
    114, 131, 143
Intersubjectivity, 194
Interventions, impact on self-esteem,
    17–18
Isolation, 48, 129

Jacobson, E., xviii–xix, 36, 97
Jaynes, J., xv–xvi, xxx, 4
Jealousy, 119

Kafka, F., 58
Kahn, E., xxvi
Kernberg, O., 61
Kohut, H., xi, xv–xvi, xviii–xx, xxii–xxiv,
    xxix, 3–5, 8–9, 11–12, 14, 19–24, 29,
    35–36, 41–42, 47, 55, 57–59, 61–64, 67,
    72–74, 76–77, 84, 87–88, 97, 99, 101,
    103–107, 111, 114, 115, 117–118,
    120–124, 129, 131–132, 136, 138–139,
    143, 154, 166, 168, 170, 171–172, 174,
    179–180, 183
Kramer, P., 64
Kris, E., 22, 24
Kubie, L.S., 24

Lachmann, F., xxv, 147, 168
Laudenslager, M.L., xxviii
Libido, xvi–xviii, 23, 117
    cathexis, 65
Lichtenberg, J., xx, 36
Life, quality of, 162
Loewenstein, R.M., 22, 24
Loss, 38, 97, 108–109, 142
Love, 75–76, 115
Love object, *see* Object love
Lust, 118

Mahler, M.S., xxi, 6, 36, 61, 64, 75–76,
    123, 152

Mania, 152
Marriage, as a replay of childhood, 89
Masochism, xxiii, xxix, 14, 109, 152, *see*
    also Sadism
    child's identification with, 77
    defense against, 54
    narcissistic rage and, 60, 70–72
    omnipotent grandiosity and, 7
    sadomasochistic tendencies, 26
    somatization and, 185
Maturity morality, xxii, 42, 47
    case example, 45–46
Memory traces, 168
Miller, A., xxii–xxiii, 60, 123, 128, 178
Mirroring, 20, 103, 105
    case example, 29, 31, 45, 112, 122,
        127–128
    child's need for, 11–13
    dealing with narcissistic rage and, 69,
        72–73
    from the spouse, 126
    grandiosity and, 57–60
    healthy exhibitionism and, 104
    older adult and, 172
    provided by the therapist, 8
    to support phallic ambition, 120
Mixed neurosis, 26
Modell, A.A., 41
Mother-child interaction, *see* Parent-child
    interaction
Mourning, unresolved, 32–33, 108–109
Myths, 73

Narcissism, xv, xxiii
    definition of normal, xvi
    higher forms of, 11
    idealized, 96
    pathological, 57
    primary, 5–6
Narcissistic personality disorder, xvi
Narcissistic rage, xvi, xxix, 114
    aggression and, 14, 24
    child abuse and, 156–157, 160–161
    directed at the therapist, 59–60, 62–63,
        66–73, 174
    faux pas and, 138–139, 141
    fear of, 126
    fragmentation of the self and, 84
    grandiosity and, 57–60
    idealized parent imago and, 8
    insomnia and, 100
    loss and, 32
    revenge and, 73
    self-fragmentation and, 6
    somatization and, 64
    survivor guilt and, 123–124
    turned against oneself, 193

wish to destroy unempathic other and, 87–88
Narcissistic transference, xxiv, 6
Negative therapeutic reaction, 13–14, 34, 121, 150–154, 178
Neurosis, 26, 152
Neutrality, analytic, xxvi, 131–132, 176
Nuclear self, xix–xx, 11, 48, *see also* Self
　chances to realize the potentialities of, 104–105
　fragile, 145–146
　grandiosity and, 58
　group pressure and, 170
　need for validation of the, 106
　nondestructive aggressiveness and, 23
　twinship compensatory structure for, 114–115
Nuclear war, xxiv–xxv, xxix–xxx, 19, 57
　sadistic parenting and, 73

O'Neill, E., 58
Object cathexis, xvii–xviii
Object constancy, xviii
Object love, xvi–xvii, 75, 115, 159
　child's burgeoning affect and, 180
Object relations, 47–48, 54, 74
　acceptance of differences in others and, 19
　intergenerational continuity and, 116
Object-representations, xviii–xix, 159, 168
Obsessional neurosis, 152
Oedipal complex, 47, 49, 51–52, 116–119, 168
　case examplee, 119–132
　empathic parents' reaction to, 180
　unresolved, 26
Oedipal defeat, 70
Older adults, group therapy and, 168–171
Olinick, S., 152
Omnipotence, 30, 98
　fantasies of, 183, 186
Optimal frustration, 8, 86, 99
Ornstein, A., xxiii, 36
Ornstein, P., xxiv, 13, 59
Overstimulation, 134, 143, 148, 154

Panic states, 22
Paranoid distrust, 153
Parent-child interaction, xx–xxi, 36, *see also* Children; Infants; Mirroring
　aggression and, 21–22
　anger at sickness and, 66
　competition with the same-sex parent, 117–119, 131
　empathy and, 12
　idealized parent imago and, 8–11, 76–77, 86, 97–98, 171

intergenerational continuity and, 116, 118, 130–132
　need for positive recognition and, 11
　primary narcissism and, 5–6
　selfobject transactions between mother and child, 180
Patients
　entitled to joy in life, 177
　expectations toward the therapist, 160
　goals, 47–48
　gratification, 39–41, 54–57
　idealization of the therapist, 85–86, 88, 96, 98, 100–102
　late or missed sessions and, 175–176
　need to control the therapist, 152
　need to fail, 152
　rage at the therapist, 59–60, 62–63
　selfobject needs of, xxvi
　shame over needing treatment, 6–8
　therapeutic touching gesture and, 55–56
Pelletier, K.R., xxvi
Peterfreund, E., 24
Phallic stage, 62, 70
Phobias, 165, 167
Physical abuse, *see* Child abuse
Physically handicapped, 181
Power, 90
Power struggles, 26
Primary narcissism, 5–6
Projection, 95
Promiscuous behavior, 89
Psychic disequilibrium, xxiv, 134
Psychoanalysis, 42
　objectivity and, 35
Psychoanalysts, 39, *see also* Therapist
Psychopathology, differences in, xxv
Psychosis, xvi, 58, 143
Psychosomatic illness, 193
Psychotherapy, ambiguity and, 174–175

Quality of life, 162

Rage, narcissistic, *see* Narcissistic rage
Reaction formation, 24, 123, 163
Reality, 186
Reality testing, 161
Regression, 18, 98
　grandiosity and, 61, 82, 86, 90, 122, 129
　to an infantile symbiotic state, xvii
Reliving of catastrophic events, 139
Repetition compulsion, 81
Repression, 94
Rescue fantasy, 28, 30–31, 82
Resistance, 17, 30
　defenses and, 136
　narcissistic, 152
　negative therapeutic reaction and, 121

therapist's empathic failure and, 20
Resurrection fantasies, 183–184
Revenge 73, 90
Riviere, J., 152
Rogers, C., xxvi
Rosenblatt, A.D., 24

Sadism, xxix, 11, *see also* Masochism
    parenting and, 73
    sexual fantasies of, 133–134
Sadomasochistic tendencies, 26
Sander, L., xx
Sargent, S.S., 161
Self, *see also* Nuclear self
    affect as the center of, 179–180
    bipolar, 13, 103–105, 119, 123, 128, 166,
        172
    ego functioning and the, xviii–xx
    as the first diagnostic criterion, 47
    fragmentation of the, 4–5, 52–53, 84, 87,
        131
        affective needs and, 179
        defenses as a way to halt, 136
        dream symbolism of, 148
        Oedipus complex and, 118
        overstimulation and, 154
        traumatic states and, 143
    love and, xvi–xviii
    rage at the, 64–66
    rehabilitation of the, 106
    rejected and hated, 192–193
    social factors and the, xxii–xxv
    supraordinate, xix, 63, 103–106
    tripolar, 11, 85, 103, 107, 111
Self-aggression, 166
Self-esteem, 82
    capacity for humor and, 3
    child abuse and, 156–159
    conflicts with authority and, 127
    ego functioning and, 116
    faux pas and, 138–142
    as the foundation for love, xviii
    fragmentation of self and, 4–5
    immune system and, xi
    mirroring and, 11
    older adults and, 166
    therapeutic intervention's impact on,
        17–18
Self-feelings, outcome of illness and, xxvii
Self-mutilations, 64–65
Self-preservation, xvi
Self psychology, xiii, xv
Self-representations, xvii–xix
Self-state dreams, 142–150
Self-structure, need for more, 135
Self-validation, 137

Selfobject, xx, 13–14
    child's need to idealize the, 76
    fear of depending on, 142
    the group as multiple, 169–171
    idealized, 98
    infant interaction and, xx–xxi
    integration of affect and, 179
    internalization of a good, 41
    needs of child abusers, 160–161
    oedipal phase and, 117
    sexualization of the need for, 89
    as a source of self-sustaining emotions,
        36
    therapist internalized as, xxiii, 24, 70–72
    therapist's failure to understand needs
        of, 154
    three lines of development of, 103
    "twinship" relationship and, 32–33
Separation, 152
Separation anxiety, 9, 64
Separation-individuation, 75
Sex, 50, 54, 56, 138
    need for affection and, 89
    oedipus complex and, 116–119, 126,
        131–132
    older adults and, 166
    sadistic fantasies of, 133–134
Sexual abuse, case example, 79–84, 87, 90,
        95–96, *see also* Child abuse
Sexual acting out, 134–138
Sexual transference, 39
Shame, 97, 123
    slip of the tongue and, 139
Sickness, *see* Illness
Sleep disorders, 98–99
    insomnia, 100–101, 133–134
Slip of the tongue, 139–140
Socarides, D.D., 179
Social environment, 131–132
Somatization, 63–64, 94
    masochistic, 185
Soothing, 99–100
Spector, H., xxvii
Speech development, 99–100
Spitz, R., xx, 36, 100, 123
Stepansky, P.E., xxiii, 35, 115, 168
Stern, D., xx
Stolorow, R., xxv, 19, 147, 152–154, 168,
        179, 194
Straus, E.W., 61
Stress, xxvi, 163
Suicide, 60, 64–65, 139
    rate for older adults, 161
Superego
    benign, 24
    ideal, 98, 101

oedipal struggle and, 116
Supraordinate self, xix, 63, 103–106
Survivor guilt, 123–124
Symbiosis, xvii, 76, 165

Tension arc, 105
Tension-regulating structures, 22
Termination phase, xxv, 171
  depression at approaching, 152
  premature, 67
Therapeutic reaction, negative, 13–14, 34,
    121, 151–154, 178
Therapist
  analytic neutrality and, xxvi, 131–132,
    176
  attitudes toward older adults, 162
  attuned with patient's feelings, 178, 180
  coping with narcissistic rage, 59–60,
    62–63, 66–73
  empathic failure and, 20, 22, 25, 43–45,
    174, 179
  failure to understand selfobject needs,
    154
  gratifying the patient and, 39–41, 54–57
  handling late or missed sessions,
    175–176
  idealization of the, 11, 85–86, 88, 96, 98,
    100–102
  inner experience of humanity and,
    176–178
  internalization of the, 114, 130–132, 143,
    166
    as a benign superego, 100–102
    as a patient's selfobject, xx, xxiii, 24,
      71–72
  patient's aggression and, 15–18, 21–34
  patient's dependency on the, 93–94
  patient's expectations toward, 160
  patient's feelings and, xiii
  patient's need to control the, 152
  retaining joy in the work of, 178–179
  role of the, 195
  task of the, 36
  touching the patient, 55–56
  traumatic states and, 151

unempathic reactions to difficult
    patients, 21
Thickstun, J.T., 24
Tolpin, M., xx, 36, 143
Tolpin, P., xx, 143
Transference, 16–17, 137, *see also*
    Countertransference; Idealization,
    Mirroring; Twinship
  aggression and, 25
  development of a stable selfobject and,
    33–34
  empathy and, 40
  grandiosity and, 86
  lack of trust and, 109
  need for mirroring and, 58
  negative, 20–21
  oedipal problem and, 120
  sexual, 39
  as unconscious oedipal competition, 26
Transference neurosis, xvii
Transmuting internalization, 8, 99–102,
    114, 130, 143
Traumatic states, 134–135, 137
  empathy and, 154
  faux pas and, 138
  self-state dreams and, 143–144, 150
  in the therapist, 151
Triangulation, 53–54
Tripolar self, 11, 85, 103, 107, 111
Trust, 14, 27, 45
  barriers to, 109–110
  fear of, 88
  idealization and, 81–82
  premature termination and, 67
Twinship selfobject relationship, 32–33,
    103, 105–110, 114–115, 137–138

Unconscious, 139

Values, 11, 123, 128
Vertical split, 70–71

Weiner, M.B., 21, 53, 123, 127
White, M.T., 21, 53, 102, 123, 127
Wolf, E., v, xxvi, 40, 166